New Casebooks

WORDSWORTH

EDITED BY JOHN WILLIAMS

MACMILLAN

First published 1993 by
THE MACMILLAN PRESS LTD
Houndmills, Basingstoke, Hampshire RG21 2XS
and London
Companies and representatives
throughout the world

ISBN 0–333–54903–1 hardcover
ISBN 0–333–54904–X paperback

A catalogue record for this book is available
from the British Library.

Reprinted 1994

Printed in Hong Kong

Contents

Acknowledgements

The editor and publishers wish to thank the following for permission
to use copyright material:

John Barrell, excerpt from *Poetry, Language and Politics* (1988)
by permission of Manchester University Press;

Geoffrey H. Hartman, excerpt from *Wordsworth's Poetry 1787–
1814* (1964). Copyright © 1964 and 1971 Geoffrey H. Hartman,
by permission of Harvard University Press;

John Lucas, excerpt from *England and Englishness: Ideas of
Nationhood in English Poetry 1688–1900* (1990), Hogarth Press,
by permission of Random Century Group;

Mary Jacobus, excerpt from *Romanticism, Writing, and Sexual
Difference: Essays on The Prelude* (1989). Copyright © 1989
Mary Jacobus, by permission of Oxford University Press;

Nicholas Roe, excerpt from *Wordsworth and Coleridge: The
Radical Years* (1988). Copyright © 1988 Nicholas Roe, by permission of Oxford University Press;

Roger Sales, excerpt from *English Literature in History 1780–
1830: Pastoral and Politics* (1983), Hutchinson, by permission of
Unwin Hyman Ltd;

Gayatri Chakravorty Spivak, excerpt from *Post-Structuralist Readings of English Poetry*, ed. Richard Machin and Christopher
Norris (1987), by permission of Cambridge University Press;

D. Simpson, excerpt from *Wordsworth's Historical Imagination:
The Poetry of Displacement* (1987), Methuen & Co., by permission of Routledge;

Ross Woodman, 'Wordsworth's Crazed Bedouin: *The Prelude* and the Fate of Madness', *Studies in Romanticism*, 27 (Spring 1988), by permission of *Studies in Romanticism*.

Every effort has been made to trace all the copyright holders but if any have been inadvertently overlooked the publishers will be pleased to make the necessary arrangement at the first opportunity.

General Editors' Preface

The purpose of this new series of Casebooks is to reveal some of the ways in which contemporary criticism has changed our understanding of commonly studied texts and writers and, indeed, of the nature of criticism itself. Central to the series is a concern with modern critical theory and its effect on current approaches to the study of literature. Each New Casebook editor has been asked to select a sequence of essays which will introduce the reader to the new critical approaches to the text or texts being discussed in the volume and also illuminate the rich interchange between critical theory and critical practice that characterises so much current writing about literature.

The series itself, of course, grows out of the original Casebook series edited by A. E. Dyson. The original volumes provide readers with a range of critical opinions extending from the first reception of a work through to the criticism of the twentieth century. By contrast, the focus of the New Casebooks is on modern critical thinking and practice, with the volumes seeking to reflect both the controversy and the excitement of current criticism. Because much of this criticism is difficult and often employs an unfamiliar critical language, editors have been asked to give the reader as much help as they feel is appropriate, but without simplifying the essays or the issues they raise.

The project of the New Casebooks, then, is to bring together in an illuminating way those critics who best illustrate the ways in which contemporary criticism has established new methods of analysing texts and who have reinvigorated the important debate about how we 'read' literature. The hope is, of course, that New Casebooks will not only open up this debate to a wider audience, but will also encourage students to extend their own ideas, and think afresh about their responses to the texts they are studying.

John Peck and Martin Coyle
University of Wales, Cardiff

Introduction

JOHN WILLIAMS

I

In 1879 Matthew Arnold published an anthology of Wordsworth's poems. It was this anthology, edited by one of the foremost Victorian men of letters, that was primarily responsible for fixing the nineteenth-century image of Wordsworth in the public mind. Arnold was providing a collection of poems, a set text, to accompany the influential critical assessment he was developing of Wordsworth elsewhere, an assessment eventually summed up in *Essays in Criticism: Second Series* (1888).

Arnold claimed that the spiritual intensity with which Wordsworth's finest poetry celebrated nature was capable of consoling and reassuring a readership beset by social and religious upheaval. Time and again he stressed the universality of Wordsworth's 'extraordinary power' in this respect: 'Wordsworth tells of what all seek, and tells of it at its truest and best source, and yet a source where all may go and draw for it.'[1] The 'source' is nature, with Wordsworth's poetry acting as an antidote to all the worst manifestations of modern 'science' in society. In an earlier essay, *The Function of Criticism in the Present Time* (1865), Arnold makes it clear that the best poetry is equally an antidote to modern political theory inspired by the French Revolution.

Wordsworth's greatness as a poet lay in his underlying commitment to an organic society very different from the fragmenting one Arnold saw around him in industrial Britain. It was a vision sustainable only if the divisive forces of modern society could at least be

1

momentarily set aside in favour of the poet's celebration of 'the simple primary affections and duties' he perceived enshrined in 'nature'.[2] To present Wordsworth in this light, Arnold needed to select from among his poems carefully. Like other nineteenth-century critics, he was well aware that Wordsworth possessed a darker and more troubled side to his personality; this was not, however, what qualified Wordsworth as a 'great' poet.

Arnold rejected the poet's own system of classification for his poems as ill-conceived, and in the anthology of 1879 he constructed a confident, visionary Wordsworth, using for the most part his shorter, lyric poems. The result was very different from the body of work which in Wordsworth's own lifetime had frequently been ridiculed as just plain silly, when it wasn't being taken to task for being politically subversive.

Certain aspects of Arnold's Wordsworth barely survived the century. The 'pure and sage master'[3] whose poetry elevates us above the transient squabbles of the everyday world was, before long, the subject of biographical research. In consequence Wordsworth the radical republican and passionate lover of the 1790s began to engross a number of critics, to the point where Arnold's poet of nature was in danger of reading like a hypocritical old windbag. Wordsworth had embraced republican principles wholeheartedly, and then, it seemed, much at the same time as he was disentangling himself from the embraces of his French mistress, Annette Vallon, and hushing up the birth of their child, he had turned his back on his radical idealism. Before long he was accepting a government sinecure and campaigning for the return of a Tory MP in Westmorland.

Biographical study was highlighting a profoundly complex if not contradictory personality. At the same time, careful textual study was beginning to show a poet who wrote, rewrote, revised, altered and tampered endlessly with his poetry (and in the case of *The Prelude* with his life story through his poetry). What, arguably, was happening, was the replacement of Arnold's poet of 'Nature' by a restless, insecure Wordsworth better suited to the demands of a post-Freudian, twentieth-century readership.

In other important respects, Arnold's influence has remained deeply embedded in Wordsworth scholarship well on into the twentieth century. This relates in particular to the idea of Wordsworth as a poet who drew uniquely on nature to achieve a power and intensity of inspiration. Behind this still lies the vague but evidently attractive notion of a 'universal' Wordsworth; a poet who perceived the interrelatedness of all things as 'inevitable' (a word Arnold stressed), and as such gave expression to a kind of transcendental confidence.[4]

Helen Darbishire's work in the 1920s and after was, together with that of Ernest de Selincourt and Emile Legouis, instrumental in revealing a biographically and textually reconstructed Wordsworth. What remained unaltered, however, was Darbishire's image of Wordsworth as a poet in supreme control of his inspirational powers. In the following extracts from her essay of 1926 on *The Prelude* (written to welcome Selincourt's publication for the first time of the original 1805 text), we should note her emphasis on the purity, strength and power of the poet's experiences, and on Wordsworth's firm belief in the value of what he writes. Darbishire's style verges on the evangelical: she never doubts Wordsworth's 'belief', Wordsworth never doubts his own 'creed'. In the final sentence we recognise, for all its vagueness, that the 'creed' she refers to is one of universalism, a perpetuation in twentieth-century form of Arnold's position:

> The inspiration of Wordsworth's poetry had its vitalising source in the power with which he realised a peculiar experience . . . The core of the experience was an intense consciousness of Nature passing through his senses to his mind . . . The experience was peculiar simply in its intensity. So pure and strong was the life his senses led that it passed, on a tide of feeling, into the life of his spirit. . . . That bold trust in feeling meant a belief also in the value of sensation out of which such feeling springs. . . .
>
> He had only to speak . . . of the soul that 'passing through all Nature rests with God', and he had uttered the first article of his creed.[5]

The extracts in this New Casebook reveal a significant shift in critical opinion since the time when Darbishire was writing. They cover a period of some thirty years, beginning in the 1960s with Geoffrey H. Hartman's *Wordsworth's Poetry 1787–1814*. Whatever else they illustrate by way of changing critical procedures in recent years, they all identify a tendency to treat as suspect the image of Wordsworth as a confident visionary; the 'universal' Wordsworth is fragmented and arguably, therefore, becomes all the more interesting. Universality is no longer a triumphant creed, it sounds increasingly like the expression of a cry for help.

Before discussing how the extracts present their various critical perspectives, however, I want to look closely at one of Wordsworth's

best known poems, 'Resolution and Independence' (1802), to see
how textual analysis can support the view that the poet's inspiration
derived not from a confident vision of universality, but from a fear
that the vision was flawed, that it was anything but 'inevitable'.

The fortunes of Wordsworth in respect of critical opinion cannot
be divorced from the much broader debate which has surrounded the
concept of Romanticism in recent years. Before looking at the poem,
therefore, it will be helpful to conclude the first section of this essay
with some brief comments on the context within which the merits of
Wordsworth's poetry have been discussed.

The coincidence of a generation of writers and artists in this
country broadly defined as Romantic with a period of social and
political unrest and revolution, has often tended to blur the relationship of the one to the other. The political theories which the American colonists used to justify their struggle for independence in the
1770s, and which provided a rationale for the far more profound
revolutionary upheavals in France after 1789, were the product of
eighteenth-century Enlightenment thinking. That is to say that they
were theories grounded in a spirit of empirical rationalist enquiry. In
France the so-called *Philosophes*, in England writers such as Thomas
Paine and William Godwin, campaigned for political justice in the
name of common sense; they had behind them a century which had
developed scientific methods of enquiry to a point where progress
towards perfectibility might seem assured. The time had come to
apply rational enquiry to outmoded and unjust political systems.

One explanation still frequently given for the lack-lustre quality of
much eighteenth-century art and literature is the dominance of the
spirit of reason at the expense of imagination and inspiration. The
roots of British Romanticism are discernible in the caricatures of
rational behaviour that occur throughout the century. Henry Field-
ing's Parson Adams in *Joseph Andrews* (1742) acts with a generous
spontaneity designed to contradict and negate his profession to be a
man of impeccable common sense. From these beginnings Romanticism eventually emerged as a movement seriously questioning the
intellectual tradition which underpinned the political philosophy of
British radicals and French revolutionaries. Yet it was the libertarian
spirit of the French in 1789 that most dramatically inspired the
Romantic sensibilities of Blake, Wordsworth, and many others.

Put this way, it is not difficult to understand why, where the
literature of the Enlightenment period claims order, control, clarity
and certainty of purpose as merits, Romantic literature makes a

necessary virtue of restless inquiry, vacillating moods and images of transience; much of the time it is a literature of fragments. What critics, however, had subsequently to decide was whether they were dealing with the death-throes of the Enlightenment tradition – discredited not by the determination of the French to cast off their oppressors, but by their misconceived method of doing so which resulted in anarchy and mass murder – or whether the Romantic Movement marked the birth of a new cultural order that was to play a positive role in building a new society in succeeding years. Was Wordsworth presiding over a wake or a baptism?

If the answer was the former, then culture and society were launched on an era of fragmentation and disorder. Arnold, as we have seen, chose to take as positive a view of Romanticism as he could, even if this required him to edit the evidence heavily. What in fact he was doing was using Romanticism to make a particular kind of sense of eighteenth- and nineteenth-century history; and the Romantic Movement understood as a positive intellectual alternative to the Enlightenment was crucial to the maintenance of a positive interpretation of post-Enlightenment, post-eighteenth-century history.

In the twentieth century that positive view has become progressively less easy to sustain. In what is now frequently referred to as a post-industrial era, the demise of the old order created by the Industrial Revolution has made a re-evaluation of the relative significance of Romantic and Enlightenment thought imperative. Many critics have now moved towards the view that the Romantic Movement, with Wordsworth at its centre, not only gives expression to a crisis of confidence in our ability to maintain a common cultural life, but also that this crisis of confidence has its origins in an essentially eighteenth-century debate. A central feature of this debate is understood to involve a growing awareness of the ambivalent function of language, where discourse was designed to be an expression of rational thought. The part which linguistics plays in much contemporary criticism is in no small way a consequence of the tendency now to see the Enlightenment, rather than Romanticism, as the formative prelude to the political, intellectual and cultural evolution of modern society.

Changing the critical perspective on Romanticism changes the critical perspectives on Wordsworth. As a poet he cannot be ignored; as a Romantic he cannot remain true to the image of the great poet first designed for him in the nineteenth century. The critical problem is also the poet's 'problem', as many of the essays in this collection make clear. And the debate continues to be relevant, for Wordsworth's crisis of literary and social identity is equally our continuing crisis of national, cultural and political identity.

II

'Resolution and Independence' was first drafted in May 1802; it was revised before publication in 1807 in *Poems in Two Volumes*, and yet further changes were made for subsequent editions. In the *Poems* of 1807 Wordsworth first began to work on a systematic grouping of his poems, indicating that he felt they should be read, under his guidance, together. 'Resolution and Independence' is the final poem in a sequence which also includes the short lyric 'To a Sky-Lark', the two ballads 'Beggars' and 'Alice Fell', and a sonnet. In scale, 'Resolution and Independence' is very different from the others; the implication is that it develops more fully the themes and the different voices displayed in the lyric, ballad and sonnet forms.

The title suggests a confidence on the poet's part of which Arnold happily approved; he praised the poem for its 'grandeur' in his *Essay* of 1888. The final stanza leaves us with Wordsworth's determination to emulate the firmness of mind he has encountered in the leech-gatherer described in the poem. There is a great deal between the title and the conclusion, however, to suggest that the poet's 'resolution' has been won at considerable cost. Just what that cost may have involved will now be discussed, taking as a starting point a consideration of the fact that Wordsworth has frequently been criticised for an obsessive concern with detail in many of his poems.

Resolution and Independence[6]

There was a roaring in the wind all night;
The rain came heavily and fell in floods;
But now the sun is rising calm and bright;
The birds are singing in the distant woods;
Over his own sweet voice the Stock-dove broods;   5
The Jay makes answer as the Magpie chatters;
And all the air is filled with pleasant noise of waters.

All things that love the sun are out of doors;
The sky rejoices in the morning's birth;
The grass is bright with rain-drops; on the moors   10
The Hare is running races in her mirth;

And with her feet she from the plashy earth
Raises a mist; which, glittering in the sun,
Runs with her all the way, wherever she doth run.

I was a Traveller then upon the moor;   15
I saw the Hare that rac'd about with joy;
I heard the woods, and distant waters, roar;
Or heard them not, as happy as a Boy:
The pleasant season did my heart employ:
My old remembrances went from me wholly;   20
And all the ways of men, so vain and melancholy,

But, as it sometimes chanceth, from the might
Of joy in minds that can no further go,
As high as we have mounted in delight
In our dejection do we sink as low,   25
To me that morning did it happen so;
And fears, and fancies, thick upon me came;
Dim sadness, & blind thoughts I knew not nor could name.

I heard the Sky-lark singing in the sky;
And I bethought me of the playful Hare: 30
Even such a happy Child of earth am I;
Even as these blissful Creatures do I fare;
Far from the world I walk, and from all care;
But there may come another day to me,
Solitude, pain of heart, distress, and poverty.   35

My whole life I have liv'd in pleasant thought,
As if life's business were a summer mood;
As if all needful things would come unsought
To genial faith, still rich in genial good;
But how can He expect that others should   40
Build for him, sow for him, and at his call
Love him, who for himself will take no heed at all?

I thought of Chatterton, the marvellous Boy,
The sleepless Soul that perished in its pride;
Of him who walk'd in glory and in joy   45
Behind his plough, upon the mountain-side:
By our own spirits are we deified;
We Poets in our youth begin in gladness;
But thereof comes in the end despondency and madness.

Now, whether it were by peculiar grace,   50
A leading from above, a something given,
Yet it befel, that, in this lonely place,
When up and down my fancy thus was driven,
And I with these untoward thoughts had striven,
I saw a Man before me unawares: 55
The oldest Man he seem'd that ever wore grey hairs.

My course I stopped as soon as I espied
The Old Man in that naked wilderness:
Close by a Pond, upon the further side,
He stood alone: a minute's space I guess   60
I watch'd him, he continuing motionless:
To the pool's further margin then I drew;
He being all the while before me full in view.

As a huge Stone is sometimes seen to lie
Couch'd on the bald top of an eminence;   65
Wonder to all who do the same espy
By what means it could thither come, and whence;
So that it seems a thing endued with sense:
Like a Sea-beast crawl'd forth, which on a shelf
Of rock or sand reposeth, there to sun itself.   70

Such seem'd this Man, not all alive nor dead,
Nor all asleep; in his extreme old age:
His body was bent double, feet and head
Coming together in their pilgrimage;
As if some dire constraint of pain, or rage   75
Of sickness felt by him in times long past,
A more than human weight upon his frame had cast.

Himself he propp'd, his body, limbs, and face,
Upon a long grey Staff of shaven wood:
And, still as I drew near with gentle pace,   80
Beside the little pond or moorish flood
Motionless as a cloud the Old Man stood;
That heareth not the loud winds when they call;
And moveth together, if it move at all.

At length, himself unsettling, he the Pond   85
Stirred with his Staff, and fixedly did look
Upon the muddy water, which he conn'd,
As if he had been reading in a book:
And now such freedom as I could I took;
And, drawing to his side, to him did say,   90
'This morning gives us promise of a glorious day.'

A gentle answer did the Old Man make,
In courteous speech which forth he slowly drew:
And him with further words I thus bespake,
'What kind of work is that which you pursue?   95
This is a lonesome place for one like you.'
He answer'd me with pleasure and surprise;
And there was, while he spake, a fire about his eyes.

His words came feebly, from a feeble chest,
Yet each in solemn order follow'd each,   100

With something of a lofty utterance drest;
Choice word, and measured phrase; above the reach
Of ordinary men; a stately speech!
Such as grave Livers do in Scotland use,
Religious men, who give to God and Man their dues.   105

He told me that he to this pond had come
To gather Leeches, being old and poor:
Employment hazardous and wearisome!
And he had many hardships to endure:
From pond to pond he roam'd, from moor to moor,   110
Housing, with God's good help, by choice or chance:
And in this way he gain'd an honest maintenance.

The Old Man still stood talking by my side;
But now his voice to me was like a stream
Scarce heard; nor word from word could I divide;   115
And the whole body of the man did seem
Like one whom I had met with in a dream;
Or like a Man from some far region sent;
To give me human strength, and strong admonishment.

My former thoughts return'd: the fear that kills;   120
The hope that is unwilling to be fed;
Cold, pain, and labour, and all fleshly ills;
And mighty Poets in their misery dead.
And now, not knowing what the old man had said,
My question eagerly did I renew,   125
'How is it that you live, and what is it you do?'

He with a smile did then his words repeat;
And said, that, gathering Leeches, far and wide
He travelled; stirring thus about his feet
The waters of the Ponds where they abide.   130
'Once I could meet with them on every side;
But they have dwindled long by slow decay;
Yet still I persevere, and find them where I may.'

While he was talking thus, the lonely place,
The Old Man's shape, and speech, all troubled me: 135
In my mind's eye I seem'd to see him pace
About the weary moors continually,
Wandering about alone and silently.
While I these thoughts within myself pursued,
He, having made a pause, the same discourse renewed.   140

And soon with this he other matter blended,
Chearfully uttered, with demeanour kind,
But stately in the main; and, when he ended,
I could have laughed myself to scorn, to find

> In that decrepit Man so firm a mind   145
> 'God,' said I, 'be my help and stay secure;
> I'll think of the Leech-gatherer on the lonely moor.'

'He with a smile did then his words repeat'. Among the things which still tend to puzzle, if not infuriate, readers of Wordsworth, is his tendency to labour points of seemingly inconsequential detail. The most notorious case in point is probably the description of the pond in 'The Thorn' from *Lyrical Ballads*:

> I've measured it from side to side:
> 'Tis three feet long, and two feet wide.[7]

This, we should appreciate, is not 'Wordsworth' speaking, it is the voice of a narrator whom Wordsworth himself described as 'credulous and talkative from indolence' and 'prone to superstition'.[8] Wordsworth, however, wrote the words, and many have never quite been able to forgive him.

If the reader has a problem here, it is equally true that Wordsworth himself is registering a difficulty, albeit of a different order. Taking the reader first, we find that Geoffrey Hartman provides us with a clue to the nature of the problem. Wordsworth's 'open and natural style', he suggests, 'can be so plain as to be anti-literary'.[9] Behind this lurks the fundamental issue of how we come to have a view on 'literariness' in the first place. Wordsworth does frequently offend our 'literary' expectations, and when he does so it is more often than not because of a perverse attention to detail. The acrimonious correspondence that ensued from the circulation of a draft copy of 'Resolution and Independence' is a case in point.

The draft poem was sent to Mary and Sara Hutchinson and, in a letter now lost, they expressed only moderate satisfaction with it; this drew from Wordsworth a vigorous defence of both the poem and the 'new system of poetry' he was attempting. Sara was told that what she was criticising as 'tedious' was in fact an intentional style of 'naked simplicity'. Wordsworth was attempting to challenge current poetic conventions, and was thus offending Sara's received notions of literariness. Dorothy tried to explain that this was because her brother was primarily concerned to 'illustrate a particular character or truth', while Wordsworth went on to explain an important aspect of this 'truth': 'the necessities which an unjust state of society has entailed upon him [the leech gatherer]'.[10]

The pursuit of 'truth', both moral and political, in all its naked simplicity, had resulted in a seemingly pointless rehearsal of trivial detail verging on doggerel. The draft poem includes the following lines:

> . . . in winter time
> I go with godly Books from Town to Town
> Now I am seeking Leeches up & down
> From house to house I go from Barn to Barn
> All over Cartmell Fells & Blellan Tarn.[11]

The point at issue here for the reader relates to the 'literary' consequences of Wordsworth's endeavour to restructure poetic language.

The point at issue here for the poet – that of shifting the language of poetry away from established structures of literary convention to reveal the 'naked simplicity' of his vision – is arguably more disturbing. If the poetry loses its reader, the reader may respond by observing the demise of the poet. Wordsworth, driven to abandon literary convention and established structures of feeling, faces the possibility of being a poet bereft of language itself. It was a problem, he suggests, that had already taken its toll on British poets. Robert Burns, 'who walk'd in glory and in joy/Behind his plough' (ll.45–6), and Thomas Chatterton, 'The sleepless Soul that perish'd in its pride' (l.44), were both poets whose deaths were understood to be directly attributable to the incompatability of their imaginative, creative selves with an unsympathetic 'real' world. It was not just a loss of language that was at stake here, it was potentially a loss of sanity, even of life: 'therefore comes in the end despondency and madness' (l.49).

To the concern for structure, therefore, is added the experience of fear, a real, palpable fear of mental dissolution without resolution. Faced with this prospect, attention to detail may well constitute a means of retaining a hand-hold on 'reality'. Fear becomes an essential part of poetry which explores the extremities of consciousness, the borderlands between 'truth' and how through language we attempt to realise that truth.

The letter from Mary and Sara, unwelcome as it was, jolted Wordsworth into abandoning the obsessive detail of 'Town to Town . . . house to house . . . Barn to Barn . . . Cartmell Fells and Blellan Tarn'; he evidently could be made to see that in this instance the reader had a right to protest. Equally, it remains clear that the subject of the poem he was writing was not a subject which even two readers who knew him well were expecting. Wordsworth's capitulation in this instance was, however, more accurately an act of strategic withdrawal which allowed him still to address the frightening prognosis of a fragmented structure of literary form and feeling.

> Close by a Pond, upon the further side,
> He stood alone: a minute's space I guess
> I watch'd him, he continuing motionless:
> To the pool's further margin then I drew;
> He being all the while before me full in view.
> (ll.59–63)

Though less overtly banal than the stanza Wordsworth was prepared to cut, these lines remain open to the charge of tediousness.

The first three lines are irritatingly 'motionless', 'upon the further side' adding unnecessary detail to 'Close by a Pond'. To be told the length of time the poet watches also seems over-specific, especially as it is, after all, only a 'guess'; the actual encounter is further postponed by learning of the route which brought Wordsworth close to the old man: 'He being all the while before me full in view'.

To try and understand what is at stake for Wordsworth here, and what consequently leads him to describe the encounter in the way he does, it will be helpful to recall a comment he made to Isabella Fenwick in the early 1840s concerning childhood memories: 'I was often unable to think of external things as having an external existence. . . . Many times . . . I grasped at a wall or tree to recall myself from this abyss of idealism to the reality. At that time I was afraid of such processes.'[12] In 'Resolution and Independence' the status of the encounter with the leech-gatherer is in doubt; Wordsworth endows it with increasingly dream-like properties as the poem progresses. The pause we have seen in the forwarding of the narrative is concluded by the insistence that the man remained in full view, which is to say his physical *reality* is being insisted upon. Here, surely, we have Wordsworth grasping at 'external existence' to steady himself, to recall himself from the 'abyss of idealism'.

As the poem progresses it becomes increasingly clear that for Wordsworth what is of significance in his encounter with the leech-gatherer is an experience that exists beyond language; an experience that in any commonly conceived notion of what is 'real', exists beyond knowing. Wordsworth therefore needed a structure that would point up the moment when the 'real' encounter ceased to have 'an external existence' and became a mystical experience, rendering it essentially inexplicable: an 'abyss of idealism'. The moment when the 'real' is on the point of dissolving is for him that moment of 'naked simplicity'; its very 'unliterary' nature was a source of power that could generate a glimpse of the divine; at the same time it could equally be a terrifying glimpse into an abyss of incomprehension. 'Naked simplicity' is therefore both the route by which he advances into the realm of what cannot rationally be known, and his means of escaping from it to tell the tale.

When we read 'Resolution and Independence' with these thoughts in mind, we can begin to appreciate how the poem is structured in order to provide that vital hand-hold on physical, material reality. It is not sufficient for us to be told that 'The Hare is running races in her mirth', in the following stanza we therefore read:

> I saw the Hare that rac'd about with joy;
> I heard the woods, and distant waters, roar
> (ll.16–17)

Again: 'I heard the Sky-lark singing in the sky'; and in due course, 'I saw a Man before me unawares'. 'Saw . . . heard . . . saw', '. . . all the while before me full in view'. Wordsworth is supplying evidence of 'being' in these lines congenial to an Enlightenment, common-sense, eighteenth-century tradition of knowledge, and it is this knowledge that the meeting in the poem confronts and challenges: 'I saw a Man before me unawares'. For all the detail establishing a concrete visual image for this moment, 'unawares' signals a breakdown in the narration, an arrival at something unknowable. Specifically, the leech-gatherer is unaware of Wordsworth's location of the encounter in time and place. The language is allowed a wayward contra-dictoriness: 'he continuing motionless'. The stillness of the man is a rebuke to the activity observed and experienced before the encounter; motion is redefined as an alternative, ghostly process, a stillness which 'continues'.

The old man now conjures up an even more disturbing image for the would-be writer:

> . . . he the Pond
> Stirred with his Staff, and fixedly did look
> Upon the muddy water, which he conn'd,
> As if he had been reading in a book.
> (ll.85–8)

This is a very different kind of reading in a very different kind of book! Knowledge in this poem is no longer controlled or structured by the language of books, though the poem itself, of course, is – has to be – sustained in that medium. The man's words 'came feebly', and yet they paradoxically become 'lofty utterance . . . Choice word . . . a stately speech' (ll.101–3). Eventually the words disappear without loss of meaning as we enter a realm of knowledge beyond language, of knowledge beyond the poem, '. . . his voice to me was like a stream / Scarce heard; nor word from word could I divide' (ll.114–15); and at this point the grasp on precise location is loosened:

> And the whole body of the man did seem
> Like one whom I had met with in a dream.
> (ll.116–17)

If Wordsworth's problem here is a fear of what the transition to a dream state could imply, the reader's problem is once more rather different. No matter how intellectually or emotionally affected we may be by this invitation to doubt the concrete reality of the conscious world, our response will be unlikely to match the intensity of the creative mind driven to produce the poem. Donald G. Marshall has argued for more than fear as a central driving force behind Wordsworth's inspiration; he puts it at terror: 'Imagination's power to draw the self into an autonomous, "apocalyptic" transcendence terrified Wordsworth.'[13] 'Autonomous . . . transcendence' means that the self enters an imaginative realm where control depends only upon the experiencing individual. Here judgement has no comparative yardstick; the metaphor is redundant, comparisons carry no weight; in rational terms there can therefore be no formal structured way of 'knowing'. For all the previous insistence on detail in the poem, the climax is the point at which all metaphors dissolve:

> Now, whether it were by peculiar grace,
> A leading from above, a something given.
> (ll.50–1)

The 'grace' is 'peculiar', unique; the leading is 'from above' (not therefore seen); what is given is 'a something'. The experience, like those formative moments in childhood and early manhood we are given in *The Prelude*, is both immeasurably valuable and frightening.

In the following two passages from Book I of the 1805 *Prelude* Wordsworth remembers stealing a bird caught in someone else's trap, and climbing the cliffs on a birds-nesting expedition. In both cases we recognise the language of 'Resolution and Independence' as fear manifests itself through encounters with formlessness, structures of feeling which are 'undistinguishable', 'undetermined' and 'unknown':

> . . . the bird
> Which was the captive of another's toils
> Became my prey . . .
> I heard among the solitary hills
> Low breathings coming after me, and sounds
> Of undistinguishable motion . . .
>
> . . . on the perilous ridge I hung alone,
> With what strange utterance did the loud dry wind
> Blow through my ears; the sky seemed not a sky
> Of earth, and with what motion moved the clouds![14]

In both these passages we encounter once more a motion that defies description. Similarly, after an excursion in a stolen rowing boat, Wordsworth recalls an 'undetermined' fear:

> . . . for many days my brain
> Worked with a dim and undetermined sense
> Of unknown modes of being.[15]

The French Revolution offered a translation of abstract idealism into social and political reality; but in Book X the Revolution likewise proves to be 'written in a tongue he cannot read'. As before the 'tongue' is located with language heard through the medium of a dream, the terror of which is openly admitted:

> . . . ghastly visions had I of despair,
> And tyranny, and implements of death,
> And long orations which in dreams I pleaded
> Before unjust tribunals, with voice
> Labouring, a brain confounded . . . [16]

Much has been made of Wordsworth's anxiety, expressed in 'Tintern Abbey' (1798), that at the very moment of discovering his poetic voice, he found himself threatened by silence because his creative powers seemed to be on the wane. This anxiety should be more properly understood as a recognition on his part that the true subject of his and every poet's art seemed to lie beyond words, forever unattainable. 'Tintern Abbey' was first published in *Lyrical Ballads*, and many of the shorter poems in that volume bear witness to the same anxiety. In 'The Thorn' Wordsworth renders the language of orthodox literary convention offensive by its lack of sensitivity. The subject of the poem resides in the untold, concealed narrative of Martha Wray. In 'The Idiot Boy', 'We Are Seven' and 'Anecdote for Fathers' articulate adults are humbled before verbally unsophisticated children. In 'The Complaint of the Forsaken Indian Woman', a poem imbued with fear and terror, the subject resides in the final silence of death.

As part of his attempt to retrieve language as a medium for poetry, Wordsworth began to work out a formal theory of language in his Preface to the second edition of *Lyrical Ballads* (1800). We should always remember that Wordsworth was not in the first instance motivated by the need to write in his defence against the hostility of the reviewers; in 1800 that particular battle was only just about to commence. The Preface was as instrumental as poems like 'Simon Lee' and 'The Idiot Boy' in provoking it. The tone of the 1800 Preface hovers midway between public and private statement; precisely the dichotomy that John Lucas addresses in his essay (4) in this New Casebook by way of analysing the tensions in Wordsworth's poetry. In many respects the Preface is a very private document, in which the poet talks to himself and a few friends.

The central principle is the same as that used in his letter defending 'Resolution and Independence': 'I have said that each of these poems has a purpose . . . it is to follow the fluxes and refluxes of the mind when agitated by the great and simple affections of our nature.' Within the principle of simplicity – notably when applied to 'utterance' – lay a universalising, synthesising power capable of articulating 'in what manner language and the human mind act and react on each other'.[17]

'I wish to keep my Reader in the company of flesh and blood', he writes. What he sees is fragmentation; language failing to retrieve 'the general passions and thoughts and feelings of men'. To be 'in the company of flesh and blood' is to be in the company of a range of universal 'moral sentiments and animal sensations'. Human experience no longer answers to a universal language, the 'organic sensibility' he craves is being dissipated by 'revolutions not of literature alone but likewise of society itself'.[18] As the narrator of 'Resolution and Independence', he struggles when it comes to hearing the profound, non-verbal message the leech-gatherer offers; his 'organic sensibility' is impaired and all language can do is to construct banal questions, 'how is it that you live, and what is it you do?' (l.126). Both in the letter to Mary and Sara defending 'Resolution and Independence', and in the Lyrical Ballads Preface, therefore, he argues that 'an unjust state of society' must bear a significant portion of blame for the demise of a language which makes 'real' the 'visionary gleam'.[19]

Throughout the Preface there is an emphasis on the need for language to articulate universal truths, to act as a point of connection between otherwise disparate areas of experience (our 'literary' and our 'political' selves); in consequence we have references to 'the primary laws of our nature', 'essential passions', and to 'elementary feelings' and to poetry as 'the breath and finer spirit of all knowledge; it is the expression which is in the countenance of all science'.[20]

Because 'Moral Sentiments' of this universal kind are organically linked to 'animal sensations', poetry 'sheds no tear "such as Angels weep", but natural and human tears'. In other words, we need not be afraid of an 'autonomous, "apocalyptic" transcendence', so long as we understand that simplicity ('natural . . . animal sensations') brings us to the threshold of that which is transcendent. Wordsworth's aim is to set down in writing a theoretical structure for the imagination capable of giving substance to that which seems least likely, or able, to respond to rationality, or to a 'literary' rendering. The poet, Wordsworth insists, must carry 'sensation into the midst of the objects of the science itself'. What may seem abstract('sensation'), even 'miraculous', must be scientifically addressed, 'for it is a fact':

> the power of the human imagination is sufficient to produce such changes even in our physical nature as might almost appear miraculous. The truth is an important one; the fact (for it is a fact) is a valuable illustration of it.[21]

In his three Essays Upon Epitaphs (1810), Wordsworth continued to search for a language that would 'readmit . . . into the soul . . . universally received truths'. The tone, however, is far less optimistic than in the *Lyrical Ballads* Preface. The epitaph's job is to encapsulate universal truths and emotions; joy, sorrow, faith, all should be present, yet Wordsworth has become preoccupied with how dangerous the medium of language is: 'Words are too awful an instrument for good and evil to be trifled with.' Used wrongly, language may 'derange . . . subvert . . . lay waste . . . dissolve'. Much as we might wish it otherwise, the effect of language will generally be to diminish what is in 'the heart and the imagination'.[22] In 'Resolution and Independence' words can ultimately offer us only a pious cliché, 'God . . . be my help and stay secure', over against the profound knowledge that remains outside the poem, yet still constitutes the poem's subject.

Wordsworth's disillusionment with language was bound up with his verdict on 'the taste, intellectual power, and morals of a country';[23] the contempt he felt for the conduct of England's political and military leaders had remained unchanged since his initiation into radical politics in the 1790s, though his personal political allegiance only briefly (and probably superficially) lay with Jacobinism.[24] In a country where the fight for political justice had been perverted from its spiritual course by the materialistic values of the age, 'thoughts cannot . . . assume an outward life without a transmutation and a fall'.[25]

Wordsworth had been deeply motivated to espouse political radicalism, but its very volubility was evidence of a lack of sincerity, of a superficiality and an inability to unite 'intellectual power, and morals' with political action worthy of the cause. From Book IV of *The Excursion* we learn that in the hour of defeat the promise of redemption belongs with silence: 'peace', 'tranquility', observation, feelings:

> . . . the wise
> Have still the keeping of their proper peace;
> Are guardians of their own tranquility.
> They act, or they recede, observe, and feel;
> Knowing that the heart of man is set to be
> The centre of the world . . .[26]

The political theme is particularly evident in 'Character of the Happy Warrior' which appeared in the 1807 *Poems in Two Volumes*. It was a poem inspired by what for Wordsworth was the poetic depravity of the many jingoistic elegies circulating to mark the death of Nelson at Trafalgar. Here certainly was evidence of language 'tainted by the artifices which have overrun our writings in metre since the days of Dryden and Pope'.[27]

Wordsworth's warrior is unfashionably introverted, his 'high endeavours are an inward light'. He is ready to do battle as much with the temptations which exist within the state for those in high office, as with the enemies of the state; he 'makes his moral being his prime care' and 'Finds comfort in himself and in his cause'; as with *The Excursion* 'the heart of man is set to be / The centre of this world'. Yet like Wordsworth, the happy warrior knows that there must be dialogue between the condition of the recluse who seeks moral purity, and that of the socially, politically responsible individual. The image of Wordsworth as a poet frequently inspired by fear, if not terror, owes its origins in no small part to the work that has been done on evidence relating to his eventful political life.

There are few critics, if any, who have not, at some point and in some way, identified a less than confident side to Wordsworth's personality and art; but the suggestion that D. D. Devlin made in 1980 that he went so far as to write 'against art, against literature, against language itself'[28] signifies the arrival of a new Wordsworth in the course of the last thirty or so years. It is now time to consider briefly the contributions to this New Casebook, all of which to some degree illustrate the tendency to challenge a Wordsworth made easy – and indeed often rendered tedious – by labelling him a poet of 'nature'. Walter Pater, writing in 1874, supposed that Wordsworth's life was 'divided by no very profound incidents', and he went on to describe the poet in a way which, though now manifestly anachronistic, still lingers to haunt the commonly perceived notion of Romantic poetry, and indeed of a poem like 'Resolution and Independence' in particular:

> This placid life matured a quite unusual sensibility, really innate to him, to the sights and sounds of the natural world – the flower and its shadow on a stone, the cuckoo and its echo. The poem of 'Resolution and Independence' is a storehouse of such records.[29]

III

Donald G. Marshall claims that the publication of Geoffrey Hartman's *Wordsworth's Poetry 1787–1814* in 1964 'marked an epoch in the study of that poet and of romanticism generally'.[30] Few would wish to dissent from this assessment, and it is wholly appropriate that this collection of essays should begin with part of a chapter from a book which continues to be an indispensable text for students of the period. The 1971 edition carried a very helpful 'Retrospect' (reprinted in the current 1987 edition) in which Hartman reflects on his underlying thesis. In just a few sentences it becomes clear that Hartman's reading of Wordsworth as a visionary poet is a product, at least in part, of the tradition to which Helen Darbishire and Ernest de Selincourt belonged.

It is equally apparent that in his concern to understand what kind of visionary poet Wordsworth was, he is breaking new ground. I suggested earlier that Darbishire's description of Wordsworth's poetry had an evangelical tone; vision was achieved through a universalising 'sympathy with Nature'.[31] 'Nature' in this reading is a concept of God, and to the extent that he was questioning this view, Hartman had to deal with what in effect constituted a charge of blasphemy from a critic of Darbishire's generation:

> One critic, quite upset, reduced the book to the interesting if bloody-minded argument that Wordsworth needed to kill or violate nature in order to achieve his moments of visionary poetry.

'Poetry', Hartman agrees, 'can exact a price, but I would not put it so high.' Wordsworth, he suggests, is discovering a visionary role for the poet that differs profoundly from the puritan Christian tradition which had produced John Milton's *Paradise Lost* in the seventeenth century:

> Wordsworth, deeply wary of visionary poetry of Milton's kind, foresaw a new type of consciousness, satisfied with nature, or at least not obliged to violate it in imagination.

The phrase 'satisfied with nature' implies that Milton's search for a God beyond and above nature has been set aside. The consequence of this for Hartman was to begin to reveal and concentrate on a poet who, far from being 'satisfied', found himself frequently perplexed by and fearful of vision, or, in Hartman's revisionary terminology, the process of 'coming-to-consciousness': 'Wordsworth was haunted, certainly, by the fear that coming-to-consciousness was connected with the sense of violation or trespass'. He summarises his position by explaining that 'the difficult humanising of imagination is what I chiefly followed in Wordsworth'.[32]

The word 'humanise' is a key term throughout *Wordsworth's Poetry*, and the process by which Wordsworth attempts to 'humanise' his vision clearly dominates Hartman's reading of 'Michael' included in this volume. Hartman is concerned with the literary process of communicating imaginative insight, and he stresses in a way others have not the fact that this process of 'coming-to-consciousness' was evidently fraught with problems and uncertainties.

In the discussion of 'Michael', therefore, it is characteristic that Hartman begins by arguing that the presence of a 'human intermediary' acts as a synthesising, healing power. We are taken by Wordsworth to 'a strangely inhuman place (a heap of stones) which his story humanises'.[33] It is through this reading of Wordsworth as a poet who humanises vision that Hartman remains linked to a critical tradition which sees Wordsworth as a 'universal' poet, but universalism is being recast in specifically twentieth-century terms. Hartman's work has been greatly influenced in this respect by his interest in phenomenology, a school of philosophy initiated by Edmund Husserl, and subsequently developed by his pupil Martin Heideggar in the 1920s.

Phenomenology comprises the search for a trustworthy knowledge of phenomena, it seeks to know the essence of things even as Wordsworth might be understood to be in search of a visionary glimpse of the essence of the objects he encounters. Heideggar in particular stressed the importance of appreciating the organic relationship of the individual to nature (in 'Michael' the relationship of Michael's story to the heap of stones). Much of what Hartman writes about 'Michael' draws on a phenomenological vocabulary, and a feeling for the way it helps more generally to explain the processes of Romantic poetry. To humanise is to heal, and in keeping with the Romantic quest for a synthesis of nature and humanity, Hartman explains that 'care of nature is also a care of the human'. 'Nature' is endowed with immense power in Hartman's critical vocabulary, but it remains undefined ('unviolated' as he claimed in his defence); it is at once both transcendental and 'real'. We are intended to appreciate that it somehow answers the phenomenological question by translating individual experience into universal essence.

Having said that, Hartman keeps firmly before us the fact that 'the labour necessary to achieve' this 'ideal vision' has about it all the fear of 'violation or trespass' described so graphically in those extracts from *The Prelude* discussed earlier.[34]

An important feature of Hartman's project has been the way he has 'humanised' Wordsworth himself, but this has been achieved in a very specific way, concentrating on the poetry, and on the interplay of language and ideas to be found in the poetry. This effectively sets Hartman's work apart from a large body of contemporary criticism influenced by biographical research and an interest in the signi-ficance of social and political context, and in the way that context comes to be interpreted by subsequent critics.

The second essay in this book, taken from Nicholas Roe's *Wordsworth and Coleridge: The Radical Years* (1988), is indicative of one way in which historical research has been integrated with the reading of Wordsworth's poetry. It is particularly suited to follow Hartman's essay because it reveals how Hartman's approach has had an influence on the way the historical perspective may be applied. The essay argues for a progression from 'Jacobin' poetry towards a poetry of the 'inner life'.[35] The 'political' text matures into a 'literary' text with roots that remain embedded in the business of social and literary protest. In a piece which bristles with contemporary political and literary points of reference, Roe is in fact primarily concerned to establish the timelessness and universality of Wordsworth's poetry; the logic behind this critical method is effectively to distance Wordsworth's mature art from its immediate historical context. We see this disengagement beginning to happen in Roe's text at the point when the literary references move dramatically outside Wordsworth's own period to Chaucer, Spenser and Milton; Hartman makes use of Spenser for a similar purpose in the first extract in this volume.

Roe's terminology serves to remind us of the continuing influence of Northrop Frye's *Anatomy of Criticism*, first published in 1957, and of great significance in Hartman's development. Frye's theory of criticism centred on a study of certain recurring, archetypal motifs in mythology, and from this he claimed to be able to identify and categorise essential, universal features within art. The recognition of these motifs thus became a critical tool making it possible to distin-guish between great art and what was merely superficial or transient. Frye's influence is clearly present in Nicholas Roe's comment on the way Wordsworth describes a discharged, mendicant soldier in Book IV of *The Prelude*. Here is an image that could be seen in terms of contemporary comment on war and poverty; for Roe it is more to the point that the soldier 'shares the permanent significance of all the deathly archetypes mentioned above'.[36]

David Simpson, whose essay oﬁ 'Wordsworth's 'Simon Lee' follows Nicholas Roe's discussion of 'Jacobin Poetry', is also very
clearly making considerable use of history. Simpson would argue,
however, that he is a 'New Historicist', and as such is developing an
approach as distinct from Roe as it is from Frye or Hartman.

The New Historicists are particularly sensitive to the danger of
literary criticism becoming bound by the methodology of historical
scholarship, its 'researches and argumentations', as Marjory Levinson
has put it in an important discussion of what historicism is.[37] Simpson
is primarily concerned to integrate the various means of critical
insight available to the modern reader, and his thesis of what he calls
'displacement' illustrates a new and challenging approach both to
Wordsworth and to critical practice in general.

What 'displacement' meant for Wordsworth, Simpson suggests,
was the search for a 'language' (by which he means the structures
of the poems) through which he could convey subjects that were
psychologically too painful for him to address directly. Wordsworth's
poetry is a 'symptom of social as well as theological or psychic
alienation'.[38] The poet's motivation is still fear, but understanding
the source of his fear involves historical research as much as it does
psychoanalysis. There remains, however, a very real respect for
Wordsworth's 'transcendence'. Simpson's reading of 'Simon Lee'
relies heavily on establishing a psychological structure of feeling for
the poem, but equally he insists that the images in 'Simon Lee' have
a 'social and historical density'. Evidence is produced to show that
the 'fiction' of the poem comes about as a rewriting of historical fact.
Simpson's method requires him to give us 'facts' of a kind which
renders his approach very different from that of Hartman.[39]

In 'The Country Dweller: William Wordsworth' by John Lucas
(essay 4, which follows Simpson's essay), we can identify a third
distinct historical approach to Wordsworth. The model is a Marxist
one which refers (and defers) regularly to other critics who share this
approach (Raymond Williams, Heather Glen, V. G. Kiernan and
Paul Hamilton). The idea of a poetry of the 'inner life' found in Roe
is recognised, but never for a moment are we allowed to forget that
'the self cannot be constructed apart from history'.[40]

Despite the breadth of Lucas's literary perspective, the ties between Wordsworth's poetic achievement and the immediate social
and political debate remain clear, along with his place in a broader
process of social tension and evolution. Wordsworth's pastoralism is

therefore seen as evidence of the poet's conservatism, a falsification of 'the actual relationships of non-city communities'. Lucas demystifies literary categories by using political analysis: thus to be 'private' is not the act of withdrawal the poetry may make it seem, it is to identify 'with certain forces, interests, which between them compose a social and cultural orthodoxy'.[41]

In common with all the other readings represented here, Wordsworth is seen as a poet facing 'an acute crisis'; it is a crisis of poetic voice, behind which lies the much larger issue tackled in Lucas's book, the way in which nationhood in England after 1688 could be identified and understood; specifically what poets 'made of a distinctively modern or modernising nation'.[42]

In the fifth essay, Roger Sales pushes the Marxist critique of Wordsworth much further. Three important texts to note here are *Culture and Society* (1958) and *The Country and the City* (1973) by Raymond Williams, and E. P. Thompson's *The Making of the English Working Class* (1963). What Williams and Thompson did was to examine the specific political, social and economic conditions within which writing took place, and to read poetry as 'cultural production', art moulded by the the ideologies and events of the time. In keeping with this view, Sales renders transcendentalist, religious insights irrelevant and self-indulgent. Criticism grounded in structures of 'literariness', or in language theory which foregrounds the text at the expense of context, is criticism designed to evade the central truths about literary texts, how they work, and what they really mean.

The controlling theoretical model here is the Marxist one of 'base and superstructure'. The 'base' is described by Raymond Williams as residing in 'the real social conditions'. Hartman's 'base' is nature, essentially a mystery; in Marxist theory this is in fact a 'superstructure' consisting of imagery, symbols, myths and ideas, the stuff of constantly shifting literary conventions. 'Michael' is therefore a poem to be read as inextricably 'based' not in nature, but in the changing processes of history:

> The relationship between the making of a work of art and its reception is always active, and subject to conventions, which in themselves are forms of (changing) social organisation and relationship.[43]

The historicising tendency of this approach removes the poet, and the poet's problems, from the centre of the critical stage. The romanticised image of the artist, along with the 'literary' language of criticism, becomes untrustworthy in the light of their subjective individualism.

Sale's journalistic style is intentionally, strategically different from orthodox critical discourse. Its implicit claim is to be more direct, more 'democratic' in that it uses a more 'common' language, and indeed uses popular culture as a source of allusion ('a simple story of farming folk') rather than a 'high culture' source (Hartman describes 'Michael' as 'Homeric'). Mary Jacobus uses the same strategy in the final essay of this collection to challenge a traditionally male-oriented view of *The Prelude*. Commenting on the love story of Vaudracour and Julia which concludes Book IX of the 1805 text, she explains that 'Vaudracour loses his liberty, his manhood, and his marbles because his noble father objects to a middle-class marriage'.[44] This is alternative scholarship, and it employs alternative rhetoric to signal a new, robust honesty.

Sales writes to expose a political agenda which Wordsworth is smuggling in under cover of poetry; Wordsworth's use of a pastoral literary convention marks him down as bent on deceit, and Sale's 'common sense' language – itself a ploy – is there to dramatise the poet's crime of 'trying to play the oldest trick in the crooked pastoralist's cooked book. He wants to suggest that early eighteenth century rural society was a pre-capitalist utopia'.[45]

With the sixth essay we move to a consideration of a quite different kind of contemporary critical analysis. Ross Woodman describes Wordsworth's fearful realisation that his commitment to nature was not a celebration of vision, but an admission that he had 'surrendered' to 'the language of sense', leaving behind any memory he might have had of 'the soul's "celestial light"'.[46] Here once more is the 'haunted' Wordsworth of Hartman, but Woodman's approach requires him to rescue the poet in a different way. Informing his critical method and vocabulary is the technique of 'deconstruction' pioneered by the two sources he regularly refers to, Jacques Derrida and Paul de Man, and it is primarily through this essay that the principles of this linguistic approach to criticism may be grasped.

Deconstructive criticism, as Terry Eagleton explains, shows 'how texts come to embarrass their own ruling systems of logic',[47] and Woodman pursues the constant, restless interplay of meaning within Wordsworth's text that makes a 'ruling system' for it so illusive. Where Hartman sees the humanising presence of the poet acting as a 'ruling system' reconciling Wordsworth to the fear that 'coming-to-consciousness' involves 'violation or trespass', Woodman finds no such fixed position outside the poem (outside language) able to provide that kind of stable reading. He argues instead that Wordsworth had to recognise and learn to live with the situation.

For all its concentration on the text, Woodman's argument does have a strong sense of historical context, but rather than the political and ideological context used by the previous contributors, here we are directed to the significance of eighteenth-century language theory, specifically as it was influenced by the work of John Locke (1632–1704). This article is therefore also an excellent illustration of the point made earlier in this Introduction that Romantic writing is being reinterpreted in the light of a revived interest in Enlightenment ideas, particularly by 'deconstructionists'.

Woodman's terminology is consequently for the most part derived from the practice of grammatical rather than historical analysis: the 'world of radical instability' he refers to is one not of political instability, but of linguistic instability, a problem primarily of 'metaphor'. The passage from *The Prelude* that forms the centrepiece of the discussion is appropriately a dream sequence, where problems of credibility in every respect will occur, the most serious of which must be the nightmare that – no matter how vivid the experience – there is in fact nothing there, the *'mise en abyme'*.[48]

A commitment to the centrality of language theory in critical analysis is also present in the seventh essay, 'Tintern Abbey', by John Barrell. Barrell's work, however, reintroduces a specific left-wing perspective, in this instance allied to the issue of gender, 'The Uses of Dorothy'.

Barrell's reference to Donald Davie's *Articulate Energy* (1953) is particularly helpful in explaining how a deconstructionist critique denies a 'ruling system of logic' for the text. References to concrete natural objects seem to give a poem like 'Tintern Abbey' a sense of place and an ultimate, knowable 'meaning'; this is, however, an 'optical illusion':

> He [Davie] begins by pointing out that 'Wordsworth's world is not preeminently a world of "things" . . . it is often supposed that his own verse is full of such phenomena rendered in all their quiddity and concreteness'. This, argues Davie, is 'a sort of optical illusion. What Wordsworth renders is not the natural world but . . . the effect that world has upon him . . . Wordsworth's words have meaning so long as we trust them.'[49]

Of 'Tintern Abbey' Barrell writes that 'the poem's success . . . is achieved not *in spite of* its failure to define the meaning of its abstract nouns, but absolutely *because* of its failure or refusal to define them'.[50]

Barrell applies the process of deconstruction to the political issues of class and gender, as do Gayatri Chakravorty Spivak and Mary Jacobus in the two essays that follow. 'Ruling systems' in society are as arbitrary and illusive as they are in the texts. Barrell argues that Wordsworth eventually rescues his poem by using Dorothy as a participant in it, and casting her in the traditional role of an inferior intellectual partner, complementing his own more sophisticated male consciousness. It is a 'strategy', Barrell suggests, which enables the supposedly superior poet to resolve the contradiction that his 'articulate and artificial language is still securely tethered to the nature which he has escaped from and transcended'.[51]

The final two essays in this New Casebook are indicative of the way feminist criticism, the product of a necessarily very specific agenda, has evolved to encompass a comprehensive range of social, political and linguistic issues. Spivak and Jacobus use deconstructive techniques to illustrate the pervasive influence of gender politics on all aspects of political change, and to pursue a more specific attack on the traditional procedures of literary criticism. An energetic, abrasive, and hugely entertaining essay on this latter issue constitutes Spivak's third footnote, and should be considered required reading for all Wordsworth scholars.

Mary Jacobus begins her essay with a critical look at the idea of 'genre', the means whereby literature is classified (for example, poetry, novel, drama and biography), and the controlling effect such a 'law of genre' can have on critical method. Her discussion of the Vaudracour and Julia story (included in the 1805 *Prelude*, but excluded from the 1850 text) provides her with a gender issue capable of deconstructing genre theory.

One of the first points Spivak makes is that the text of *The Prelude* is not chronological, and that 'narrative consecutivity' has been 'imposed by an authorial decision'. Any idea that we should expect somehow to arrive at a stable meaning for *The Prelude* is firmly rejected. 'Whatever the "truth" of Wordsworth's long life', Spivak writes, Books IX to XIII of *The Prelude* '*present* the French Revolution as the major crisis of the poet's poetic formation' [my italics]. We have seen the solemnity of Hartman (and others) being undermined by Sales in order to expose political hypocrisy; Spivak and Jacobus do the same in order to highlight the operation of gender politics. All three critics identify the problematic in discourse, and therefore attempt a radical revision of critical style. Barrell, without feeling the need for a radically altered discourse, never the less develops the same idea. It is an exercise in demystification. Spivak reminds us that all we have is the text (any text) as an unavoidable condition of reading and analysis; the quest for universals, for 'origins', is a chimera.[52]

The text is therefore accepted at its face value in the knowledge that we are dealing with the surface. We may duck beneath the surface while we continue at the same time to play along with the author. We are invited to take part in a game rather than a solemn quest. In doing so we knowingly adopt a 'position' as we might put on fancy dress.

One important consequence of deconstruction when applied to literature in this way, is to redefine 'history' as simply another 'text'; it exists as something else that has been written down or verbalised many times and in various ways. Both Jacobus and Spivak therefore have a very different sense of what history does for literary criticism from Roe, Sales and Lucas; Simpson, as a New Historicist, is taking up a position which endeavours to be of all parties, while slave to none. In Spivak's essay history is clearly another fiction at the mercy of language. Quoting what Wordsworth *wrote* about the French Revolution, Spivak refers us not to the facts, but to 'the text of the September Massacres'.[53] There is no transcendental, unifying structure. Davie's observation, quoted by John Barrell, remains a pertinent insight: 'Wordsworth's words have meaning so long as we trust them.'

In Spivak and Jacobus, therefore, we can detect all the various tools of critical analysis represented in this collection: psychoanalysis, close reading of the text, history, 'historicism', transcendentalism, biography, genre and gender. But none of them is allowed to lead to a formal closure, a concluding paragraph of the kind that formal education habitually tends to require of its well-educated students.

The discussion of 'Resolution and Independence' in this essay rested its case chiefly on the thesis that Wordsworth, because he was who he was, writing when he did, was inspired by fear. One consequence of this fear was that it led him into a kind of writing that emphasised the particular; without mundane details to cling to he was in immanent danger of losing all sense of reality, of disappearing into a world of meaning beyond language where meaning consequently evaporated. This was, and continues to be, a danger that has an existence beyond Wordsworth's poetry; in the course of the twentieth century it has surfaced in the context of the practice of criticism and fragmented the concept of the study of literature as a 'discipline'. The critics represented in this New Casebook are in consequence contributing both to the development in various ways of Wordsworth studies, and to the contemporary debate on the future of literary studies. The latter is a peculiarly Wordsworthian project, and helps to explain why discussion of a poet of the late eighteenth and early nineteenth centuries has remained such an active battle-ground for contesting critical approaches.

NOTES

1. Matthew Arnold, 'Essays in Criticism: Second Series' in *Matthew Arnold Selected Prose*, ed. P. J. Keating (Harmondsworth, 1970), p. 381.

2. Ibid., p. 381.

3. Ibid., p. 385.

4. Ibid., p. 381.

5. Helen Darbishire, 'Wordsworth's *Prelude*', *The Nineteenth Century*, xcix (May 1926), in *Wordsworth: The Prelude*, ed. W. J. Harvey and Richard Gravil (London, 1972), pp. 83–91.

6. William Wordsworth, *Poems in Two Volumes, and Other Poems 1800–1807*, ed. Jared Curtis (New York, 1983), pp. 123–9.

7. William Wordsworth, *Lyrical Ballads*, ed. R. L. Brett and A. R. Jones (London, 1963), p. 71, ll.32–3.

8. Ibid., pp. 7–8.

9. Geoffrey Hartman, 'Wordsworth Revisited', in *The Unremarkable Wordsworth*, ed. Donald G. Marshall (London, 1987), p. 10.

10. *The Letters of William and Dorothy Wordsworth: The Early Years 1787–1805*, ed. Ernest de Selincourt, 2nd edn, revd Chester L. Shaver (Oxford, 1967), pp. 366–7. See also Stephen Gill, *William Wordsworth: A Life* (Oxford, 1989), pp. 203–4.

11. *Poems in Two Volumes, and Other Poems 1800–1807*, ed. Jared Curtis (New York, 1983), p. 323.

12. *Prose Works of William Wordsworth*, ed. A B. Grosart, 3 vols (London, 1876). Quoted in John Purkis, *A Preface to Wordsworth* (London, 1982), p. 150.

13. Donald G. Marshall, 'Foreword', to *The Unremarkable Wordsworth* (London, 1987), pp. vii–viii.

14. William Wordsworth, *The Prelude 1799, 1805, 1850*, ed. Jonathan Wordsworth, M. H. Abrams and Stephen Gill (London, 1979), Book I, ll.326–31, 347–50. See also Timothy Bahti, 'Wordsworth's Rhetorical Theft', in *Romanticism and Language*, ed. Arden Reed (London, 1984), pp. 100–22.

15. William Wordsworth, *The Prelude, 1799, 1805, 1850*, ed. Jonathan Wordsworth, M. H. Abrams and Stephen Gill (London, 1979) Book I, ll.418–20.

16. Ibid., Book X, ll.374–8.

17. *The Prose of William Wordsworth*, ed. W. J. B. Owen and Jane Worthington Smyser (Oxford, 1974), vol. 1, p. 126, ll.133, 137–8; p. 120, ll.40–5.

18. Ibid., p. 130, l.212; p. 142, ll.497–9; p. 120, ll.40–5.

19. William Wordsworth, 'Ode: Intimations of Immortality', in *Poems in Two Volumes, and Other Poems*, ed. Jared Curtis (New York, 1983), p. 272, l.54.

20. *The Prose of William Wordsworth*, 3 vols, ed. W. J. B. Owen and Jane Worthington Smyser (Oxford, 1974), vol. 1, p. 124, l.74, 77, 80; p. 141, ll.441–2.

21. Ibid., p. 134, ll.200–9; p. 141, l.460; p. 150, ll.422–5.

22. Ibid., vol. 2, p. 83, ll.119, 134–5; p. 84, ll.178–9; p. 85, ll.187–8.

23. Ibid., p. 85, ll.191–2.

24. See John Williams, *Wordsworth: Romantic Poetry and Revolution Politics* (Manchester, 1989), pp. 142–4.

25. *The Prose of William Wordsworth*, 3 vols, ed. W. J. B. Owen and Jane Worthington Smyser (Oxford, 1974), vol. 2, p. 85, ll.198–9.

26. *The Poetical Works of William Wordsworth*, 5 vols, ed. E. de Selincourt and Helen Darbishire (Oxford, 1974), vol. 5, p. 118, ll.320–5. See John Williams (above) pp. 60–1.

27. *The Prose Works of William Wordsworth*, ed. W. J. B. Owen and Jane Worthington Smyser (Oxford, 1974), vol. 2, p. 84, l.18.

28. D. D. Devlin, *Wordsworth and the Poetry of Epitaphs* (London, 1980), p. 48.

29. Walter Horatio Pater, 'Wordsworth' (1874), in *Wordsworth: The Prelude*, ed. W. J. Harvey and Richard Gravil (London, 1972), pp. 67–8.

30. Donald G. Marshall, 'Foreword' to *The Unremarkable Wordsworth* (London, 1987), p. vii.

31. Helen Darbishire, 'Wordsworth's *Prelude*', in *Wordworth: The Prelude*, ed. W. J. Harvey and Richard Gravil (London, 1972), p. 87.

32. Geoffrey H. Hartman, *Wordsworth's Poetry 1787–1814* (London, 1987), pp. xi–xx.

33. See p. 34 below.

34. Geoffrey H. Hartman, *Wordsworth's Poetry 1787–1814* (London, 1987), p. xi. See pp. 35–6 above.

35. See p. 53 below.

36. See p. 59 below.

37. Marjory Levinson, *Wordsworth's Great Period Poems* (Cambridge, 1986), p. 1

38. David Simpson's book includes a very lucid account of historicist theory – see pp. 1–21; this quote, p. 19.

39. See p. 65 below.

40. See p. 83 below. See Heather Glen, *Vision and Disenchantment: Blake's Song and Wordsworth's Lyrical Ballads* (Cambridge, 1983); Paul Hamilton, *Wordsworth* (Brighton, 1986); V. G. Kiernan, 'Wordsworth and the People', in *Marxists on Literature* (Harmondsworth, 1975); Raymond Williams, *Culture and Society* (London, 1988). See also Christopher Norris, *Derrida* (London, 1988), p. 19, on the relevance of deconstruction to Lucas's approach.

41. See p. 89 below.

42. See p. 88 below. See also John Lucas, *England and Englishness: Ideas of Nationhood in English Poetry 1688–1900* (London, 1990), p. 1.

43. Raymond Williams, *Problems in Materialism and Culture* (London, 1980), p. 47.

44. See p. 192 below.

45. See p. 96 below.

46. See p. 112 below.

47. Terry Eagleton, *Literary Theory* (London, 1983), p. 133.

48. See p. 136 below.

49. See p. 143 below.

50. See p. 149 below.
51. See pp. 168–9 below.
52. See p. 173 below.
53. See p. 176 below.

1

Wordsworth's Poetry: The Major Lyrics 1801–1807

GEOFFREY HARTMAN

The lyrics composed between 1801 and 1807 were gathered in a collection called *Poems in Two Volumes* (1807). Here some of Wordsworth's most familiar pieces are found: poems on the Solitary Reaper, the Cuckoo, the Daisy, the Daffodils; 'ballads' on Alice Fell and the Sailor's Mother; the better-known sonnets, and such larger-scaled lyrics as 'Resolution and Independence' and the Intimations Ode. It would be wrong to treat this collection as a natural unity. It is, as the title indicates, a composite volume written over a number of years and with no single aim. In this it differs from the *Lyrical Ballads*, many of which, composed in one fervid year, are consciously innovative. Yet the *Poems* of 1807 do have some distinguishing characteristics, and many of them were actually composed in a short period of time, the spring of 1802. I propose to consider individually, yet in the approximate order of their composition, several of the poems spanning the period between the 1800 *Lyrical Ballads* and the *Poems* of 1807, hoping to salvage some gradations that would be lost if the two collections were compared only generally.

'MICHAEL'

'Michael', the last poem to enter *Lyrical Ballads*, was finished December 1800, and is one of Wordsworth's great poems of fo tude. It can set the tone for the group of lyrics on which our consideration will centre: 'Resolution and Independence' (1802), the Intimations Ode (1802–04), the 'Ode to Duty' (1804) and the 'Elegiac Stanzas . . . on Peele Castle' (1805 or 1806).[1] 'Michael' is somewhat of an anomaly, for it might have been as appropriate for *The Prelude* as for *Lyrical Ballads*. It is a 'ballad' in that it begins with a heap of stones with which no one but Wordsworth could have shaped a story, is unenriched by strange events, and intends to delight only a few 'natural hearts'. Forty lines of prologue apologise mildly for its 'homely' and 'rude' character. Yet the prologue also resembles those frames of authorial comment in *The Prelude* which allow episodes to point their own meaning yet link them thematically to the growth of a poet's mind. 'Michael' may have been conceived as Wordsworth was thinking back to his youth and composing drafts for the poem on his own life. It supplements Book V of *The Prelude* and covers the time when children, though still careless of books, begin to develop their sympathetic imaginations by listening to tales like 'Michael'.

As in 'The Thorn', Wordsworth opens in the person of a guide who leads us to a strangely inhuman place (a heap of stones) which his story humanises. 'The Thorn', of course, maintains a tension between inhuman and human significancies. Here the resolution is clearer. The stones are shown to have been the site of a covenant, the birthplace and grave of a human hope. When we have finished the story, they are no longer an accidental or indifferent part of nature, a 'spot . . . shut out from man', but in a landscape where, had we but eyes to see, 'All things . . . speak of Man'.[2] That Wordsworth begins in the person of a guide is apt, for just as nature (or this tale) had originally guided and expanded his imagination, so he intends to lead *our* imaginations to an equal humanity of vision.

Though the story, once we come to it, is cleanly told, with the least intervention of the author, the poet begins by insisting that it is not an object made for its own sake. The story had a function in his life; it is this function he means to explain and perpetuate. He establishes, in fact, a strange identity between himself and his main character. Both Michael and Wordsworth wish to save the land, the one for Luke, the other for the imagination. Michael desires Luke to inherit a land 'free as the wind/That passes over it'; and Wordsworth ͢lls Michael's story for the sake of 'youthful Poets, who *among these ʼs* / Will be my second self when I am gone'. The underlying ͜ern, conscious in Wordsworth as shepherd-poet, is for the

human imagination, which cannot be renewed unless it has a nature
to blend with, not any nature, but *land* as free and old as the hills:

> Those fields, those hills – what could they less? had laid
> Strong hold on his affections, were to him
> A pleasurable feeling of blind love,
> The pleasure which there is in life itself.[3]

Thus 'Michael' is a Pastoral in the most genuine sense: its care of
nature is also a care of the human (as distinguished from super-
naturalistic) imagination. The urgency of its task is heightened by the
spirit of the time. Industrialisation is causing great changes, changes
affecting also the minds of men; and Wordsworth, writing toward
the beginning of this epoch, is not less than prophetic. The Industrial
Revolution, in his eyes, is divorcing man from the earth as effectively
as a debased supernaturalism. He sees that what is happening is
indeed a revolution, cutting men off from their past, and their
imagination from its normal food. The popularity of gothic novel
and German ballad are only two examples of the 'craving for extraordinary incident' and the frantic thirst for novelty which he
decries in the 1800 Preface to *Lyrical Ballads*. He therefore begins his
story with the simplest object imaginable, the most recalcitrant to a
novelty-seeking mind. A truly great, unblunted imagination, Henry
James said, is better served by the minimum of valid suggestion than
by the maximum.

The care of nature is everywhere in 'Michael', at the level of
property and the level of words:

> And when by Heaven's good grace the Boy grew up
> A healthy Lad, and carried in his cheek
> Two steady roses that were five years old;
> Then Michael from a winter coppice cut
> With his own hand a sapling, which he hooped
> With iron, making it throughout in all
> Due requisites a perfect Shepherd's Staff,
> And gave it to the Boy; wherewith equipt
> He as a Watchman oftentimes was plac'd
> At gate or gap, to stem or turn the flock;
> And, to his office prematurely called,
> There stood the Urchin, as you will divine,
> Something between a hindrance and a help;
> And for this cause not always, I believe,
> Receiving from his Father hire of praise.

The description of how Michael makes the boy a staff is Homeric in its respect for weapon or implement; while the staff itself, given at a certain age, is a mark of new or coming dignity, as well as a necessary tool. That Michael cuts it with his own hand bespeaks his direct relation to the lad, and is as significant as when he later asks Luke to lay one stone of the sheepfold 'with thine own hands'. Labour, or the products of labour, are not yet alienated from man as they will be through the Industrial Revolution. The fold, again, is no impersonal object but associates son and flock in the same way as parental affection and love for the land are fused in Michael's heart.[4] The 'patrimonial fields' are made dearer by Luke's presence.

The chaste and natural diction of the narrative is standard; there are greater passages in 'Michael' but none falls below this in its pastoral care for words. We find, of course, slight heightenings; a kind of alliteration and doubling as in 'gate or gap', 'hindrance and a help', 'turn or stem'; but these are colloquial not latinate in origin, and probably echo the old northern tradition of alliterative verse. In respecting them, Wordsworth continues a living idiom in touch with the past. He also diverges slightly from natural word order, just enough to give sinew to the line, and to postpone by the interposition of an adverbial phrase the object (sometimes the subject) of the verb. This serves to throw the emphasis steadily forward in a kind of self-qualifying conversational movement:

> And when by Heaven's grace the Boy grew up
> A healthy Lad,

and so we feel the mind still thinking, still alive, while it narrates. The interpositions, at the same time, by diminishing the transitive effect of the verbs (there is a considerable proportion of intransitive verbs and copulas in any Wordsworth passage), equalise the energy of the various parts of verse-line and sentence. Verbs are naturally strong, emphasising action or event; but the poet works against this to build up the dignity of every phrase in a manner almost formulaic:

> He / as a Watchman / oftentimes / was plac'd
> At gate or gap, / to stem or turn / the flock.

But when we add to this muting of the 'verb active' that the plot of 'Michael' is very slight – the focus is totally on the way Michael's feelings for his son are blended with his feelings for nature, and when

Luke is sent to the city it is to keep the land free, and Luke's fall is treated as quietly as the Boy of Winander's death – a certain doubt may mingle with our admiration for the story. Does not Wordsworth give us a picture of suffering rather than of significant action, and does this not falsify his purpose of expanding the human imagination? The food of hope, as he himself remarks in a poem close to this time, is 'meditated action',[5] yet here there is an absence of action.

It is clear, however, that the story touches on a kind of loss and suffering which occurs in some form to everyone. The changes wrought by the Industrial Revolution are only the occasional cause for the disaster. The *universal* aspect of the loss suffered by Michael is of a hope which has attached itself to a person and seems to die with that person. Through Luke the old man's heart was born again; after Luke's defection, one wonders whether Michael can continue to live. It is then that Wordsworth shows in what way nature is essential to human actions and meditations. His picture of the old man is not simply of suffering or muted despair, but of natural resilience and the habit of fortitude. The inalienable sources of vigour in a man who has lived 'in the strength of nature' are brought out: there is not a hint of the need for or even possibility of a specifically religious consolation. We feel, of course, how close to heartbreak the old man comes; we feel it in the absolute tact with which the poet begins to describe him after the disaster, when Wordsworth is like one who may not come near the quick of the grief, and approaches his subject by generalisation and indirection:

> There is a comfort in the strength of love;
> 'Twill make a thing endurable, which else
> Would overset the brain, or break the heart:
> I have conversed with more than one who well
> Remember the Old Man, and what he was
> Years after he had heard this heavy news.

Yet Michael does not break; he continues his habitual labours, still looks up to sun and cloud, listens to the wind, and will live 'the length of full seven years'.

Though we are told about the seven years in connection with Michael's unfinished labours at the sheepfold, there remains his persistence which suggests an immemorial covenant between man and the land. Michael does not hasten the end, and abides his time without abandoning the land even in imagination. Like the Old

Cumberland Beggar he dies as he has lived: 'in the eye of Nature'. His patriarchal strength, his strange and lonely fidelity, make him the poem's centre. Yet Michael is not an obsolete possibility of the human spirit: the covenant that holds the mind of man to the earth springs only from such as he. Abraham was not unlike Michael. He needed Isaac, his only child, the child of his old age, to perpetuate a similar fidelity. But the land cannot retain its hold on Luke's imagination. Can it, then, retain its hold through Wordsworth, who is restoring the covenant once more by wedding the mind of man and this goodly earth? The poet is Michael's true heir. 'I look into past times', says Wordsworth in a related fragment, 'as prophets look into futurity.'[6]

'RESOLUTION AND INDEPENDENCE'

In February 1801, having sent Charles Lamb the new second volume of *Lyrical Ballads*, and received Lamb's criticisms, Wordsworth dispatches a strong reply to his correspondent. It must have been a pompous, not to say condescending letter, such as he could write only too well. We know of it through Lamb's good-natured report:

> I lately received from Wordsworth a copy of the second volume . . . with excuses for not having made any acknowledgment (of my play) sooner, it being owing to an 'almost insurmountable aversion to letter-writing.' This letter I answered in due form and time . . . adding unfortunately that no single piece had moved me so forcibly as the *Ancient Mariner*, *The Mad Mother*, or the *Lines at Tintern Abbey*. The Post did not sleep a moment. I received almost instantaneously a long letter of four sweating pages from my Reluctant Letter-Writer, the purport of which was, that he was sorry the 2nd vol. had not given me more pleasure (Devil a hint did I give that it had *not pleased me*), and 'was compelled to wish that my range of sensibility was more extended, being obliged to believe that I should receive large influxes of happiness and happy Thoughts' (I suppose from the L. B.) – With a deal of stuff about a certain Union of Tenderness and Imagination, which in the sense he used Imagination was not the characteristic of Shakespeare, but which Milton possessed in a degree far exceeding other Poets: which Union, as the highest species of poetry, and chiefly deserving that name, 'He was most proud to aspire to.'[7]

What concerns us is mainly that 'deal of stuff about a certain Union of Tenderness and Imagination'. Wordsworth uses some such formula repeatedly after this time, often varying the specific terms but always reflecting a distinction similar to that of 'sublime' and 'pathetic'. The formula can guide us in an approach to 'Resolution and Independence', which was composed in May 1802, in the midst of a new surge of poetic activity equalled only by that of 1797–8. It is not difficult to translate Wordsworth's terms into those generally used in this book: the desired union is that of the supernatural and the naturalised (or sympathetic) imaginations. The covenant of mind and nature, the marriage of heaven and earth, centre on the possibility of converting, yet not subduing, the one imagination to the other. The reason why Wordsworth ascribes that union to Milton rather than to Shakespeare is that he saw in Milton his own greatest predecessor, a religious poet who had succeeded in weaning his imagination from sublime and terrible without abandoning them. Shakespeare, however, was a 'human and dramatic' rather than meditative and religious poet. The distinction is openly made in the preface to the *Poems* of 1815. 'The grand store-houses', says Wordsworth, 'of enthusiastic and meditative Imagination, of poetical, as contra-distinguished from human and dramatic Imagination, are the prophetic and lyrical parts of the Holy Scriptures, and the works of Milton; to which I cannot forebear to add those of Spenser.'[8]

Now it is actually Spenser who is more helpful than Milton in clarifying the mode of 'Resolution and Independence'. Its basic situation is Spenser modified. The poet walks out into the country on a beautiful day; he is depressed (in Wordsworth's case depression has given way to joy only to turn back into depression) and comes upon a mysterious sight which restores him. This is the very scheme of Spenser's *Prothalamion*; though what is important here is not the *Prothalamion* but what Spenser has done with the type it represents.[9] Behind Spenser's mode there lies the dream-vision converted so calmly yet daringly into a waking vision that dream blends with reality and an autonomous product is created which we rather helplessly define as 'allegory'. Spenser walking along the Thames near London's bricky towers is no dreamer, unless we adduce Goethe's definition of the poet as one who dreams with open eyes. For without any 'methought I saw' he views in open sight a marriage procession in which the bridesmaids are water-nymphs:

> All lovely daughters of the flood thereby
> With goodly greenish locks all loose untyde,

and the brides-to-be are swans floating down the Thames as fair and white as Leda. This is a direct exercise of the mythopoeic imagination in the context of a realistic scene, and no facile retranslation of the swans into the barges that carried the Lady Elizabeth and the Lady Katherine Somerset can undo the metamorphosis. It is Spenser's courage we admire, his passing from personal cares at court to a magnificence which redeems the courtly life, but which stands or falls with his unashamed direct exercise of the poetical faculty. Behind this faculty, however, here so personally exerted, is the 'prothalamic' imagination in general, which brings together not only man and woman, but also myth and reality, human and divine, nature and human nature.

This 'union' is also achieved by 'Resolution and Independence' in very different circumstances. On the deserted moor, a man appears to Wordsworth ' unawares', and the sight is ghostly enough to make him suspect a divine apparition. Yet though he tends toward apocalyptic thoughts, a precarious intermingling of vision and matter-of-fact is all the while maintained. Wordsworth's mode differs, of course, from that established by Spenser's fiat. It is not even a mode, strictly speaking, but an uncertain consolidation of thoughts. Spenser's refrain, for example, 'Sweet Themmes, runne softly, till I end my song', is the very emblem of literary and natural continuity, and indicates by its steady return how much time is at man's disposal, how everything will flow along in order and degree, and how the world is too well established on the flood for any 'end' to be feared. But Wordsworth's greatest lyrics are acts of a living mind open to the terror of discontinuity. His encounter with the Leech-gatherer is unrelieved by myth or allegory or any steadying indulgence. The waters do not flow easily; the strange repetitions (sts XVII ff.) have no aim that is not mental and precarious; and the continuity, even on the level of rhythm (that last, draggle-tailed alexandrine), is uncertain. We feel the poet's distraught perplexity, as if this could not be, or could not last.

How open Wordsworth's mind is in 'Resolution and Independence', how receptive to new thought even during composition, can be shown more specifically. Though he begins with an emotion recollected in tranquillity, the tranquillity soon disappears and his mind not only recalls the past but also responds once more to what it has recalled. The past event is not so totally in the past, not so determinate, that it cannot confront the poet in a new way. This new and further confrontation must then be honoured in addition to the old. There is the question of the poet's original recognition, and then of his insight as he tells, so to say, his story back to himself. The two do not coincide in all respects.

Wordsworth's earlier and formal recognition is found in the concluding stanzas of the poem and is expressed in part as an absorbing mental echo (st. XVI) and image (st. XIX). I quote the latter:

> While he was talking thus, the lonely place,
> The old Man's shape, and speech, all troubled me:
> In my mind's eye I seem'd to see him pace
> About the weary moors continually,
> Wandering about alone and silently.
> While I these thoughts within myself pursued,
> He, having made a pause, the same discourse renewed.

An *after-image* of this kind plays an important role in many of Wordsworth's poems. It expresses the possibility of the renewal (or at least recurrence) of a certain experience by including that possibility in the very structure of the experience. As a mental reflex, the after-image elongates the encounter, and as an image of something, it may also suggest an indefinitely extended action. Not any action, of course: it is the image, itself repeated, of a repeated and persistent action which moves the Leech-gatherer closer to the figure of the Wandering Jew and brings about Wordsworth's recognition of his firmness.

The after-image or echo may occur at a distance from the original experience, and still be part of it. If in 'The Solitary Reaper' the inward echo follows immediately on the actual hearing of the girl's song, in 'I wandered lonely as a cloud' the daffodils flash in the mind some time after the poet has seen them. The lapse of time seems to be a relatively unimportant factor, since Wordsworth's point is that the renewal of the image – or of the inner person through the image – occurs despite time. The overcoming of time can be shown by either a delayed or an immediate response. When Wordsworth says of the cuckoo, hailing its return, 'I have heard, / I hear thee and rejoice', the doubling (reflecting) is immediate. Yet since in listening to its call the poet *begets again* the golden time of his youth (st. VII), the simple repetition of 'hear' together with the tense change from past to present, indicates in one formula his inward response, and the renewal of the past in the present – in short, the gentle and immediately renovating influence of nature.

The after-image could be defined as a re-cognition that leads to recognition. It is found as early as 'The Ruined Cottage', in which the poet describes the echoes left in him by the pedlar's story.[10] The *Lyrical Ballads* also show the poet or his personae responding to the very incidents they describe, yet no such *formalised* structure of recognition appears. Only one lyric before 1802 depicts the after-image as a formal part of the structure of experience, yet does this so well that chronology seems unimportant. 'The Two April Mornings', in which again an old and a young man meet, is totally conceived in terms of a contrast between recurrence in nature and recurrent powers of feeling. An April dawn brings back the memory of another April dawn thirty years ago, when Matthew met a girl resembling his dead daughter yet 'did not wish her mine'. The poem, like 'Tintern Abbey', is realistic (compared to the lighter lyrics) in its acknowledgement of time, for it seems to indicate a limit to nature's renovating influence. But it ends with a beautiful reflective doubling similar to that which concludes Wordsworth's meeting with the Leech-gatherer:

> Matthew is in his grave, yet now,
> Methinks I see him stand,
> As at that moment, with his bough
> Of wilding in his hand.

I come, then, to the second kind of insight, in which the mind moves under the renewed (recollected) rather than original impact of an experience.[11] Though the after-image is often delayed, and so approaches the second kind of recognition, some distinctions can be made. The second kind of recognition is based on an experience to which the mind has already formally reacted. Moreover, while this initial reaction (an after-image) helps to dissolve the finiteness of the experience, the renewed recognition is more complex, and suggests both its continuity with the after-image (thus increasing the sense of infinite repercussion) and a possible discontinuity. The second type of recognition is, in fact, an unpredictably organic movement of the poet's mind in the very moment of recollection, yet Wordsworth allows it to enter into the experience he is remembering. Before an event which includes his first insight has been fully described, a second insight forestalls and even transcends it. The most dramatic instance of such displacement is *Prelude VI*.592 ff., and in 'Resolution and Independence' we find a similar, though less dramatic re-vision:

There was a roaring in the wind all night;
The rain came heavily and fell in floods;
But now the sun is rising calm and bright;
The birds are singing in the distant woods;
Over his own sweet voice the Stock-dove broods;
The Jay makes answer as the Magpie chatters;
And all the air is fill'd with pleasant noise of waters.

All things that love the sun are out of doors;
The sky rejoices in the morning's birth;
The grass is bright with rain-drops; on the moors
The hare is running races in her mirth;
And with her feet she from the plashy earth
Raises a mist; that, glittering in the sun,
Runs with her all the way, wherever she doth run.

I was a Traveller then upon the moor;
I saw the hare that rac'd about with joy;
I heard the woods, and distant waters, roar;
Or heard them not, as happy as a Boy:
The pleasant season did my heart employ:
My old remembrances went from me wholly;
And all the ways of men, so vain and melancholy.

In line 3 the poet crosses spontaneously from the past tense to the present and does not return to the past till stanza III, 'I was a Traveller then upon the moor'. His mind, rejoicing in the beautiful dawn like birds, sky and hare, seems to have imperceptibly entered its own conception.[12] This crossing over, from past to present, happens during composition, and shows that time itself can still dissolve at the touch and even the mere memory of nature.

Yet in the original incident the poet's extreme joy was followed by a reversal: 'As high as we have mounted in delight / In our dejection do we sink as low' (st. IV). Knowing this, Wordsworth cannot entirely liberate himself from the fear of a reversal even in the moment of recollection. If he passes with line 3 beyond mutuality, for his mind can still dissolve time, or the barriers between past and present, his verses continue to reflect a slight hemming which is expressed by the repeatedly end-stopped (semicolon) lines. In stanza II, with the picture of the hare, the mood overflows and is close to breaking down the end-stopped line; but it is still restrained by residual stops and a certain syntactical heaviness. In stanza III, then, the semicolons return (they lessen in frequency but continue to dominate the rhythm till stanza VIII); the past tense is reinstated; and we sense – fully now – the burdened mind, as it revolves heavy thoughts and anticipates the reversal of which it eventually speaks. When the present tense returns momentarily in stanza v ('Even such a happy Child of earth am I . . .') it does not betoken a spontaneous transcendence of time but reports the speech of a man vainly reasoning with himself.

'Resolution and Independence' is the most characteristic of Wordsworth's greater lyrics because of this openness of mind which makes it in mode what it is in subject: a self-confrontation. Though it is proper to refer to the *Prothalamion* as the nearest literary model, Wordsworth restores the archaic situation from which both his and Spenser's poem derive. Behind the dream-sight is the prophetic situation, the 'chance' omen sent against a man whether or not he can interpret it. The uncertainties of interpretation in Wordsworth's case are remarkable; I can only repeat that though a steadying recognition is gained from his meeting with the Leech-gatherer – an open meeting indeed, beside a pool 'bare to the eye of heaven', and radically Protestant in its sense that nothing stands between man and man except God – the possibility of reversal, of recognition turning into peripety, is never absent.[13] It can be urged that the poem's high point comes not at the end but at the beginning, when the heart *is* renewed toward nature and enters the recollected image.

THE INTIMATIONS ODE

Once more, to the poet of the Intimations Ode, a thought of grief comes on a fine spring morning. And, again as in 'Resolution and Independence', instead of saying immediately it was this or that which grieved him, Wordsworth goes on to think aloud, as if thinking and grief had now an intimate link, and the one would always issue, at some point, in the other. This time, however, the recognition that restores him is elusive. There is no Leech-gatherer: it is all a dialogue of the soul with itself in the presence of nature. The joy must spring from deep within thought; the consolation perhaps from the very grief he feels. We sense the constant possibility of reversal even more than in 'Resolution and Independence.'

The irregular rhythms, a privilege of the ode form, work independently of specific stanza or stage of argument to express the flux and reflux of a mind for which reversal is no longer simply the structure of experience but its own structure, its very *style* of thought. Wordsworth does mention in the third stanza a 'timely utterance' which gave him relief, but what happened is kept vague, and the event, in any case, could not have been determining, since the grief returns in the next stanza. There is, finally, again encouraged by the ode (the sublimest of the lyric genres), a larger pattern of influx and reflux: even though each stanza tends to mingle rising and falling rhythms, stanzas III and IV are, as it were, a 'Counter-turn' to stanzas I and II, while stanza V is a kind of epode or 'stand' in which the passion seems to level out into a new generalisation or withdrawal from personal immediacy.[14] Related to this larger pattern is the Ode's admixture of reflection, question, invocation, petition, and praise, which approaches the Psalms in sublimity, and also recalls the confessional style of St. Augustine.

The subject of the Ode, Lionel Trilling has said, is growing up. Yet though it is true that the subject is conceived, except for the organ- ising myth, in naturalistic terms, Wordsworth's high style and the religious intensity of his emotions must be considered. There is a Hebrew prayer which praises God's mercy in restoring the soul every morning to its body, even as He restores it to the dead. Some of the terror of discontinuity behind the gratitude of this prayer is also in Wordsworth's Ode. The poet fears a decay of his 'genial' responses to nature, and he fears that this decay has affected his powers of renovation. Growing up is not enough; the development of abstract sympathies is not enough; these must be linked, else they cannot be actualised, to the renewal of earlier feelings, to *joy* in nature.[15] It is easy to gain the world and to lose one's soul.

This deeper concern with renewal explains why Wordsworth is so affected by what appears to be a very little thing: a wrong echo. On this May morning, his heart responds with a thought of grief instead of equal gaiety. All other creatures have the proper harmonic echo, the immediate internal response to nature's influence. The young lambs bound 'As to the tabor's sound' – there is no tabor, but Wordsworth sees their joy as a responsive joy. He calls them and the other participants in nature's jubilee 'blessed Creatures': 'And God created . . . every living creature that moveth . . . and God saw that it was good. And God blessed them, saying, Be fruitful and multiply.' God responded to them, God *recognised* them, but the poet's heart is dull. We remember the opening of 'Resolution and Independence', where everything echoes and responds: the Jay to the Magpie, the Stockdove to its own call, and even the glittering mist to the hare wherever the latter runs.

That Wordsworth should take a momentary grief as an omen questioning his power to be renewed, to be 'naturally' renewed, is typical of his spiritual state at this time. *The Prelude* also begins with a failed response (overcome more lightly), and the fear that his 'genial spirits' might be decaying was already quietly expressed in the meditations of 'Tintern Abbey'. We have to do with a recurrent, not an unusual, fear. The Ode, in fact, begins with a general statement, and only then proceeds to mention the particular moment which perhaps was the occasion of that generality.[16] Each failure of joy, each feeling of indifference or alienation, newly accuses the poet. Much later in his life, when he seems to be more resigned to what he here still resists, and an 'Evening of Extraordinary Splendour' surprises him, he will querulously demand: 'This glimpse of glory, why renewed?'[17] But in the Ode he rises to an answering vigour of imagination.

There is first the 'timely utterance' which frees him for other utterances:

> The Cataracts blow their trumpets from the steep,
> No more shall grief of mine the season wrong.

The second verse is surely the inner call by which, in this restored continuum of inner and outer events, he replies to the cataracts. It is followed by a movement like the Psalmist's 'Awake the dawn', when he accepts the fact that the initiative is with him, and indicates his readiness to join 'in thought' what others may feel at heart. 'Thou Child of Joy / Shout round me, let me hear thy shouts . . . ' 'Then, sing ye Birds, sing, sing a joyous song'. There are, finally, those 'intimations of immortality' which remind him of actual continuities and permanent points of relation with the Nature he has known.

These affirmative movements are interrupted, of course, by renewed questionings and qualifications (extending even into imagery and rhythm), so that the continuity of the Ode is as precarious as the 'natural piety' which is its subject. But though this precariousness is just – the Ode is prayer as well as celebration – one contradiction seems not to have been expressed clearly enough by Wordsworth, which may perhaps explain why so many have felt the Ode to be confused, or not completely unified. There are, if we look closely, two quite different 'intimations of immortality'. Whereas one implies the mortality of nature:

> questionings
> Of sense and outward things,
> Fallings from us, vanishings;
> Blank misgivings of a Creature
> Moving about in worlds not realised . . .

the other implies its immortality:

> the primal sympathy
> Which having been must ever be.

In stanza IX especially, when Wordsworth says that his thanksgivings are less for the visionary gleam than for the visionary dreariness, and goes on to describe the latter as:

> those first affections,
> Those shadowy recollections,
> Which, be they what they may,
> Are yet the fountain light of all our day,
> Are yet a master light of all our seeing;

it is hard to follow him. He seems to be wilfully confusing moments of darkness and fear in which nature seemed alien to the child with moments of splendour and beauty which first developed the child's affections and drew them to nature in a more intimate way.

The confusion is wilful, I think, and may be resolved; but not by the Ode alone. It needs an understanding of Wordsworth's conception of the progress of the soul. Wordsworth shares with St. Augustine the knowledge of a personal mercy which is part of a mercy to mankind. Both have been rescued 'unto life'; but life for Wordsworth is the freeing of his soul from solipsism. Before the child is naturalised, and sporadically at later times, its soul moves in another world than 'nature', or if in nature, then one that is coloured by a sublime and terrible imagination. The soul's eventual turning to nature is therefore a real conversion, and proof of self-transcending powers. Man's growth into humanity is founded on this conversion. A child is an 'Alien scatter'd from the Clouds', but the strength which its imagination exhibits in going out of itself and blending with a lesser nature is the source of all further strength: it is for Wordsworth *the* act of re-generation. Every step in growing up is but an extension of this constitutive sympathy. The mature man, therefore, bases his faith in self-transcendence on the ease or unconsciousness with which the apocalyptic imagination turned in childhood toward life. Then the crisis was to go from self-love (unconscious) to love of nature, and now it is to go from self-love (conscious) to love of man. Each transition is precarious; but the second cannot occur without the first, and the first is the sign that the second is possible. 'The Child is the father of the Man.'

By the time the poet understands nature's role, only intimations of his unself-conscious powers of relationship remain. The nature to which he appeals in his great envoi:

> And oh ye Fountains, Meadows, Hills, and Groves,
> Think not of any severing of our loves!

is dying to him; and the perilous progress of the Ode comes from Wordsworth's resistance to this appearance of death. I say 'appearance', because, were nature really lost to him, the excursive or self-renewing vigour of his soul might be impugned. Wordsworth cannot give up nature without giving up his faith in renovation. The whole issue turns on faith and hope.

From Geoffrey Hartman, *Wordsworth's Poetry, 1787–1814* (London, 1987) pp. 259–77.

NOTES

[Geoffrey Hartman's criticism is based on the premise that Wordsworth's poetry reveals a preoccupation with relating the numinous power of imagination, or vision, to the physical world. The success of *Wordsworth's Poetry 1787–1814* in unveiling the tensions at work when Wordsworth sought thus to 'humanise' visionary experience, played a significant part in establishing the agenda for Wordsworth criticism after the mid 1960s. *Wordsworth's Poetry* displayed a new sensitivity to the text, detailing nuances of meaning brought about by the subtleties of word play and shifts in grammatical form. The importance of historical context for literary analysis was marginalised; what Hartman stressed was the humanising presence of the poet in the text. He developed this idea as a means of exploring the relationship between natural objects conjured up in Wordsworth's 'visionary gleams'. Hartman's own description of his critical aim is 'to describe Wordsworth's "consciousness of consciousness"' ('Retrospect', in *Wordsworth's Poetry*, p. xiii). Ed.]

1. The 'Ode to Duty' and 'Elegaic Stanzas' are discussed in the next section of Hartman's book (pp. 277–91) which is not included here for reasons of space. [Ed.]

2. See fragments printed in *The Poetical Works of William Wordsworth*, ed. E. de Selincourt and Helen Darbishire (Oxford, 1940–9), vol. 2, pp. 479–80, vol. 5, p. 401.

3. So 1832; the version of 1800 is more crudely emphatic, and reads: 'These fields, these hills, / Which were his living Being, even more / Than his own Blood.' Unless otherwise stated, in this chapter all extracts from the poems of 1800 are quoted from the version of 1800, and all extracts from the 1807 *Poems* from the version of 1807.

4. See also Wordsworth's letter to Thomas Poole, 9 April 1801: 'I have attempted to give a picture of a man, of strong and lively sensibility, agitated by two of the most powerful affections of the human heart; the parental affection, and the love of property, *landed* property.' *The Early Letters of William and Dorothy Wordsworth*, ed. E. de Selincourt (Oxford, 1935), p. 266.

5. *The Poetical Works of William Wordsworth*, ed. E. de Selincourt and Helen Darbishire (Oxford, 1940–9), vol. 5, p. 287 (*Excursion* IX. 20f.), originally in MS 18a.

6. Ibid., vol. 2, p. 480.

7. *The Letters of Charles Lamb*, ed. F. L. Lucas (London, 1935), vol. 1, p. 246.

8. *The Poetical Works of William Wordsworth*, ed. E. de Selincourt and Helen Darbishire (Oxford, 1940–9), vol. 2, pp. 439–40.

9. Dorothy and William spent the morning of 25 April 1802, reading the *Prothalamion*; his poem was begun 3 May. The stanza form, of course, though not un-Spenserian in mood, is not that of the *Prothalamion*: Chaucer and also Chatterton's 'Balade of Charitie' may have exerted some influence on it. For the Chaucerian influence, and the allegorical prototype in general, see E. M. Conran, in *PMLA*, 75 (1960), 66–74. A. F. Potts suggests Spenserian influences on other poems of the period in *Studies in Philology*, 29 (1932), 607–16.

10. See especially *The Poetical Works of William Wordsworth*, ed. E. de Selincourt and Helen Darbishire (Oxford, 1940–9), vol. 5, p. 400, fragment 1. Both *Prelude* VI. 592 and *Prelude* XIV. 63, which are studied in detail in Part II [of Hartman's book], could be considered as after-images, and become 'spots of time' in so far as they reach through intermediate tracts of time. The Snowdon vision itself is, moreover, almost a paradigm case of doubling. I leave the question of after-image, mirror-image, and eidetic image to a further essay. Cf. Gerhard Hensel, *Das Optische bei Wordsworth* (Marburg, 1930), and pp. 165–8 [of Hartman's book].

11. This means, unless the occasion is an actual revisiting of the scene as in 'Tintern Abbey', the mind is moved more by itself, by its own recollection, than by the original event. Even in 'Tintern Abbey' the mind is really comparing two reactions and being moved toward a self-recognition, an omen of its progressive destiny.

12. A similar thing occurs in stanza II of the Intimations Ode. The sudden rise in feelings of 'Liberty and Power' as Wordsworth comes to the moon indicates also a dissolving of barriers between past and present, or a return of the childhood power to go out and participate in the life of things. 'The moon is treated', says Cleanth Brooks, 'as if she were the speaker himself in his childhood, seeing the visionary gleam as she looks round her with joy' (*The Well Wrought Urn* [New York, 1947], ch. 7). But the child's participation in the life of nature is, of course, unself-conscious: cf. stanza III of the present poem: 'I heard the woods and distant waters roar; / Or heard them not, as happy as a boy.'

13. Peripity: a sudden change of fortune; in this case the possibility that the 'steadying recognition' might as easily turn into a disconcerting sense of strangeness and alienation. [Ed.]

14. My comment, because of the complexity of the transitions, is only roughly correct. Stanza VI, for example, is a subtle counter-turn to stanza V; so that, in a sense, there is no 'stand'. (The edition of 1807, by the way, has no stanza numberings.) 'The ode was intended for such readers only as had been accustomed to watch the flux and reflux of their inmost nature, to venture at times into the twilight realms of consciousness, and to feel a deep interest in modes of inmost being' (Coleridge, *Biographia Literaria*, ch. 22).

15. Coleridge, in his dialogue with the Intimations Ode, uses 'joy' to mean the feeling that enables or accompanies a living, regenerative contact with nature (see the Dejection Ode).

16. The supposition that the first two stanzas are the 'utterance' mentioned in stanza III is strongly supported by Hirsch, *Wordsworth and Schelling* (New Haven, 1960), pp. 150–1.

17. *The Poetical Works of William Wordsworth*, ed. E. de Selincourt and Helen Darbishire (Oxford, 1940–9), vol. 4, p. 12, *Evening Voluntaries*, IX (composed 1817).

2

Protest and Poetry 1793–1798: 'Jacobin' Poems?

NICHOLAS ROE

I have seen the Baker's horse
As he had been accustomed at your door
Stop with the loaded wain, when o'er his head
Smack went the whip, and you were left, as if
You were not born to live, or there had been   5
No bread in all the land. Five little ones,
They at the rumbling of the distant wheels
Had all come forth, and, ere the grove of birch
Concealed the wain, into their wretched hut
They all return'd. While in the road I stood   10
Pursuing with involuntary look
The Wain now seen no longer, to my side
[   ] came, a pitcher in her hand
Filled from the spring; she saw what way my eyes
Were turn'd, and in a low and fearful voice   15
She said – that wagon does not care for us –
The words were simple, but her look and voice
Made up their meaning, and bespoke a mind
Which being long neglected, and denied
The common food of hope, was now become   20
Sick and extravagant, – by strong access
Of momentary pangs driv'n to that state
In which all past experience melts away,
And the rebellious heart to its own will
Fashions the laws of nature.[1]   25

Wordsworth's 'Baker's Cart' fragment was probably composed between late 1796 and March 1797. It immediately precedes work on
'The Ruined Cottage' and anticipates some details and circumstances
of the later poem. A first glance might also suggest that Wordsworth's
fragment corresponds to Coleridge's account of 'helpless Women
. . . "Bold from despair and prostitute for Bread" ' in *On the Present
War*.[2] But the 'Baker's Cart' has no political or social purpose
comparable to Coleridge's lecture or to Wordsworth's own earlier
poetry of protest. The wain is 'loaded' as usual, the land is evidently
one of plenty, and the horse is 'accustomed' to stop at the door of the
hut. It is the violation of customary routine – 'Smack went the whip'
– that prompts Wordsworth's interest, which turns upon the figure
left behind 'as if [She] were not born to live, or there had been / No
bread in all the land'. '[A]s if': Wordsworth gestures towards famine
as a possible explanation for what has happened, but apparently by
way of showing that it is not so in this case. The 'Five little ones'
come out expectantly when the wagon is heard, and silently retire
into their hut before it has disappeared again. Their pathetic appeal,
which in 1793 Paine, or Frend, or Cooper, or Wordsworth might
have used for protest, now elicits no comment at all.[3]

Up to line 10, the poem describes a routine inexplicably upset as
the wain moves off, drawing after it Wordsworth's 'involuntary
look'. The following lines mediate between the poet's blank confusion and the woman's state of mind, so that the poem as a whole
moves from incidental disruption to inner derangement. The 'Smack'
of the whip drives off the horse, but it finds a further report in the
woman's 'sick and extravagant' mind,

> driv'n to that state
> In which all past experience melts away,
> And the rebellious heart to its own will
> Fashions the laws of nature.

Her wilful fashioning of those 'laws' appears in her simple words
'– that wagon does not care for us –', irrationally attributing her own
desolation to the wain's desertion of routine. But in doing so she also
identifies Wordsworth's 'law of nature' in the human kindness or
'care' which her existence has been denied.

The 'Baker's Cart' opens with an incident that apparently has
potential for protest: "Tis against that / Which we are fighting',
Beaupuy might have said. Rather than finding its meaning in famine
or poverty, though, it turns inwards to discover a heart goaded into

strife against its own nature. This imaginative involution from external circumstances to inner life is a paradigm for Wordsworth's larger development between 1793 and 1796 from poet of protest to poet of human suffering. It also offers a clue to understanding the perplexed response to some of the poems Wordsworth wrote during the next two years, when they were published in the first edition of *Lyrical Ballads* in September 1798.

Dr Burney reviewed *Lyrical Ballads* for the *Monthly Review* in June 1799. He was confused by most of the poems, but 'The Last of the Flock' caused him particular difficulty. 'We are not told how the wretched hero of this piece became so poor', Burney says:

> He had, indeed, ten children: but so have many cottagers; and ere the tenth child is born, the eldest begin to work, and help, at least, to maintain themselves. No oppression is pointed out; nor are any means suggested for his relief. If the author be a wealthy man, he ought not to have suffered this poor peasant to part with *the last of the flock*. What but an Agrarian law can prevent poverty from visiting the door of the indolent, injudicious, extravagant, and, perhaps, vicious? and is it certain that rigid equality of property as well as of laws could remedy this evil?[4]

It is easy to laugh at Burney, but his misreading of 'The Last of the Flock' does help to define the relation of some of Wordsworth's ballads to contemporary ideas of 'Jacobin' poetry. Three points that Burney makes are correct: 'We are not told how the wretched hero . . . became so poor', he says. 'No oppression is pointed out; nor are any means suggested for his relief.' His mistake was to anticipate Wordsworth's concern with 'oppression' and 'relief', and that the poem would advocate a 'levelling' Agrarian law: he was looking for a protest poem, and was puzzled to find that Wordsworth's ballad resisted his expectations.[5]

Burney's comments on 'The Last of the Flock' may well have been influenced by an article upon 'Jacobin Poetry' in the second issue of the *Anti-Jacobin; or, Weekly Examiner* which appeared on 27 November 1797. The purpose of this discussion was to define a particular treatment of suffering figures characteristic of 'Jacobin' poetry, by way of ridiculing the political motives of the poet:

> A human being, in the lowest state of penury and distress, is a treasure to a [poet] of this cast – He contemplates, he examines, he turns him in every possible light, with a view of extracting from the variety of his wretchedness, new topics of invective against the pride of property. He

indeed (if he is a true Jacobin) refrains from *relieving* the object of his compassionate contemplation; as well knowing that every diminution from the general mass of human misery, must proportionably diminish the force of his argument.[6]

The *Anti-Jacobin* took Southey's 'Widow' as an example of this 'Jacobin' mode, and parodied its clumsy and inappropriate sapphic metre in 'The Friend of Humanity and the Knife-grinder'. Like Wordsworth's beggar in 'An Evening Walk', Southey's widow is described with melodramatic relish and then abandoned to her misery and death. The *Anti-Jacobin* parody indulges a comparable wish to contemplate wretchedness, and wittily frustrates it. The poem forms a dialogue in which the Friend of Humanity repeatedly interrogates the knife-grinder to extract his 'Pitiful story',

> 'Tell me, Knife-grinder, how you came to grind knives?
> Did some rich man tyranically use you?'

– but his solicitude is rebuffed by the knife-grinder's tale of tavern brawls and the stocks, and by his concluding remark: 'for my part, I never love to meddle / With Politics, Sir.' The Friend of Humanity reproaches him as a 'Wretch! whom no sense of wrongs can rouse to vengeance', overturns his grinding-wheel, *'and exit in a transport of republican enthusiasm and universal philanthropy'*.[7]

The *Anti-Jacobin* parody of 'The Widow' is amusing and, in this instance, rightly sends up Southey's experiments with metre. It is also particularly astute for identifying a treatment of human suffering that is common to 'Jacobin' or protest poetry, and Wordsworth's 'tragic super-tragic' in *The Prelude*, Book Eight:

> Then, if a widow staggering with the blow
> Of her distress was known to have made her way
> To the cold grave in which her husband slept,
> One night, or haply more than one – through pain
> Or half-insensate impotence of mind –
> The fact was caught at greedily, and there
> She was a visitant the whole year through,
> Wetting the turf with never-ending tears,
> And all the storms of heaven must beat on her.[8]

'The fact was caught at greedily': in 'An Evening Walk' 'distress' is the material for sensational elaboration not compassionate understanding, and in protest poetry it feeds 'invective against the pride of property'. In each case the human experience is subordinate to an ulterior motive, but in 'The Last of the Flock' this is apparently not so – hence Dr Burney's bafflement. The shepherd is in 'the lowest state of penury and distress' as the *Anti-Jacobin* required. Wordsworth's encounter with the weeping man leads to the questions expected of a friend to humanity,

> I follow'd him, and said, 'My friend
> What ails you? wherefore weep you so?'[9]

– apparently to 'extract . . . the variety of his wretchedness'. But no political 'invective' follows. In 'The Last of the Flock' Wordsworth seems deliberately to conform to the *Anti-Jacobin* pattern of protest poetry, only to disappoint the anticipated attack on 'pride of property'. As in the earlier 'Baker's Cart' fragment, Wordsworth's concern in 'The Last of the Flock' appears where he diverges from the circumstantial 'fact' of distress towards an imaginative understanding of the shepherd's existence.

Burney's literal observation that 'the author . . . ought not to have suffered this poor peasant to part with *the last of the flock*' may, as Mary Jacobus says, be a 'naïve' index of Wordsworth's success 'in making us respond to the poetry of passion as if to passion itself'.[10] But when read in the light of contemporary expectations about political poetry, his comment is the less simplistic for indicating Wordsworth's success in the poems of 1797–8 in realising the imaginative potential of protest. Clearly, this approach is effective for only some of the poems Wordsworth published in *Lyrical Ballads*; it is not possible to read 'The Idiot Boy' or 'The Complaint of a Forsaken Indian Woman' as modified social protest, although the emotional and imaginative concerns of both poems might be related back through 'The Ruined Cottage' and 'The Female Vagrant' to the compassionate politics of earlier years. The milieu of protest does have a bearing, though, on a poem Wordsworth wrote at about the same time as the 'Baker's Cart' late in 1796 or early 1797, 'Old Man Travelling':

> The little hedge-row birds,
> That peck along the road, regard him not.
> He travels on, and in his face, his step,
> His gait, is one expression; every limb,
> His look and bending figure, all bespeak   5
> A man who does not move with pain, but moves

With thought – He is insensibly subdued
To settled quiet: he is one by whom
All effort seems forgotten, one to whom
Long patience has such mild composure given,   10
That patience now doth seem a thing, of which
He hath no need. He is by nature led
To peace so perfect, that the young behold
With envy, what the old man hardly feels.
– I asked him whither he was bound, and what   15
The object of his journey; he replied
'Sir! I am going many miles to take
'A last leave of my son, a mariner,
'Who from a sea-fight has been brought to Falmouth,
'And there is dying in an hospital.'   20

As with his comments on 'The Last of the Flock', Burney misreads
'Old Man Travelling' as a poem of protest – this time against the war
with France. '[F]inely drawn', he says, 'but the termination seems
pointed against the war; from which, however, we are now no more
able to separate ourselves, than Hercules was to free himself from the
shirt of Nessus' – and he adds by way of a final perverse hint: 'The
old traveller's son might have died by disease.'[11] The mariner is
evidently 'dying in an hospital' of war wounds, but his father's mild
words are not explicitly 'pointed against the war' at all. Burney is
wide of the mark, but his comments once again suggest how 'Old
Man Travelling' is related to protest poetry, while transcending the
political and social focus of that genre.

The shepherd in 'The Last of the Flock' and the woman in the
'Baker's Cart' are consumed and distracted by their experiences; like
Mortimer in *The Borderers* they are beings 'by pain and thought
compelled to live'. Wordsworth's old man resembles Mortimer as 'a
shadowy thing', but he has passed the boundary of anguished consciousness to exist in profound passivity, 'insensibly subdued / To
settled quiet'. His self-resignation leads to transcendence of self, 'by
nature led' Wordsworth writes,

To peace so perfect, that the young behold
With envy, what the old man hardly feels.

His quietus is enviable but it is not explicable. Wordsworth's questions, 'whither . . . and what / The object of his journey', seek a
rational understanding of the old man's existence, and his reply
yields a few circumstantial details that are irrelevant to the preceding

imaginative 'sketch'. The same might be said of 'The Discharged
Soldier' and 'The Leech-gatherer' in each of which an imaginative
comprehension of the solitary figure is accompanied by what Jonathan
Wordsworth has called 'the border compulsion to ask questions':

> While thus we travelled on I did not fail
> To question him of what he had endured
> From war & battle & the pestilence[12]

– and, in the later poem,

> 'How is it that you live, and what is it you do?'[13]

Such questioning may reflect Wordsworth's intuition that the old
man, the soldier, and the leech-gatherer possess an ultimate wisdom
beyond the bourn dividing life and death, but his interrogation might
formerly have been designed to 'extract' a tale comparable to those
of the sailor and Female Vagrant in 'Salisbury Plain'. Looking back
over Wordsworth's development after 1793, the most characteristic
perceptions and strategies of his imaginative poetry can be seen to
have evolved out of political and social protest, as much as from
eighteenth-century literary precursors such as Langhorne, Goldsmith,
Thomson. In that process the political imperative is succeeded by
imaginative receptivity as the dominant mode of Wordsworth's writing, and the social victim gradually transformed into a figure of
monitory wisdom. So it is that Thomas Cooper's unhappy conscript,
'cut off from his peaceful habitation and domestic Society' and put
to 'murdering his fellow Creatures', returns as if from another world
in the ghostly form of Wordsworth's discharged soldier:

> He was in stature tall,
> A foot above man's common measure tall,
> And lank, and upright. There was in his form
> A meagre stiffness. You might almost think
> That his bones wounded him. His legs were long,
> So long and shapeless that I looked at them
> Forgetful of the body they sustained.
> His arms were long & lean; his hands were bare;
> His visage, wasted though it seem'd, was large
> In feature; his cheeks sunken; and his mouth
> Shewed ghastly in the moonlight. From behind
> A mile-stone propp'd him, & his figure seem'd
> Half-sitting & half-standing. I could mark
> That he was clad in military garb,

Though faded yet entire. His face was turn'd
Towards the road, yet not as if he sought
For any living thing. He appeared
Forlorn and desolate, a man cut off
From all his kind, and more than half detached
From his own nature.[14]

The conscript who was forcibly separated from his family is trans-
figured in Wordsworth's soldier as 'a man cut off / From all his kind',
and almost abstracted from 'his own nature' altogether. His ghastly
figure has acquired an emblematic presence beyond the 'simple fact'
of his personal history, placing him in a distinguished line that
includes the 'olde man' resting at the stile in Chaucer's 'Pardoner's
Tale':

'Thus walke I, lyk a restelees kaityf,
And on the ground, which is my moodres gate,
I knokke with my staf, bothe erly and late,
And seye "Leeve mooder, leet me in!
Lo how I vanysshe, flessh, and blood, and skyn!
Allas! whan shul my bones been at reste?"'
(ll.728–33)

– And Spenser's 'dead-living swaine' Malegar in *The Faerie Queene*:

As pale and wan as ashes was his looke,
His bodie leane and meagre as a rake,
And skin all withered like a dryed rooke . . .
(II.xi.22)

Finally, as has often been pointed out,[15] the soldier's 'uncouth shape'
recalls Milton's Death at the gates of Hell in *Paradise Lost*,

If shape it might be called that shape had none
Distinguishable in member, joint, or limb,
Or substance might be called that shadow seemed
(II.667–9)

– but, as Wordsworth was well aware, Milton had also embedded a
republican barb in his description of this figure:

black it stood as night,
Fierce as ten Furies, terrible as hell,

And shook a dreadful dart; what seemed his head
The likeness of a kingly crown had on.
(II.670–3)

Milton would have claimed the authority of Revelations 6:2 for Death's 'kingly crown', although his anti-monarchist jibe at the Restoration is obvious and might also extend to a grisly joke at the expense of Charles I who had lost his crown along with his head. Wordsworth's discharged soldier shares the permanent significance of all the deathly archetypes mentioned above. No longer the focus of protest, he is a symbolic figure uniting the kingly perpetrators and manifold victims of war in a common destiny: 'the great day of wrath' promised in Revelations 6:17. But for Wordsworth the encounter with the soldier also served to waken, 'in [his] own despite', memories of the shock and disappointment that followed his return from France in December 1792. As he contemplates the soldier, Wordsworth's 'mingled sense / Of fear and sorrow' arises, in part, from that recollection. It also betrays his recognition of the soldier as a harbinger of 'the day of vengeance' for which he had prayed when war began exactly five years previously in February 1793:

> I left the shady nook where I had stood
> And hailed the Stranger. From his resting-place
> He rose, & with his lean & wasted arm
> In measured gesture lifted to his head
> Returned my salutation.[16]

With the soldier's 'measured' acknowledgement the poet of social protest first emerges as prophet of apocalypse, translating 'Effort, and expectation, and desire' from the revolutionary milieu of 1792–3 as a prerogative of the imagination 'And something evermore about to be'.[17] 'I returned / The blessing of the poor unhappy man', Wordsworth writes, 'And so we parted': his strange meeting with the soldier was in fact a benediction, an unexpected earnest of his own future calling as a writer.

From Nicholas Roe, *Wordsworth and Coleridge: The Radical Years*, (Oxford, 1988), pp. 135–44.

NOTES

[Nicholas Roe's work is shaped by his painstaking research into the literary and political context of Wordsworth's poetry; this places *Wordsworth and Coleridge: The Radical Years* within a long tradition of contextual criticism, whose concern it has been to trace relationships between creativity and ideology, between culture and society.

The epithet 'Jacobin' denoted sympathy with the radical political aims of Maximilien de Robespierre and his followers at the time of the French Revolution, and implied tacit approval of the violent means by which the Jacobins sought to realise those aims. To what extent were Wordsworth's poems of the mid 1790s examples of Jacobin polemic? Although Roe's conclusion may well seem to be essentially negative, the important point is that the question has been considered worth asking in that form. The influence of Hartman on Roe's critical response is clear, as I suggested in the Introduction, but we can equally appreciate how very different is the route Roe has travelled in order to arrive at his conclusions. Ed.]

1. Jonathan Wordsworth, *The Music of Humanity* (London, 1969), pp. 5–6.

2. S. T. Coleridge, *Lectures 1795 on Politics and Religion*, ed. L. Patton and P. Mann, CC i (Princeton, NJ, 1971), p. 69.

3. Thomas Paine (1737–1809): author of the most substantial and influential radical pamphlet published in England at this time, *The Rights of Man* (1791–2). Wordsworth's familiarity with Paine's ideas and rhetoric is evident from his unpublished *Letter to the Bishop of Llandaff* (1793). William Frend (1757–1841): unitarian dissenter and reformist, an important early influence on Coleridge's political and religious thought. In 1793 Frend was deprived of his fellowship at Jesus College, Cambridge, and banished from the University because of his outspoken political views. Thomas Cooper (1759–1840): a founder member of the radical Manchester Constitutional Society. He travelled to France with James Watt (son of the inventor) in 1792, and delivered a 'fraternal address' to the Jacobin Club at Paris.

4. *Monthly Review*, xxix, June (1799), 207.

5. Back in 1793 Wordsworth explained his attitude to Agrarian law in his *Letter to the Bishop of Llandaff*: 'I am not an advocate for the agrarian law', he said, 'but I contend that the people amongst whom the law of primogeniture exists, and among whom corporate bodies are encouraged and immense salaries annexed to useless and indeed hereditary offices, is oppressed by an inequality in the distribution of wealth which does not necessarily attend men in a state of civil society' (*The Prose Works of William Wordsworth*, ed. W. J. B. Owen and Jane Worthington Smyser (Oxford, 1974), vol. 1, pp. 43–4).

6. *Anti-Jacobin; or, Weekly Examiner* (London, 1799), vol. 1, p. 70.

7. Ibid., vol. 1, p. 72. For 'The Widow' and 'An Evening Walk', see Jonathan Wordsworth, *The Music of Humanity* (London, 1969), p. 63.

8. William Wordsworth, *The Prelude, 1799, 1805, 1850,* ed. J. Wordsworth, M. H. Abrams and J. Gill (New York, 1979), p. 294, ll.533–41.

9. William Wordsworth, 'The Last of the Flock', in *Lyrical Ballads 1798 and 1800,* ed. R. L. Brett and A. R. Jones (London, 1963), ll.15–16.

10. Mary Jacobus, *Tradition and Experiment in Wordsworth's Lyrical Ballads* (Oxford, 1976), p. 205.

11. *Monthly Review,* xxix, June (1799), 209.

12. Jonathan Wordsworth (ed.), *Bicentenary Wordsworth Studies* (Ithaca and London, 1970), p. 436, ll.136–8.

13. Ibid., p. 436, ll.119. [For a further discussion of this poem, see pp. 6–15 above, Ed.]

14. Ibid., p. 434, ll.41–60.

15. For example in Jonathan Wordsworth, *The Borders of Vision* (Oxford, 1982), p. 13, and, more recently, L. Newlyn, *Coleridge, Wordsworth, and the Language of Allusion* (Oxford, 1986), p. 30.

16. Jonathan Wordsworth (ed.), *Bicentenary Wordsworth Studies* (Ithaca and London, 1970), p. 435, ll.85–9.

17. William Wordsworth, *The Prelude, 1799, 1805, 1850,* ed. J. Wordsworth, M. H. Abrams and S. Gill (New York, 1979), Book VI, p. 216, ll.541–2.

3

Wordsworth's Historical Imagination: 'Simon Lee', the Poet as Patron

DAVID SIMPSON

Simon Lee,

the old Huntsman, with an incident in which he was concerned

In the sweet shire of Cardigan,
Not far from pleasant Ivor-hall,
An old man dwells, a little man,
I've heard he once was tall.
Of years he has upon his back,
No doubt, a burthen weighty;
He says he is three score and ten,
But others say he's eighty.

A long blue livery-coat has he,
That's fair behind, and fair before;
Yet, meet him where you will, you see
At once that he is poor.
Full five and twenty years he lived
A running huntsman merry;
And, though he has but one eye left,
His cheek is like a cherry.

No man like him the horn could sound,
And no man was so full of glee;
To say the least, four counties round
Had heard of Simon Lee;

His master's dead, and no one now
Dwells in the hall of Ivor;
Men, dogs, and horses, all are dead;
He is the sole survivor.

His hunting feats have him bereft
Of his right eye, as you may see:
And then, what limbs those feats have left
To poor old Simon Lee!
He has no son, he has no child,
His wife, an aged woman,
Lives with him, near the waterfall,
Upon the village common.

And he is lean and he is sick,
His little body's half awry
His ancles they are swoln and thick
His legs are thin and dry.
When he was young he little knew
Of husbandry or tillage;
And now he's forced to work, though weak,
– The weakest in the village.

He all the country could outrun,
Could leave both man and horse behind;
And often, ere the race was done,
He reeled and was stone-blind.
And still there's something in the world
At which his heart rejoices;
For when the chiming hounds are out,
He dearly loves their voices!

Old Ruth works out of doors with him,
And does what Simon cannot do;
For she, not over stout of limb,
Is stouter of the two.
And though you with your utmost skill
From labour could not wean them,
Alas! 'tis very little, all
Which they can do between them.

Beside their moss-grown hut of clay,
Not twenty paces from the door,
A scrap of land they have, but they,
Are poorest of the poor.
This scrap of land he from the heath
Enclosed when he was stronger;
But what avails the land to them,
Which they can till no longer?

Few months of life has he in store,
As he to you will tell,
For still, the more he works, the more
His poor old ancles swell.
My gentle reader! I perceive
How patiently you've waited,
And I'm afraid that you expect
Some tale will be related.

O reader! had you in your mind
Such stores as silent thought can bring,
O gentle reader! you would find
A tale in every thing.
What more I have to say is short,
I hope you'll kindly take it;
It is no tale; but should you think,
Perhaps a tale you'll make it.

One summer-day I chanced to see
This old man doing all he could
About the root of an old tree,
A stump of rotten wood.
The mattock tottered in his hand;
So vain was his endeavour
That at the root of the old tree
He might have worked for ever.

'You're overtasked, good Simon Lee,
Give me your tool' to him I said;
And at the word right gladly he
Received my proffer'd aid.
I struck, and with a single blow
The tangled root I sever'd,
At which the poor old man so long
And vainly had endeavour'd.

The tears into his eyes were brought,
And thanks and praises seemed to run
So fast out of his heart, I thought
They never would have done.
– I've heard of hearts unkind, kind deeds
With coldness still returning.
Alas, the gratitude of men
Has oftner left me mourning.

(*Lyrical Ballads*, 1798)

I turn now to another representation of rural poverty, one that will
be found to be even more revelatory of hitherto unnoticed personal-

historical anxieties: 'Simon Lee', first put before the public in the 1798 *Lyrical Ballads*. Much of the commentary on this poem has concentrated on the way in which it is a 'test' of the reader's ability to sympathise with a poetry devoid of gaudy and inane phraseology and loudly declared messages.[1] This critical emphasis is entirely consonant with Wordsworth's own, as he speaks of 'placing my Reader in the way of receiving from ordinary moral sensations another and more salutary impression than we are accustomed to receive from them'.[2] Challenging us with the declaration that the ideal reader will find a 'tale in every thing', 'Simon Lee' seems to fulfil Wordsworth's anti-authoritarian mandate in transcribing a poet who is a man speaking to men, rather than a sage gifted with superior insight. Invited to 'make' our own tale out of the raw materials of this incident, we at once accede to a creative stature and admire a poet who is prepared to record events that are inconclusive and even potentially inconsequential. In his assertion of the ordinary event as of great poetic importance, Wordsworth is mounting the sort of attack upon decorum that offended so many of the readers of his early work, and still offends others today.

We may wonder, none the less, whether Wordsworth is here making virtue of necessity, and inviting the reader's response as a way of displacing something that is not, in the last analysis, open to any comfortable aesthetic or moral control. This question must be pursued, once again, by tracing the clues that lead to the unfolding of a social and historical density to the images that Wordsworth as speaker seems to seek to evacuate or to displace. We may begin with Isabella Fenwick's account of the poet's recollection of the raw materials that gave rise to the poem:

> This old man had been huntsman to the Squires of Alfoxden, which, at the time we occupied it, belonged to a minor. The old man's cottage stood upon the common, a little way from the entrance to Alfoxden Park. But it had disappeared. Many other changes had taken place in the adjoining village, which I could not but notice with a regret more natural than well-considered. Improvements but rarely appear such to those who, after long intervals of time, revisit places they have had much pleasure in. It is unnecessary to add, the fact was as mentioned in the poem; and I have, after an interval of 45 years, the image of the old man as fresh before my eyes as if I had seen him yesterday. The expression when the hounds were out, 'I dearly love their voices' was word for word from his own lips.[3]

The Fenwick note pays homage to many of the archetypes of Wordsworth's poetics. The emotion is recollected in tranquillity, but becomes almost as intense, after an interval of forty-five years, as if it were being experienced in the present. And Wordsworth authenticates the diction of the poem as in part a transcription of what the old man actually said, which is thus reported without the deviant glosses of poetic diction.

But this more or less exhausts the claims to documentary exactitude that can be made for this poem. Mark Reed dates its composition to the period March–May 1798, and the meeting with the old man to the autumn of 1797. The Wordsworths were a long way from Cardigan, and were in fact living at Alfoxden House, in Somersetshire; and the old man's name was not Simon Lee but Christopher Tricky. Moorman reports that Tricky and his wife lived at the dog pound just outside the grounds of the house, and that the Wordsworths first made his acquaintance by asking him about the navigability of the local rivers, thus contributing to the spy rumours that were circulating in the neighbourhood about the new tenants and their odd friends – Poole, Coleridge and most notoriously of all, radical John Thelwall, who visited the Wordsworths between autumn 1797 and the writing of the poem.[4] Thelwall actually had plans to settle near Alfoxden, but was dissuaded from doing so as a result of the Wordsworth circle's concern about the spy rumours: he moved on to Llyswen Farm, in Brecknockshire.

The Wordsworths were not, then, at all comfortably integrated into the local community of which Christopher Tricky was the most closely contiguous representative. It was a time of national paranoia, focused on the possibility of a French invasion, and it is not surprising that the educated democrats from afar should have been the objects of gossip and suspicion. Exchanges between the Wordsworths and the Trickys must have been somewhat tense and embarrassed.

So: the real Christopher Tricky became the fictional Simon Lee, renominated into a generic, pseudo-biblical identity (his wife's name is Ruth), rehoused in his cottage (if he had ever had one – the Trickys were living at the dog pound), and shunted out of the Alfoxden landscape into the 'sweet shire of Cardigan'. Why Cardigan? The simplest explanation of such a displacement would rest with the shared syllabic patterning of Alfoxden and Cardigan, and invoke the principle of casual poetic licence. But there are a good many clues that suggest a more coherently motivated choice of location.

To the best of my knowledge Wordsworth had never been in south-west Wales; but in his account of the Celtic revival, David Solkin has pointed out the implications of the image of Wales for eighteenth-century men of letters.[5] Among them was a strong tradition identifying Wales as a bastion of that much-vaunted entity, 'British liberty'. As the Welsh mountains had once kept out the invading Romans, so they were, from the 1760s, imagined to be keeping out also the more subtle modern corruptions of commerce and luxury. Wales became the locus of a picturesque feudalism, what Solkin calls the 'patrician rural ideal'. As one might expect, this image persisted in despite of evidence that the actual economic condition of Wales was one of extreme poverty and hardship. (We have already seen that the Lake District was to provide Wordsworth with some of the same images.) Solkin quotes John Shebbeare, writing in 1756:

> Not long since on a journey into . . . Wales . . . I found more remains of ancient vasselage amongst the common people, and a greater simplicity of manners, than is to be met with in England . . . The peasants, as free by law as those in England, yet retain a great deal of obedience to their landlords, which was paid the Barons of old.[6]

This is a more explicitly hierarchical image of rural society than that Wordsworth was to claim as typical of the Lake District, but it speaks forth the same virtuous traditionalism. As Prys Morgan has put it, the 'image of Wales was of a quaint back-of-beyond where gentlemen with hardly a shirt to their backs reeled off endless family trees going back to Aeneas from Troy'. Morgan suggests that the Welsh were very far behind with fashions, still wearing in the 1790s what had been current in England in the 1620s; and that the atmosphere in Wales in the 1790s was fiercely anti-revolutionary. At the same time, things *were* changing owing to the attractions of the metropolis and the abandonment of the old ways.[7]

This explains something of the implications of Wordsworth's removal of Simon Lee's cottage to the 'sweet shire of Cardigan', a place that was the site of the first recorded eisteddfod and thus perhaps closely associated with the old traditions.[8] In his mention of 'pleasant Ivor-hall', moreover, Wordsworth seems to have been calling up a precise literary allusion. Morgan's account is worth quoting at length:

> Iolo Morganwg [a Welsh poet of the late eighteenth century] was responsible for turning many obscure figures into national heroes . . . Iolo was farming in the 1780s in the marshland between Cardiff and Newport, where he came into contact with Evan Evans, then a drunken, threadbare curate at Bassaleg, and they both visited the ruins of the fourteenth-century hall of Ifor Hael (Ivor the Generous), who, tradition stated in a vague and uncertain way, had been the patron of the great fourteenth-century poet Dafydd ap Gwilym. Evans wrote a fine romantic poem about the ivy-clad ruins, and Iolo set about his first important forgeries, the imitation of the love poems of Dafydd ap Gwilym, which contained subtle little references to Glamorgan and to Ifor Hael. Iolo in his subsequent writings did much to make out Ifor as the greatest patron of Welsh literature. Ivor became a popular name in Wales, a household word for generosity. The most Welsh of the workmen's benefit societies, the Order of Ivorites, took their name from him; the inns where many of their lodges met were called Ivor Arms, and many of these still survive to this day.[9]

It is tempting to speculate that Wordsworth might have known something of this. I have found no record of his meeting or reading the works of either Evan Evans or Iolo Morganwg (Edward Williams), but he is likely to have known them. Evans (1731–89) the author of *Some Specimens of the Poetry of the Ancient Welsh Bards*(London, 1764), was born and died in Cardiganshire, a drunkard and a failure; as a writer, he had failed to make his way in the world, a predicament perhaps not too remote from the inner thoughts of the young William Wordsworth in the Alfoxden period. Morganwg, or Edward Williams (1746–1826), was a Unitarian and a member of the radical circle of Priestley and Wakefield. The author of *Poems, Lyric and Pastoral* (2 vols, London, 1794), he must surely have been known to Thelwall, as he was known to Coleridge and thence perhaps to Wordsworth. Coleridge met him in 1796 and owned a copy of the poems.[10] The name 'Ifor Hael' (Ivor the Generous) is very close to Wordsworth's 'Ivor-hall', which may thus be a convenient mistranslation, or coinage by association. Ifor Hael, according to Morganwg, lived in Glamorganshire, but it is the unfortunate Evan Evans's locality, Cardigan, that Wordsworth makes the site of his Ivor Hall. The displacement thus expresses both his wishful fantasies and his fears. In placing the incident, and thus himself, in Cardigan, he identifies himself with Evan Evans, the failed poet. And in invoking the name of Ifor Hael as Simon's former master (occluded, that is to say, by the name of the house), he laments at once the plight of the old man and his own condition as a poet without a patron.

Morganwg (Edward Williams) had made much of the liberality of Ifor Hael, whom he called 'Ivor the Liberal':

> Thy ample gate, thy ample hall,
> Are ever op'ning wide to all . . .
> The poor from thee with joy return,
> They bless thy name, they cease to mourn

Nor is it just the conventional poor who are favoured, for Gwilym himself has received the gift of a pair of gloves crammed with gold:

> Thy Bard, esteem'd the nobler guest.
> Was with distinguish'd bounty bless'd.[11]

The momentary social contract between Wordsworth and his Simon Lee thus conceals an identity within its apparent difference: in familiar Wordsworthian style, the stylistic and semantic instabilities of the poem emanate from a complex interrelation of self and other. The poet is able to come to the old man's aid, but his discomfort at so doing is a function of his own sense of displacement as well as of his guilt or embarrassment at being in better health and fortune. At the same time, he is better off than Simon, and is in this way a sort of 'proxy' of the vanished owner of Ivor Hall, able to dispense the assistance that Simon is now sorely missing. The incident thus appeals to a wishful fantasy in Wordsworth: that he himself is not in need, but in a position that enables him to dispense charity and patronage. The predicament of the apprentice poet in a world without patrons is momentarily eclipsed by an act of contingent condescension.

The odd mixture of emotional release, honest sympathy, condescension and embarrassment that critics have often found in the climactic moment of the poem can thus be coherently related to the conflicting aspirations and anxieties in the Wordsworthian psyche. Chopping the tangled root offers the poet a moment of freedom from an ongoing predicament that is all too similar to that of the old man – the predicament of one who cannot earn a living on his own.

Let us look more closely at the circumstances, apart from those of youth and good health, that enabled the poet to come to the aid of the struggling old man. The former squire of Alfoxden had maintained, we assume, his 'running huntsman merry', Christopher Tricky. But the house is now owned by a minor, and is no longer owner-occupied but let out to tenants – none other than the Wordsworths.

The poet quite literally substitutes for the squire by living in his house. Alfoxden House, moreover, was not just any old home – it was by a long way the grandest place that the family would ever occupy. Moorman rather modestly calls it 'a charming middle-sized country house; but Dorothy's account is much more rapturous.[12] Having begun only with 'some dreams of happiness in a little cottage', she describes her residence as follows:

> Here we are in a large mansion, in a large park, with seventy head of deer around us . . . The house is a large mansion, with furniture enough for a dozen families like ours . . . Wherever we turn we have woods, smooth downs, and valleys with small brooks running down them through green meadows, hardly ever intersected with hedgerows, but scattered over with trees.[13]

Here are the Wordsworths enjoying the aesthetic gratifications of living in the house of the lords of the manor – long, uninterrupted views unmarked by signs of labour or human proximity, and a deer park. Deer had become property rather than game, in the eyes of the law, and symbols of rural gentility.[14] Of course, the house is now owned by a minor, so that the Wordsworths are not occupying the place of an active squirearchy; but the sight of Christopher Tricky's poverty and physical decay could hardly have failed to make William feel uncomfortable about his own tenure of the house that had once maintained him. Perhaps, in the severing of the 'tangled root', we may see some grand, relieving gesture of making amends, as if the tangled roots of the poet's own social anxieties could similarly be struck away in a moment of resolution and independence. For Tricky, Wordsworth's timely appearance perhaps registered as the image of a long-vanished condescension from the master of Alfoxden House. Fond memories of interaction between master and man, as well as his own physical decay and the suggestion that he is all too seldom in receipt of such attentions from his other neighbours, may explain what the poem's speaker registers as an excessive gratitude. The 'long blue livery-coat' that Simon wears suggests a perfect accord of virtue and necessity. It may be the only garment he has left, in his abject poverty, but it is also the sign of his former place in the vanished social system, and of his 'belonging' to the house. As he clothes his back, he may also feed his memories and maintain his self-esteem. Of course, the Wordsworths were merely tenants, paying £23 a year for the privilege of occupying the centre of the landscape; but it is hard to image that William would not have felt uncomfortable at the interaction with Tricky, most of all at the time when he was very actively discussing the brotherhood of man with man in the company of Poole, Coleridge and Thelwall. The old order has changed, and the poet seems to have at least a lurking sympathy for its idealised features; but there is no new order yet apparent to relieve the neglect of its displaced members, nor indeed the needs of those who now function symbolically as proprietors. Being able to help an ailing working man must appeal to Wordsworth's democratic imperative, but the form and the traditions of assistance make him the symbol, only partly unwilling, of a vanished feudal order. The instability of his position makes him at once a man of the people – a man assisting a fellow man – and a proxy of the old hierarchy. Wordsworth occupies the classic bourgeois site, an unstable and amorphous middle ground which disables him from validating *any* orthodox social role in a wholehearted manner.

Once again, this is not to be seen simply as a 'generic' example of a conflict determined exclusively by social-historical conditions. As we accord these conditions a prominent causal role, we must also be aware of their compatibility with the idiosyncratic factors that had made up Wordsworth's particular life-experience. The traumas of not belonging and of disconnection must have been especially urgent to a poet who lost his mother when he was 8, and his father when he was 13. From his father's house he might even have recalled the presence of a liveried servant, an image of the bourgeois aspiration to the genteel life.[15] The bizarre mistranslation or coinage of 'Ivor-hall' may then also be a homophonal pun, 'I've a hall', a wished for, if uneasy, restitution of what he had lost – place, parents, and property. Against this paradigm of restitution, we may set the more recently acquired republican sentiments that, in the revolutionary spirit of new beginnings, might have made the ideology of *dis*connection – from place, parents, property – an appealing one. For it was precisely in its replacement of the language of inheritance, paternity and tradition by that of fraternity and equality that the rhetoric of 1789 was most striking. Wordsworth strikes through the tangled root that separates man from man in the social as well as the physical order; none other than Tom Paine, in his *Rights of Man*, had appealed to his reader to 'lay then the axe to the root, and teach governments humanity'.[16]

The conflict of desires and aspirations that are built into this poem is then to be understood in both personal and generic terms, each indeed informing and modifying the other. And, as Wordsworth's ideological and psychological personalities were thus divided within themselves, so too was his economic psyche. He was not an Evan Evans figure, completely unknown and unrewarded; but neither was he a Dafydd ap Gwilym (in Morganwg's reconstruction of him), sheltered by the generous attentions of a wealthy patron. The Calvert legacy had left him a sizeable £900, though much of it had been lent out again in an imprudent fashion. Alfoxden was not a cheap place to live, and might have seemed something of an extravagance to the Wordsworths themselves. The rent was £23 a year, almost three times as much as the £8 a year they would pay for the cottage at Grasmere shortly thereafter.[17] This was at a time when the agricultural workers of Somerset and the Vale of Gloucester were making between 1s. and 1s.6d. a day, depending on the season, i.e. between £15 and £22.10s. a year, based on a six-day week for fifty weeks.[18] The much-debated Speenhamland provision of 1793 had proposed that every poor and industrious man should have 3s. weekly, (£7.16s. p.a.), either from his own and his family's labour or from the poor rates, with an extra 1s.6d. a week for the support of his wife and any other family member.[19] The Wordsworths' expenses for a twelve-month period spanning 1797–8 were, according to Dorothy, £110.[20] The same sum would be advanced by the Wedgwoods to finance the Wordsworths' and Coleridge's trip to Germany, which they could not otherwise have afforded.[21] Wordsworth repaid the loan in 1800. Alfoxden House was clearly not a comfortable symbol of the Wordsworths' financial condition, either actual or imaginary. Wordsworth and Coleridge were to receive thirty guineas from Cottle for the copyright of the first edition of Lyrical Ballads; but even as late as 1807, as we have seen, Wordsworth was to cast the then all too predominant sonnet form as his 'scanty plot of ground', an almost exact recall of the 'scrap of land' that Simon Lee had enclosed.[22]

There is one more major element in the iconography of 'Simon Lee' that requires some attention: his identification as a 'huntsman', the right-hand man of the master of hounds, who would usually have been the squire himself. Wordsworth seems quite sensitive to the technical vocabulary of fox hunting. The midland counties of England, where fox hunting was becoming more professionalised by about 1800, were commonly known as 'the shires', and Wordsworth places his poem in a 'sweet shire'. Simon's 'long blue livery-coat' may derive from the blue coats worn by the graziers who followed the Quorn; and in Devonshire a 'cry of hounds' was the technically correct term for the pack.[23]

Under the laws of the land the fox was classed as vermin rather than as game. This meant that fox hunting was in principle open to all, and not limited to those who owned a certain amount of land. It was, in other words, not subject to the game laws which were perhaps the single most divisive presence in the English legal system, at least in rural areas. E. P. Thompson, in *Whigs and Hunters*, has shown how the rights to game were contested as part of the struggle between Whig magnates and Tory squires some years before Wordsworth was born.[24] But right through the century, there were violent confrontations between poachers and gamekeepers, the haves and the have-nots. Blackstone opined that whereas 'the forest laws established only one mighty hunter throughout the land, the game laws have raised a little Nimrod in every manor'. As such, he calls them a 'bastard slip' in the English legal system.[25] The Hammonds and Chambers and Mingay are eloquent about the intensity of the disputes over game; Dorothy Marshall remarks that 'no single factor caused such bad blood and bitter resentment in the countryside than the determination of the landowners to enforce the game laws in all their savagery'.[26]

Relations between landowners and tenants were, then, particularly contentious on the matter of the game laws. These laws seem to have gone through a particular state of crisis in the 1790s, when their enforcement came to be, for the landowners, the public symbol of an anti-Jacobin platform.[27] In Wordsworth's poem, Simon Lee is not only shifted out of Alfoxden into Cardigan, but he is upheld as an emblem of the least socially divisive element of the traditional life of the gentry. Fox hunting stands as an ideal image of co-operation between the social orders in the English countryside. The potentially inflammatory charge that the livery coat of subservience to the squirearchy might have had for some readers of 1798 is diminished by its specification as a relic of fox hunting. If the squire of Alfoxden had ever been a 'little Nimrod', then nothing in the poem hints at such a possibility.[28]

The career of 'huntsman' is a part of Simon's past, an element in that 'mellowed feudality' of which Wordsworth was so fond. Rather more puzzling is his role in the present. He functions now as an owner-occupier, one of that class of persons whom Wordsworth frequently idealises (in 'Michael', for example) as perfect citizens, and the desired analogues in ordinary life of the poetical character when it is most true to itself. Christopher Tricky had lost his cottage, if he ever had one, but Wordsworth restores Simon Lee to his, though we must wonder why. Simon can hardly stay alive, let alone work, so that he is not a very efficient image of economic self-sufficiency. Wordsworth does not play up his potential as an emblem of persistence in adversity, but rather seems to stress the pointlessness of it all. Simon's function in Wordsworth's economic ideal is thus not very clear; though we might note the ambiguity whereby the poet's gesture of unofficial charity and one-time assistance both compensates for a proper welfare provision (this would be the Burkean-Malthusian argument) and implies its necessity – for Simon's excessive gratitude surely results in part from the fact that he receives so little help of any kind from anyone. Nor should we forget the subjective appeal of this incident to the poet's imagination. Wordsworth is able to make a 'work' out of working, and this moment of climactic physical activity, of doing something whose validation is immediately apparent and beyond doubt, must have afforded him considerable psychological relief. If the hyperbole of 'Gipsies' was in part a result of the self-esteem attendant upon the glow of honest labour, then 'Simon Lee' chronicles the act of labour itself.

If this account of 'Simon Lee' and its coming into being carries any conviction, then it is not surprising that literary critics should have found themselves worrying over oddities of style and diction, which then become the formal manifestations of a serious turbulence and insecurity in Wordsworth's mind, and in the public languages available to it. Hartman finds that Wordsworth 'has trouble with the tone', although John Danby makes a good case for the purposive conversion of jest to earnest at the end of the poem.[29] Andrew Griffin, in the most thorough of the available studies of 'Simon Lee', sees in its conclusion a 'characteristically fumbling apology', and suggests that in the later revisions Wordsworth loses 'confidence or interest in the burlesque aspects of his loquacious narrators'.[30] This does seem to have been the most tangled of all the roots in Wordsworth's shorter poems, and he worked on it constantly over the years. It never achieves the comfortable mock-heroic tone of similar passages in, for example, *Benjamin the Waggoner*, but always retains elements of strong contrasts and even conflicts in style. How can this be explained, if at all?

As Danby has observed, the opening descriptions of the old man and his environs are platitudinous to say the least. Such phrases as 'sweet shire', 'pleasant Ivor-hall', 'huntsman merry' and 'cheek . . . like a cherry' have often been judged to be intrinsically vapid, at best an uncomfortable participation in the language of naïve ballad conventions, at worst a total failure of poetic intelligence. The poem passes on to a more detailed description of Simon's physical predicament, so that a contrast appears between the first and second halves. This also corresponds, as we have seen, with the distinction between the 'invented' and the reported parts of the poem's plot. But what can we make of this? Is the poet in control of these shifts? A case could be made for the fictionalising motifs of the first half as part of a parodic purpose whereby Wordsworth alludes to the 'fake' poetry of Edward Williams to expose the absurdity of middle-class ideas about what ballads are. Are we invited to mock romantic feudalism only to be later made aware that real people do suffer in real places?. Or is Wordsworth totally under the sway of his own inner insecurities that motivate the complex play upon 'Ivor-hall' in the ways that I have already described?[31] This question seems to me genuinely insoluble, and not least because of the point made in various ways by the likes of Freud, Lacan and Derrida about the implausibility of any absolute distinction between the conscious and the unconscious, most of all in the realm of language. If both are motivated energies, then patterns of coherence are going to emerge, and as such they were 'meant', and meant by Wordsworth, whether he knew it or not. And yet the 'covering over' or displacement that the poem performs has proved very efficient. Wordsworth clearly did not mean his readers to have biographies and chronologies to hand for the deciphering of his meanings. 'Simon Lee' does not clearly and openly transcribe a subject in a state of historical and biographical crisis. Not only does it continue to foreground the questions raised by the 'objective' dimension, the old man's decay and excessive gratitude; it also displaces the production of meaning onto the alerted reader. But that crisis is there none the less, and its terms are available to a careful inspection. The names of the authors did not appear on the title page of the first edition of *Lyrical Ballads*; it is significant, then, that 'Simon Lee' alludes to an idealised, pre-alienated culture in which the production of poetry by gifted individuals is rewarded by lavish recognition, reputation and wealth.

We have, thus far, looked at three of Wordsworth's shorter poems in considerable detail. 'Gipsies' has been usually judged a failure, 'Michael' a masterpiece, and 'Simon Lee' something in between. All of these poems, upon close inspection, reveal complex interactions between the subjective and objective; as they address the objective features of the rural life, so they also dramatise the unstable position of the poet reporting upon them. Christopher Tricky and the band of gypsies lived and breathed, and their reality impinges upon the messages of Wordsworth's poems, even as they are variously refigured into shapes that Wordsworth found more manipulable, comfortable or polemically convenient. The discourses that Wordsworth was addressing by way of these refigurings also had actual consequences and implications. While it is possible to establish differences of degree between the public and the private references that Wordsworth's language brings forward, it is not either possible or useful to try to create absolute distinctions of kind. The self inspecting itself in language, and putting itself forward as a poetic speaker, is already in part contemplating a third person. These poems do not faithfully *reproduce* a simple external reality, but they inevitably *reflect* it, and comment upon it. Nor, at the other extreme, do they tell us 'just' about Wordsworth. In the realm of language, and exclusively conceived, there is no such person. The subject is always and inescapably intersubjective, and the forms of that intersubjectivity can be effectively objective, active elements in a shared world and a common public space.

From David Simpson, *Wordsworth's Historical Imagination: The Poetry of Displacement* (London, 1987), pp. 149–59.

NOTES

[In recent years, 'historicist' critics of Wordsworth – of whom David Simpson is one – have sought to incorporate contemporary poststructuralist techniques with those of the historical, contextual approach. This has inevitably affected the way historical material has been used; the detail is scrupulously researched, but it then becomes the basis of an imaginative, open-ended exploration of possible textual meanings. Historical research does not therefore have the effect of locating literary 'meaning' in quite the way it tends to in the work of John Lucas, Roger Sales or Nicholas Roe, where the impact of specific political events is foregrounded.

The central thesis of *Wordsworth's Historical Imagination* is 'displacement': Wordsworth chose poetic subjects that enabled him indirectly to address personal and social issues it would have been – for whatever reason – impossible for him to confront directly. The poetic imagination is thus tethered to 'history', but equally it proceeds to expand, embellish, deconstruct and reconstruct history. Historicist criticism tends, unrepentantly, to invite a process of analytical embellishment (see, for example, note 31). Ed.]

1. See Paul D. Sheats, *The Making of Wordsworth's Poetry 1785–98* (Cambridge, Mass., 1973), pp. 88–93; James H. Averill, *Wordsworth and the Poetry of Human Suffering* (London, 1980), pp. 162–6; Andrew L. Griffin, 'Wordsworth and the problem of imaginative story: the case of "Simon Lee"', *PMLA*, 19 (1977), 392–409; John F. Danby, *The Simple Wordsworth: Studies in the Poems 1797–1807* (London, 1960), pp. 38–47. For a more general study of 'reader activation', see David Simpson, *Irony and Authority in Romantic Poetry* (London, 1979).

2. *The Prose Works of William Wordsworth*, ed. W. J. B. Owen and Jane Worthington Smyser (Oxford, 1974), vol. 1, pp. 126–8.

3. *The Poetical Works of William Wordsworth*, ed. E. de Selincourt and Helen Darbishire (Oxford, 1940–9), vol. 4, pp. 412–13.

4. Mark L. Reed, *Wordsworth: The Chronology of the Early Years* (Cambridge Mass., 1967), p. 32, 202. Mary Moorman, *William Wordsworth: A Biography. The Later Years 1803–50* (London, 1968), p. 329.

5. David H. Solkin, *Richard Wilson: The Landscape of Reaction* (London, 1982), pp. 86f.

6. Ibid., pp. 101, 102.

7. Prys Morgan, 'From death to a view: the hunt for the Welsh past in the romantic period', in Eric Hobsbawm and Terence Ranger (eds), *The Invention of Tradition* (Cambridge, 1984), pp. 45–50, 60, 80.

8. Ibid., p. 56.

9. Ibid., p. 85.

10. *The Notebooks of Samuel Taylor Coleridge. Vol. I, 1794–1804*, ed. Kathleen Coburn (Princeton, 1957), p. 174, n. 16.

11. Edward Williams, *Poems, Lyric and Pastoral* (London, 1974), vol. 1, pp. 193–4.

12. Mary Moorman, *William Wordsworth: A Biography. The Early Years 1787–1803* (Oxford, 1969), p. 325.

13. *The Letters of William and Dorothy Wordsworth. The Early Years 1787–1805*, ed. E. de Selincourt, 2nd edn, revd Chester L. Shaver (Oxford, 1967), pp. 190–1.

14. P. B. Munsche, *Gentlemen and Poachers. The English Game Laws 1671–1831* (Cambridge, 1981), pp. 107f.

15. Mary Moorman, *William Wordsworth: A Biography. The Early Years 1787–1803* (Oxford, 1969), pp. 9, 11.

16. Thomas Paine, *Rights of Man*, ed. Henry Collins (Harmondsworth, 1976), p. 80. In this context it is notable that the root that Simon is trying to sever is not attached to a flourishing (Burkean) tree but to a

'stump of rotten wood'. What is being swept away is thus a hollow or decaying growth; nor is the improver in any state of physical vigour. A more ingenious reader than myself might be able to find in this poem a place for the severed head of Louis XVI, and surely for a phallic motif in the incident itself, and in the identification of 'root' and 'stump'.

17. Mark Reed, *Wordsworth: The Chronology of the Early Years 1770–1799* (Cambridge, Mass., 1967), p. 281.

18. See Elizabeth W. Gilboy, *Wages in Eighteenth Century England* (Cambridge, Mass., 1934), pp. 80–2. Agricultural labour was notoriously irregular, so that most workers would not have had the chance to work for a full fifty weeks of the year.

19. J. L. and Barbara Hammond, *The Village Labourer*, ed. G. E. Mingay (London, 1978), p. 109.

20. Mary Moorman, *William Wordsworth: A Biography. The Early Years 1787–1803* (Oxford, 1969), p. 399.

21. Ibid., p. 409.

22. William Wordsworth, *Poems, in Two Volumes, and Other Poems 1800–1807*, ed. Jared Curtis (Brighton, 1983), p. 133. Added evidence of Wordsworth's discomfort with the Alfoxden experience appears in 'Anecdote for Fathers', written during the same period. Pressured to choose between life at Kilve (perhaps Racedown) and Liswyn Farm (perhaps Alfoxden, and an apparent identification with Thelwall's new home in Brecknockshire), the boy bursts out 'At Kilve there was no weather-cock'. The 'broad and gilded vane' that catches the boy's eye may well be an image of the uneasy splendour of Alfoxden House, an awkward contradiction of the republican plainness wishfully intimated in the poet calling his present residence (in the poem) after Thelwall's. Wordsworth was not living on a farm, within a working economy, but renting a manor house.

23. Raymond Carr, *English Fox Hunting. A History* (London, 1976), p. 85; David C. Itzkowitz, *The Peculiar Privilege. A Social History of Fox Hunting* (Brighton, 1977), pp. 34, 47.

24. E. P. Thompson, *Whigs and Hunters* (London, 1975).

25. William Blackstone, *Commentaries on the Laws of England 1765–9* (London, 1979), vol. 4, p. 409.

26. J. L. and Barbara Hammond, *The Village Labourer* (London, 1978), pp. 133f; J. D. Chambers and G. E. Mingay, *The Agricultural Revolution 1750–1880* (London, 1982), p. 138; Dorothy Marshall, *Industrial England 1776–1851* (London, 1982), p. 62.

27. P. B. Munsche, *Gentlemen and Poachers. The English Game Laws 1671–1831* (Cambridge, 1981), pp. 123f.

28. In 'The Childless Father', *Lyrical Ballads*, ed. R. L. Brett and A. R. Jones (London, 1963), p. 204, Wordsworth describes a man going out with the hunt in a gesture of rehabilitation after the death of his daughter. C. M. L. Bouch and G. P. Jones, *A Short Economic and Social History of the Lake Counties 1500–1830* (Manchester, 1961), p. 231, suggest that such participation was often required of his tenants, as a boon service, at least in the Lake District. Wordsworth avoids specifying the degree of obligation, and thus may or may not be suggesting that the burdens of customary tenancy have a silver lining.

29. Geoffrey Hartman, *Wordsworth's Poetry 1787–1814* (London, 1977), p. 148; John Danby, *The Simple Wordsworth: Studies in the Poems 1797–1807* (London, 1960), p. 47.

30. Andrew L. Griffin, 'Wordsworth and the problem of imaginative story: the case of "Simon Lee"', *PMLA*, 19 (1977), 399–400.

31. And to which may be added the sense of 'serve Ivor' in 'He is the sole survivor'. Praise or blame for this one goes to Fred See, to whom my gratitude.

4

The Country Dweller: William Wordsworth

JOHN LUCAS

In a typically incisive essay on 'Culture', his contribution to *Marx: The First Hundred Years*, Raymond Williams discusses the development of those divisions in labour which resulted in 'mental labour' being privileged over 'manual labour', especially as the former is restricted to a certain class.

> The effect is not only the undervaluation of manual labour . . . on [which] in fact the maintenance of human life still absolutely depends. The effect is also on the character of 'mental labour' itself. In its separation from the basic processes of assuring human existence it is inherently more likely to develop false conceptions of both general and specific human conditions, since it is not as a matter of necessary practice exposed to and tested by human activity in general. Even more, since the fact of the division of labour, in this basic classic sense, is not just a matter of different kinds of work but of social relations which determine greater rewards and greater respect for 'mental labour', and of these relations as established in and protected by a specifically exploiting and unequal social order, the operations of 'mental labour' cannot be assumed in advance to be exclusively devoted to 'higher' or 'the highest' human concerns, but are in many or perhaps all cases likely to be bound up, in greater or lesser degree, with propagation, ratification, defence, apologia, naturalisation of that exploiting and unequal social order itself.[1]

It might almost have been written with 'Resolution and Independence' in mind. And yet we have immediately to qualify the remark.

For Wordsworth does not so much try to ratify and defend the unequal social order as to confront the fact of its inequality, and this is essential to the poem's meaning and to its significance.

But then again, the confrontation is muted, not merely by the suppression of that 'unjust state of society', but by the odd deflections from heed of others to heed for self, and this is also significant because, great as the poem undoubtedly is in its attempt to come to terms with the privileged status of poet, and hard though it works to unpick the mystificatory process whereby 'the poet' is produced as a special type, in the last resort Wordsworth cannot bear to let go of that type. If we want further evidence of this we can look at the altogether more comic account he produces of himself as poet in 'Stanzas Written in My Pocket Copy of Thomson's "Castle of Indolence"', which was composed at exactly the time he was working on 'Resolution and Independence'. This poem also speaks of the poet – that is, Wordsworth himself – in the third person; and it makes him altogether 'unfathomably' mysterious:

> Some thought he was a lover, and did woo:
> Some thought far worse of him, and judged him wrong;
> But verse was what he had been wedded to;
> And his own mind did like a tempest strong
> Come to him thus, and drove the weary Wight along.

Given that this was not published until 1815, it may be that we should not place great weight upon it. Yet it claims that the poet is somehow the passive instrument of poetry – is driven, chosen, 'inspired' (the terms fall into place). It therefore suggests a man struggling to justify his wandering 'far from the world', even though that same man had earlier wished to justify poetry as the act of a man speaking to men. And *that* man, by refusing to endorse the 'egocentric dehumanising distancing' which Heather Glen identifies as central to his culture, had hoped that *as poet* he would be of real use.[2]

Yet no matter how far he might wander, Wordsworth could not wander from himself. At his truest, this meant discovering in himself those elements, qualities, feelings, which he had in common with others. In 'Resolution and Independence' the leech-gatherer provides the opportunity, or the enforced occasion, for such a discovery. He seems, Wordsworth says, 'like a Man from some far region sent; / To give me human strength, and strong admonishment'. This was later changed to 'To give me human strength by apt admonishment',

which perhaps unfortunately implies that the old man is a figure of
almost comically stern reproof. But it is more important to note how
often in Wordsworth's poems the word 'human' turns up in challenging, difficult contexts. At the beginning of 'Michael' Wordsworth
speaks of how as a young man he had been led to feel

> For passions that were not my own, and think
> At random and imperfectly indeed
> On Man; the heart of man and human life.

At the end of the great Immortality Ode he gives 'Thanks to the
human heart by which we live, / Thanks to its tenderness, its joys, its
fears'. In the 'Elegiac Stanzas Suggested by a Picture of Peele Castle,
in a Storm', he says that 'A deep distress hath humanis'd my Soul';
and in the third of the Lucy poems he writes:

> A slumber did my spirit seal,
>   I had no human fears:
> She seem'd a thing that could not feel
>   The touch of earthly years.

In all these cases, to be human is to be caught up in, or at the very
least made aware of, suffering, of fears which have to be met and –
somehow – accommodated in any adequate living. To be human is to
be moved out of that 'sealed' infancy, that delighted, unclouded
vision which is unapprehensive of the tragic possibilities attached
to 'human life'.

The most sensitively acute account of this movement is to be
found in Keats's famous letter to his friend John Reynolds, in which
he speaks of the chamber of maiden thought and the inevitability of
going beyond it, through

> sharpening one's Vision into the heart and nature of Man – of
> convincing one's nerves that the world is full of Misery and Heartbreak,
> Pain, Sickness and oppression – whereby this Chamber of Maiden
> Thought becomes gradually darkened, and at the same time, on all
> sides of it, many doors are set open – but all dark – all leading to dark
> passages. We see not the balance of good and evil; we are in a mist
> . . . To this point was Wordsworth come, as far as I can conceive,
> when he wrote 'Tintern Abbey,' and it seems to me that his genius is
> explorative of those dark passages.[3]

'The heart and nature of Man' – the phrase might almost be Wordsworth's. But Keats does not, I think, acknowledge the yearning in Wordsworth to be able to 'seal' the dark passages, so that the Lucy poems, for example, hope against hope for the continuation or recovery of what, in 'Elegiac Stanzas' is called 'A power' which, gone now, 'nothing can restore'. Many of the great poems are about this: they confront the loss of precisely that power whose glory has somehow prohibited or hidden the dark passages. It is even possible to read 'Old Man Travelling' as being about the need to endorse the vision of them and himself as 'sealed' against suffering: by being 'insensibly subdued / To settled quiet' and because he is 'by nature led / To peace so perfect', the old man is without 'human fears'. But then he speaks.

The leech-gatherer, the old man, the blind beggar: in their different ways they can all be seen as admonishers. But I suggest that Wordsworth became incapable of enduring their endurance, of bearing the admonishment. It not only connected him too painfully to the 'human heart', it required him to acknowledge that the connection denied him his authority as poet and as representative of certain class aspirations. In the end, therefore, the wanderer away from the world won, and the poet, as opposed to the 'poet' lost. This is the real meaning of the egotistical sublime. Autobiography becomes the means of securing selfhood, although the greatness of *The Prelude* has much to do with Wordsworth's awareness of how the world breaks in upon him, how, in other words, the self cannot be constructed apart from history.

Yet the counter movement, which Coleridge encouraged, towards the construction of the 'private' self in opposition to those 'out there', announced in the poem's opening lines, is very recognisable. It is both an element in Wordsworth's poetry, and a feature of the period. Raymond Williams has noted that such a movement anticipates a crisis in modern literature, which he explains as

> the division of experience into social and personal categories. It is now much more than an emphasis. It is a rooted division, into which the flow of experience is directed, and from which, with their own kinds of vigour, the separated kinds of life flow.[4]

Coleridge lived this division in particularly acute ways. He begins as a political radical, typically enough for an intellectual of his period, and from the early collaborative work with Southey he moves onto the great enterprise of the *Lyrical Ballads*. He and Wordsworth are to reunite divergent strains of poetry: of lyric (the personal) and ballad (the social). Yet from the outset of his career, Coleridge exhibits grave doubts and insecurities leading to a posture, a way of thinking and feeling, which seems very like paranoia. (A term which enters the language at about this time.) 'Others' represent a threat to the sense of selfhood so painfully constructed and so deeply doubted. And in Coleridge's case, this self is, of course, 'the poet'. Coleridge, we may say, almost needs to think of himself as 'a poet', where the term can be held to define a complex of given characteristics (given by Coleridge though derived from concepts we saw being linked together in Chapter 2: 'imagination', 'joy', 'inspiration'). These are then taken to be self-validating. They are also held to separate the poet from others, who in the 'Dejection' ode are lumped together as 'the poor loveless, ever-anxious crowd', and who pose a threat because they may not see the poet as he wants to see himself and to be seen. As a result, the personal and social cannot be reconciled or connected in a knowable community unless the social – whatever is 'out there' – is theorised as potentially destructive and thus requiring to be brought under control.

Whatever else *The Rime of the Ancient Mariner* is about, it is about this fear of others. As W. H. Auden pointed out, the individualised mariner is contrasted with the sailors *en masse*, who behave as an undifferentiated crowd. They live together, they die together:

> Four times fifty living men,
> (And I heard nor sigh nor groan)
> With heavy thump, a lifeless lump,
> They dropped down one by one.

The collective pronoun works here as it does in Edward Lear's limericks: 'They' signify the irresponsible but threatening crowd and as such 'they' are close to Wordsworth's presentation of the city crowd in *The Prelude*:

> The slaves unrespited of low pursuits,
> Living amid the same perpetual flow
> Of trivial objects, melted and reduced
> To one identity, by differences
> That have no law, no meaning, and no end.
> (Book 7, ll.700–4)

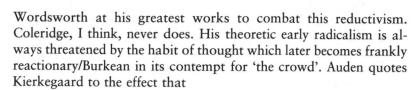

Wordsworth at his greatest works to combat this reductivism. Coleridge, I think, never does. His theoretic early radicalism is always threatened by the habit of thought which later becomes frankly reactionary/Burkean in its contempt for 'the crowd'. Auden quotes Kierkegaard to the effect that

> A public is neither a nation, nor a generation, nor a community . . . no single person who belongs to the public makes a real commitment; . . . a public is a kind of gigantic something, an abstract and deserted void which is everything and nothing.[5]

It is true that in 'This Lime Tree Bower My Prison' Coleridge struggles free of the prison of self so that the poem may end with him voicing his love for friends, and specifically for Charles Lamb, 'my gentle-hearted Charles'; and it is possible to make connections between this movement from imprisoned, internalised brooding towards social, affiliative love, and the movement of the mariner from *his* paranoid certainties to his 'blessing' the sea-creatures. It is further possible to note that in the beautiful 'Frost at Midnight' Coleridge's mind turns outward from 'Abstruser musings' to musings over his 'cradled infant'. In all these cases there is a movement from self-absorption towards that which is beyond the self. But what is beyond is not confronted as it is in Wordsworth. Vague blessings take the place of that painful, detailed encounter with the unfamiliar which distinguishes Wordsworth's radically great work. Coleridge's doubts and fears, on the other hand, are no doubt the motive power for his wanting Wordsworth to write that philosophical poem which would justify the act of poetry, of the *individual* imagination. This will explain why he complained of his friend's

> under predilection for the *dramatic* form in certain poems, from which one or other of two evils result. Either the thoughts and diction are different from that of the poet, and then there arises an incongruity of style; or they are the same and indistinguishable, and then it presents a species of ventriloquism, where two are represented as talking, while in truth only one speaks.[6]

To *complain* of the incongruity of styles is of course what gives Coleridge away. He refuses to acknowledge that such incongruity is the point. No wonder that he should have remarked to Crabb Robinson that Wordsworth 'unreasonably attached himself to the low'.[7] Fear of others now becomes a justification of separation from others, especially those who may be separated by class considerations. A consequence of all this is that the political and social commentator has to be brought into line with the literary theorist, and the result is that the many facets of Coleridge's thought are melded together by a conservatism which is affirmed as somehow 'natural'. Thus Coleridge can complain in a letter of 1809 of 'the present illogical age, which has in imitation of the French rejected all the *cements* of language', just as he can assert that the ideal statesman must not

> delude the uninstructed into the belief that their shortest way of obtaining the good things of this life is to commence busy politicians, instead of remaining industrious labourers. He knows, and acts on the knowledge, that it is the duty of the enlightened philanthropist to plead *for* the poor and ignorant, not *to* them.[8]

These unargued assertions show how far Coleridge has moved from his early radicalism towards the reactionary position into which he later hardened. And although not all aspects of his thought move at the same pace or with the same intensity, those that don't are pushed to the margins. This is why, as Paul Hamilton has excellently observed, there is an irreconcilable split between Coleridge's radical theory of the need for poetic language to be *constructive*, and that political and social conservatism which eventually means that he 'removes the conclusions of his radical philosophy to an isolated, immediate domain whenever they threaten his conservative interests in existing institutions'.[9]

That this does not make Coleridge pause to wonder whether he is entitled to speak 'for England' is evidence only of his typicality in believing that the isolated intellectual, like the poet, is properly privileged, or sanctioned, precisely because he is 'above' the crowd. Coleridge naturalises a socially constructed image of poet/intellectual in a manner that is familiar to us through the assumptions of his disciple, Matthew Arnold. This is the very opposite of that embattled commitment which other Romantic poets recognised in Milton; and it is typical of Coleridge that when he does make use of Milton it is to the Milton of *Samson Agonistes* he turns. In the 'Dejection' ode, Coleridge echoes words which the despairing Samson had addressed to his father, Manoa. Samson tells Manoa that he feels 'My genial spirits droop'. Coleridge says that he feels his own 'genial spirits fail'. The echo, whether conscious or not, is of great significance. The ode is about Coleridge's feeling himself to be no longer a 'chosen' poet.

He traces the cause of his rejection to God's displeasure at his guilty relationship with Sarah Hutchinson. (I put the matter baldly, but this is what it comes to.) Joy has been withdrawn from him. Milton's Samson similarly feels himself to be no longer a 'chosen' vessel of God. Coleridge is constructing an idea of the poet which derives from those half-developed concepts of inspiration and the sacred calling which will allow him to say something about the 'shaping spirit of imagination'. It is meant to be a contribution to, even a correction of, Wordsworth's brooding about the failure of such imagination. And this is quite deliberate.

One starting point for Coleridge's poem is the 'Immortality' ode, or as much of it as Wordsworth had written when Coleridge happened upon it at the beginning of April 1802. The relationship between the two poems is as complicated as was the relationship between the two poets.[10] But we know it was partly as a result of reading Coleridge's poem that Wordsworth wrote 'Resolution and Independence'. Wordsworth's poem is, among other things, a rebuke to that 'naturalised' and mystificatory image of the poet which his friend tried to substantiate in his 'Dejection' ode.

I draw attention to this for two reasons. First, it shows that the great Wordsworth was not prepared to rest content with Coleridge's idealist concept of the poet. Second, the other side to the coin is that Wordsworth was more affected by Coleridge's theory than might at first seem clear, or than is admitted by those who want to pretend that the poet of 'Resolution and Independence' isn't the poet of 'Sonnets Dedicated to Liberty'. And yet, here again matters are far from simple. Against the routine patriotism of 'On Returning to Dover' there is, for example, the sonnet on Toussaint L'Ouverture, whose terrible fate, although not completed by the time Wordsworth wrote his sonnet in August 1802 (Toussaint died in a French prison in 1803), is nevertheless emblematic of the reversal of events from the great days of the French Revolution. In 1801 Napoleon had reinstated in the French colonies the slavery which the Republic had abolished in 1794, and had brought to France the man who had freed the slaves of San Domingo. One can therefore understand why Wordsworth should now look to England as the land of liberty and why the cadences of many of the sonnets in this sequence should be derived from Milton, just as one can understand Landor's remark about France in 1802, when he heard of Napoleon's assuming the title of First Consul for life, that 'as to the cause of liberty, this cursed nation has ruined it for ever'.

The problem, however, is that unlike the Blake of *Poetical Sketches* and the *Songs*, Wordsworth has no way of going on from Milton. The ending of the sonnet to Toussaint, which tells him that 'thou hast great allies; / Thy friends are exultations, agonies, / And love, and Man's unconquerable mind' may be touching, but is spoken in conquered accents. These are the accents of Milton's sonnets to Fairfax and Cromwell, and 'On the Late Massacre in Piedmont', which we know that Wordsworth deeply admired. Thus the despairing 'Milton! thou shouldst be living at this hour' can do no more than ape 'Miltonics' in its account of England as 'a fen / Of stagnant waters'. In short, these are not the poems of a man speaking to men. They are more the work of a man putting on – not airs, that would be quite wrong, but putting on borrowed robes.

I would suggest that at this period Wordsworth faced an acute crisis. He hated what had happened to the French Revolution, and felt England had no option but to renew war in 1803 (he even offered his services, should they be needed). But he had lost the ability to find a poetic voice which would connect him to the radical concerns which had sustained his earlier work. The Miltonics are, then, part of a lapse into nostalgia which allows him to speak of the 'Great men [who] have been among us' as a way of writing off the present. The dilemmas of the moment left Wordsworth with insuperable difficulties when it came to finding a poetic strategy – a language – that would be equal to the occasion. The sonnets do what he rightly condemned Paley and Godwin for doing, fitting things to words rather than words to things. They are 'powerless in regulating our judgements concerning the value of men & things. They contain no picture of human life: they *describe* nothing'.[11] They are, in short, 'poetry'. From here it is a short step to the fantasising that shows through 'Rob Roy's Grave' (1803).

> And, if the word had been fulfill'd,
>   As *might* have been, then, thought of joy!
> France would have had her present Boast;
>   And we our brave Rob Roy!

The word that might have been was Rob Roy's boast that 'kingdoms shall shift about, like clouds, / Obedient to my breath'. The implausibility of this is only slightly less than the poem's soft-focus hero-worship; and this, in its anti-democratic individualism, makes possible that stance of apartness from the world whose variant expression can be aloofness: of being above the crowd. As Kiernan remarks, Wordsworth increasingly came to 'think of the mind's contact with other minds in social life as cramping and strangling, instead of moulding and fertilising'.[12] Speaking 'for' England means insisting on an unopposable authority which denies the possibility of speaking *to* or *with* those men and women who are both within Wordsworth's greatest poetry and who provide a possible constituency for its reception.

Blake, never seeking to appease a readership, ends without one. Wordsworth, seeking appeasement, ends as Poet Laureate. Blake's visions of England are liberating and tragically truthful. Wordsworth's are increasingly false. Wordsworth, of course, does what becomes accepted as orthodox and proper. He retreats to higher ground – that ground which Arnold thought all true prophets and commentators should occupy if they were to avoid being blackened by the smoke of the market place. From this prospect he can comment, in 'Miltonic' style, upon that vast and empty abstraction, 'England', while at the same time claiming the right to be a private poet.

But it is a false division. For 'private' turns out to mean identification with certain forces, interests, which between them compose a social and cultural orthodoxy. This is to be a lost leader. Nor will it do to say that Wordsworth moves towards the kind of Horatianism which Pope adopted in his later years. Too much has happened in between times for that to be possible. The choices are different and indeed became so from the moment when Wordsworth announced that a poet was a man speaking to men. The grandeur of that claim and the ambition to make it good are hardly to be denied. But Wordsworth finds it too painful to sustain them. Instead, he tries to cover over the fact that he is someone who, both as man and as poet, is implicated in the social process in ways that make for separation and thus impede the connections which a man speaking to men must wish to establish. Of course, the impediments could have become a proper part of speech, could indeed have been what that speech, that poetry, was *about*. But for that to have been so would have required Wordsworth to have stripped away what was meant by 'poet', and this he would not or could not bring himself to do. The result is that he has to mystify his role just as he has to mystify as 'inevitable' particular processes by means of which he is separated from the 'men' whom he hopes to address in communality. And it then follows that 'poet' and historical 'inevitability' are alike constructions which are used to make legitimate a withdrawal onto what is asserted as a more authoritative plane of utterance.

From his 'free' place, or 'dwelling', among the Lakes, remote from the city, the poet poses as a man speaking *for* men, and particularly for Englishmen and England. This is the ultimate, deeply conservative, ambition of pastoral. It falsifies the actual relationships of non-city communities just as much and for the same reason that it falsifies city communities. 'Merry England' stands at the opposite end of a vision of nationhood from Blake's Golgonooza. And as we have seen, neither old men travelling nor city crowds may be allowed their own voices, for these might disturb and even undermine the poet's authority. 'England' now becomes a vacant site, its custodian the poet who claims for himself the right *as poet* to interpret it in a way that denies all other interpretations. Everything now becomes mysterious.

From John Lucas, *England and Englishness: Ideas of Nationhood in English Poetry 1688–1900* (London, 1990), pp. 110–18.

NOTES

[John Lucas's critique of Wordsworth comes in the course of a comprehensive discussion of the way ideas of England and Englishness were expressed in poetry between 1688 and 1900. Lucas locates Wordsworth historically at a point of crisis for national identity: the period of the French Revolution and its immediate, Napoleonic aftermath, and the early phase of nineteenth-century industrialisation. The analysis is informed by Marxist theories of emergent class struggle and alienation.

For Lucas, Wordsworth's career encapsulates the air of uncertainty and dislocation which characterises this period, and which surfaces in the debate that developed about the function of the poet and poetry in early nineteenth-century society. A broad cultural thesis is therefore being addressed here, in the course of which new insights into the poetry become available. References to poems from *Lyrical Ballads* are taken from *Wordsworth and Coleridge, Lyrical Ballads*, ed. Brett and Jones (London, 1963); for all other references, see *The Poetical Works of William Wordsworth*, ed. E. de Selincourt and Helen Darbishire, 5 vols (Oxford 1940–9). Ed.]

1. Raymond Williams, 'Culture', in *Marx: The First Hundred Years*, ed. D. McLellan (London, 1983), p. 33.

2. Heather Glen, *Vision and Disenchantment: Blake's Songs and Wordsworth's Lyrical Ballads* (Cambridge, 1983), p. 21.

3. *Complete Works of John Keats*, ed. Buxton Forman (Glasgow, 1901), vol. 4, p. 109.

4. Raymond Williams, *Modern Tragedy* (London, 1977), p. 121.

5. W. H. Auden, *The Enchafèd Flood* (London, 1951), p. 34.

6. S. T. Coleridge, *Biographia Literaria* (London, 1817), vol. 2, pp. 150–1.

7. Quoted by Paul Hamilton in *Coleridge's Poetics* (London, 1983), p. 161.

8. For this see Coleridge, *The Friend*, 'Section the First: On the Principles of Political Knowledge', Essay 5, 'On the Errors of Party Spirit: or, Extremes Meet'.

9. Paul Hamilton, *Coleridge's Poetics* (London, 1983), p. 203.

10. There is an account in H. House, *Coleridge* (London, 1953), which has been amplified by later commentators.

11. Paul Hamilton, *Coleridge's Poetics* (London, 1983), p. 142.

12. V. G. Kiernan, 'Wordsworth', in *Marxists on Literature*, ed. David Craig (London, 1975), p. 198.

5

William Wordsworth and the Real Estate

ROGER SALES

UNWORTHY PURPOSES

Wordsworth toadied the counter-revolutionary line with the worst of them towards the end of his career. He was forever moaning away about the way in which social edifices were crumbling because tried and tested props and buttresses had not been repaired. He also lamented the lack of 'moral cement'[1] to bind the whole structure together. He felt, somewhat predictably, that self-interest was shaking the very foundations. His breathtakingly unoriginal solution was to try to persuade everybody to support their local landed aristocrat. He showed them the conservative way when he lent his support to the Lowthers in the 1818 election. Self-interest was apparently destroying civilisation. Now the Lowthers had used their substantial influence to secure Wordsworth's appointment as distributor of stamps for Westmorland in 1813. Although minor bureaucrats were not supposed to be actively involved in electioneering, Wordsworth nevertheless inflicted two almost unreadable election addresses on the unfortunate freeholders of Westmorland in 1818. It would appear that self-interest and civilisation were not exactly incompatible. Civilisation was, according to this very civil servant, a large landed estate:

> As far as it concerns the general well-being of the Kingdom, it would be easy to shew, that if the democratic activities of the great Towns and of the manufacturing Districts, were not counteracted by the

92

sedentary power of large estates, continued from generation to generation in particular families, it would be scarcely possible that the Laws and Constitution of the Country could sustain the shocks which they would be subject to. And as to our own County, *that* man must be strangely prejudiced, who does not perceive how desirable it is, that some powerful individual should be attached to it: who, by his influence with Government, may facilitate the execution of any plan tending, with due concern for the *general* welfare, to the especial benefit of Westmorland. The influence of the House of Lowther is, we acknowledge, great; but has a case been made out, that this influence has been abused?[2]

It presumably depended on whether the Lowthers used their influence wisely on your behalf, or abused it by taking action against you. Henry Brougham, who entered the electoral lists against such 'sedentary power' certainly felt that he could rest his case on the fact that the family had a whole county, not to mention a hack writer, in their political pocket. Wordsworth's election addresses ought to have sent the freeholders scampering over to Brougham, but the Lowther boys did in fact romp home. Wordsworth was entitled to vote in the election himself as Lord Lowther had helped him to buy a freehold in Westmorland in 1806. No wonder he was strangely prejudiced in favour of the landed aristocracy. They helped William to pay the bills with a handful of silver.

Angry young men become more aristocratic than the aristocracy with monotonous regularity. Wordsworth made surprisingly few twists and turns on his journey down this well-trodden path. There is only really a difference of emphasis between the 1818 election addresses and poems such as 'Michael'. Wordsworth wrote to Charles James Fox in 1801 to try to interest him in the plight of small farmers in the Lake District:

> In the two Poems, 'The Brothers' and 'Michael', I have attempted to draw a picture of the domestic affections, as I know they exist amongst a class of men who are now almost confined to the North of England. They are small independent *proprietors* of land here called statesmen, men of respectable education who daily labour on their own little properties. The domestic affections will always be strong amongst men who live in a country not crowded with population, if these men are placed above poverty. But if they are proprietors of small estates, which have descended to them from their ancestors, the power which these affections will acquire amongst such men is inconceivable to those who have only an opportunity of observing hired labourers,

farmers, and the manufacturing Poor. Their little tract of land serves as a kind of permanent rallying point for their domestic feelings, as a tablet upon which they are written which makes them objects of memory in a thousand instances when they would otherwise be forgotten.[3]

The increasing belief that small was inefficient was, according to Wordsworth, leading to the virtual genocide of this race of small proprietors and all that they stood for. These 'statesmen', like the Lowthers, handed down their estates from father to son. In this, and other respects, they merely illustrated that the great and small were inextricably connected. If these small estates were allowed to be broken up, then it was only a matter of time before the aristocratic estates and the realm of the state itself crumbled away. 'Domestic affections' and a sense of place and pride would, presumably, be replaced by mere self-interest. The argument is essentially the same whether you work downwards from the large estate, or upwards from the small one. 'Michael' and the 1818 election addresses only differ in emphasis.

'Michael' appears to be concerned with refuge.[4] It is necessary to leave 'the public way' in order to reach the 'straggling heap of unhewn stones', which, like the bones of a dead sheep, are strewn over a particular part of the landscape. This 'public way' represents orthodox interpretations of historical progress. Wordsworth establishes a contrast between such official, linear versions of history and a more private version. Michael's story is significantly 'ungarnish'd with events', in other words with what historians classify as important events. It is 'a history' or a story, rather than history. Wordsworth is not, however, just taking refuge in early eighteenth-century rural society. He is trying to suggest that the lessons which may be drawn from this simple story of farming folk might offer a more acceptable social foundation. He draws out these lessons or worthy purposes by reflecting on the relative merits of past and present. His emphasis is reflective rather than purely descriptive. He implies that the virtues of thrift, frugality, patience and perseverance, all of which he claims to have found in this early eighteenth-century society, could put the country back on the right road. Reflection has led to thoughts of rescue. His initial suggestion is that such rescue will be on a fairly limited scale:

Therefore, although it be a history
Homely and rude, I will relate the same
For the delight of a few natural hearts,
And with yet fonder feeling, for the sake
Of youthful Poets, who among these Hills
Will be my second self when I am gone.

Pastoral is an underground literature in which stories are passed on
and kept alive by the faithful few. Yet the unfinished sheep-fold
provides a warning for the present. You may not need cement to
build with dry-stone, but you must have 'moral cement' in order to
achieve anything permanent in both private and public life. If public
life is based on 'domestic affections', then there may be a chance of
rescuing it from the error of its ways. Public figures like Charles
James Fox were invited to read the poem and then act upon it. Such
attempts at social rescue are severely compromised by strains of
requiem. The farmhouse needs to be approached with due religious
care and attention. The brook may be 'boisterous', but the atmosphere at this shrine is dominated by 'an utter solitude'. The clipping
tree represents a spire and the heap of stones a bare, ruined choir.
Wordsworth has come both to praise and bury Michael. The poem
has come full circle. We start by leaving 'the public way' to find these
stones and we finish up there as well:

The Cottage which was nam'd The Evening Star
Is gone, the ploughshare has been through the ground
On which it stood; great changes have been wrought
In all the neighbourhood, yet the Oak is left
That grew beside their Door; and the remains
Of the unfinished Sheep-fold may be seen
Beside the boisterous brook of Green-head Gill.

Our beginning is also our end. This circular movement, and the
requiem which accompanies it, rules out any chance of effective
social rescue.

Wordsworth's vision of rural society is mediated and controlled
by refuge, reflection, rescue and requiem, yet the most significant
aspect of 'Michael' is the way in which it reconstructs the past. The
plough that broke this plain style of living was not actually driven by
anybody. This provides a good example of the way in which
Wordsworth is unwilling to commit himself even to general propositions about economic agency in relation to the internal structure of

rural society. The nearest he comes to it is when he raises the issue of land tenure, which was very much the grievance of grievances as far as the Lakeland farmers were concerned:

> These fields were burthen'd when they came to me;
> 'Till I was forty years of age, not more
> Than half of my inheritance was mine.

Yet fields do not burthen themselves, just as ploughs do not drive themselves. Wordsworth is deliberately vague about economic agency because he is trying to play the oldest trick in the crooked pastoralist's cooked book. He wants to suggest that early eighteenth-century rural society was a pre-capitalist utopia. Michael and his wife, Isabel, are, apparently, able to take such a pride in their work because it is their work. There is no division of labour. Cottage industry appears to take place in a vacuum:

> She was a woman of a stirring life
> Whose heart was in her house; two wheels she had
> Of antique form, this large for spinning wool,
> That small for flax, and if one wheel had rest,
> It was because the other was at work.

The cottage was a veritable hive of 'eager industry'. If this was taken away, it too would become merely a heap of useless stones. Property and possessions provided a vitalising eagerness, or what Wordsworth referred to in 'The Old Cumberland Beggar' as 'vital anxiousness'. Adam Smith and the political economists would have agreed with this equation between economic vitality and 'anxiousness'. Yet Michael and his ilk might well have been a great deal more anxious than Wordsworth implies, for cottage industry was not carried out in such splendid isolation. All the evidence, including Wordsworth's own prose works, suggests that there was an economic market-place in the Lake District itself. The products of cottage industry were bought and sold. Any mention of this in the poem would have raised questions about economic agency, so Wordsworth reconstructs the past by presenting us with a self-sufficient family unit, who are hermetically sealed off from the outside world. Their cottage stands 'single' and they too stand aloof from any economic community. It is therefore impossible for them to be attacked and destroyed by economic agents from within Lake District society itself. We learn that Michael has agreed to stand surety for his nephew. We do not learn, incidentally, whether this nephew actually lives and works in the Lake District. The implication is that he does not, for 'unforeseen misfortunes suddenly/Had press'd upon him'. This sounds like the supposedly alien commercial world with its booms and slumps rather than the natural rhythms and patterns of farming life. Michael decides to try to pay off this forfeiture by sending his son, Luke, off to work in the 'dissolute' city with another member of the family. This means that the small estate does not have to be broken up and sold off. It also means that son will be able to inherit from father. Luke leaves the cottage and begins his journey along 'the public way'. He fails to remember the virtues of the face-to-face, shoulder-to-shoulder world he has left behind. He forgets that pride and dignity in labour cement a family together. It is, then, an ill-defined and significantly distanced commercial ethos which destroys Michael's estate. This presumably drives the plough by remote control. The land is, incidentally, not bought up by a member of the Lakeland community. A stranger, who may well have made his money in the 'dissolute city', finally gets possession of the estate. As suggested, Wordsworth can only achieve this distance between commerce and the farming community by a process of reconstruction. We do, it is true, learn about other members of the family and some of the neighbours are allowed walk-on parts. Yet the overall impression conveyed by the poem is that Michael, Isabel and Luke are an island entire unto themselves. Robert Burns shows in 'The Cottar's Saturday Night' that it is perfectly possible to evoke this sense of splendid isolation without necessarily reconstructing the entire agricultural community. Saturday night is an island in a sea of commercialised agriculture. The family make a special point of returning from their various scattered occupations for this particular evening. One of the many problems with 'Michael' is that every night is Saturday night.

It is easy enough to think of products which are advertised as being both natural and historically authentic. If the advertising boys wanted us to wear old-fashioned, hand-knitted socks, they would probably show us a farmer's wife, all wrinkles, white hair and toothless smile, cheerfully at work on an antique spinning-wheel. We would probably realise, instanter if not sooner, that the natural setting and the antique, or historical, props were being used by them as hidden persuaders. Similarly, if they tried to persuade us to drink pints and pints of 'old familiar' by showing us a venerable old shepherd having a quick one as the sun went down over the clipping tree, we would probably be able to read the image without too much difficulty. What is Wordsworth trying to peddle in 'Michael'? It is substantially the same product as he was trying to sell to the freeholders of Westmorland in 1818, for he is primarily concerned to divorce real estate, or economics, from concepts of estate. He does this, as suggested, by ignoring or evading questions of economic agency. Farmers' wives do not go to market. Ploughs drive themselves and fields are mysteriously burdened with debts. Strangers snap up property and an alien commercial system casts dark shadows over the landscape. Such an image must be seen as propaganda for the local gentry and aristocracy, as it conveniently ignores even the possibility that they might have been Michael's real enemies. The historical evidence, particularly with regard to land tenure, suggests that this was more of a probability than a possibility. John Bailey described in his *General View of the Agriculture of the County of Cumberland* (1794) how the large landowners were able to extract feudal obligations from the statesmen:

> There are probably few counties, where *property in land* is divided into such small parcels as in Cumberland: and those small properties so universally occupied by the owners; by far the greatest part of which are held under the lords of the manors, by that species of vassalage, called *customary tenure*; subject to the payment of fines and heriots, on alienation, death of the Lord, or death of tenant, and the payment of certain annual rents, and performance of various services, called *Boon-days* such as getting and leading the lord's peats, plowing and harrowing his land, reaping his corn, haymaking, carrying letters, &c.&c whenever summoned by the lord.
>
> (p. 11)

Bailey estimated that two-thirds of the county was held under the feudal sway of customary tenure. Those who leased their property were even worse off, since the aristocracy and gentry of Cumberland rarely signed any binding documents or let out their property for longer than nine years at a stretch. A . Pringle's *General View of the Agriculture of the County of Westmorland* (1794) made the same complaints against customary tenure. Statesmen in the Lake District also had the lords of the manor on their backs for tithes since most of these were owned by lay impropriators.

Unlike the election addresses, 'Michael' should be seen as implicit rather than explicit propaganda for the Lowther family, since relationships between the Wordsworths and the Lowthers were cool to freezing when the poem was actually written. Wordsworth's father had acted as a political agent for the Lowthers, which ought to make us cynical of the attempts in Book Nine of *The Prelude* and elsewhere to pretend that the Lake District had once been an egalitarian republic. It was in reality more like an extensive pocket borough. The community as a whole had never been Hawkshead writ large. After his father's death, Wordsworth and the other members of the family were involved in a long wrangle to try to get the Lowthers to pay up for the services which had been rendered. This dispute was not settled until 1802. Although 'Michael' was not written specifically for the Lowthers, there was nothing in it which they, or their rivals such as the Curwens, could object to, for their role as economic agents in the community is not even hinted at. Luke is not packed off to a local town such as Whitehaven, from which the Lowthers controlled their extensive coal and tobacco empires. He is sent to an unnamed city. Thus the message that the estate is being swamped by an alien commercial spirit is not compromised by the recognition that the large estates of the Lowthers and the Curwens were built on the foundations of capitalist enterprises. If Luke had gone to Whitehaven, he might have noticed that a lot of small statesmen had been cleared off the land so that they would not impede the production and transportation of coal. Statesmen were also cleared off to make way for agrarian as well as industrial capitalism. Like most other rural areas in this period, the Lake District was subjected to a double standard. Those at the bottom of the scale were hemmed in with paternalistic, in this particular case almost feudalistic, restrictions. They also had to put up with the disadvantages of capitalism just for good measure. Those at the top of the scale were able to exploit both paternalism and capitalism to the full.[5] Wordsworth tries to peddle us an image in which paternalism is presented as individualism and capitalism as totally alien. He is thus writing propaganda for the victors.

Wordsworth told Fox that both 'Michael' and 'The Brothers' were 'faithful copies from nature'.[6] They were, of course, nothing of the kind. There may appear to be a contradiction between this assertion of authenticity and the fact that 'Michael', like other lyrical ballads, is subtitled 'A Pastoral Poem'. Yet this subtitle probably needs to be taken ironically. It is clearly stated in the 1800 Preface to *Lyrical Ballads* that conventional literary expectations are going to be turned upside down:

> It is supposed, that by the act of writing in verse an Author makes a formal engagement that he will gratify certain known habits of association, that he not only thus apprizes the Reader that certain classes of ideas and expressions will be found in his book, but that others will be carefully excluded.
>
> (p. ix)

Wordsworth and Coleridge tried iconoclastically to smash such formal engagements. As far as 'Michael' is concerned, Wordsworth assumes that the reader, like the tourist, has certain preconceived ideas about pastoral. These need to be confronted by the realities of rural life. Wordsworth's brisk, guidebook tone at the beginning of the poem needs to be seen as pastiche. The description of 'The pastoral Mountains' probably needs to be taken ironically as well, for, as a general but by no means infallible rule, Wordsworth does not describe mountains in the Lake District as being pastoral. The farms around Tintern Abbey, the downs around Salisbury Plain and the valleys around Goslar in Switzerland are described as being pastoral, but this is almost to differentiate these landscapes from the mountains, if not the valleys, of the Lake District. Wordsworth claims in Book Eight of *The Prelude* that he has always been fascinated by real rather than imaginary shepherds. Classical and Renaissance pastoral fictions were no substitute for the real thing. Although Wordsworth does claim, rather interestingly, that there were jolly English peasants who danced around maypoles, such creatures played no part in his childhood:

> . . . the times had scattered all
> These lighter graces, and the rural custom
> And manners which it was my chance to see
> In childhood were severe and unadorned.
> The unluxuriant produce of a life
> Intent on little but substantial needs.
> Yet beautiful, and beauty that was felt.
> (ll.204–10)[7]

Wordsworth's emphasis on the 'severe and unadorned' may be seen as part of a general attempt to convince us that his descriptions of Lakeland society really are faithfully copied from nature. Yet particular shepherds are so inextricably connected with the geographical and emotional landscape of childhood that the equation between 'severe' and 'faithful' or realistic, which is a shaky one at the best of times, does not hold. They emerge from the mountain mists like giants and disappear into the setting sun. A love of nature leads to a love of mankind simply because, as far as these shepherds are concerned, it is difficult to work out what the difference is. They thus become an integral part of Wordsworth's pastoral perspective. 'Michael' follows the same pattern as Book Eight of *The Prelude*. There is an attempt to juxtapose pastoral conventions with the 'severe and unadorned'. Wordsworth uses a number of devices to try to achieve this kind of authenticity. He pointed out that the poem was a true story as it was based on

> a family to whom had belonged, many years before, the house we lived in at Town-End, along with some fields and woodlands on the eastern shore of Grasmere.[8]

He tells us, in the poem itself, that the story was one he had heard in his youth. Topographical details help to sustain this illusion of authenticity. The stones are also important in this attempt to move from pastoral fictions to historical facts. If these stones actually exist, then the implication is that the story associated with them is, if not quite so tangible, then certainly real. Like Oscar Wilde, we should be suspicious of these and other documentary strategies. Vivian in 'The Decay of Lying' notices that Wordsworth has a habit of finding 'in stones the sermons he had already hidden there'.[9] We should always be on our guard against interpretative sleights-of-hand, particularly when they may be hidden behind supposedly realistic trappings. Wordsworth may not present us with a world of jolly good shepherds fleecing their flocks, but his pastoralism hides a world in which such members of rural society are fleeced by their local overseers.

CIRCUS TURNS

If all the young men like Luke have gone to become just another face in another crowd, then the writing is well and truly on the cottage wall. Wordsworth maintains, in 'Michael' and elsewhere, that the days of 'domestic affections' have been numbered. Although he does in fact try to convince Charles James Fox that these values were still just about alive and well in 1801, poems such as 'The Female Vagrant' present a rather different picture.[10] 'Domestic affections' are only kept alive by outcasts and solitaries. The vagrant's troubles are brought about by gentrification:

> . . . Then rose a stately hall our woods among,
> And cottage after cottage owned its sway.
> No joy to see a neighbouring house, or stray
> Through pastures not his own, the master took;
> My Father dared his greedy wish gainsay;
> He loved his old hereditary nook,
> And ill could I the thought of such sad parting brook.

Wordsworth is again deliberately vague about economic agency. Halls do not build themselves, just as ploughs do not drive themselves. We are also not told whether the new master is a native of the Lake District or an outsider. All the indications are that he is a stranger. So, once again, there is no consideration of the internal economic structure of the community. This new master attempts to buy out the vagrant's father. He may have suggested that a few 'domestic affections' might accidentally get broken, if the old man continued to block his view. The father is certainly 'Sore traversed in whate'er he bought and sold' and so has to leave this particular cottage. Economic sharp practice is being associated with outsiders. The family manage to set themselves up in another cottage, so father is at least able to die happy. He may not have 'One field, a flock, and what the neighbouring flood / Supplied' any more, but there was a good old cottage roof over his head. He is thus able to retain illusions about the permanence of this way of life:

> . . . My happy father died
> When sad distress reduced the childrens' meal:
> Thrice happy! that from him the grave did hide
> The empty loom, cold earth, and silent wheel,
> And tears that flowed for ills which patience could not heal.

The vagrant and her husband are forced to leave the Lake District and follow like dogs at the 'heels of war'. Tragedy strikes yet again:

> . . . All perished – all, in one remorseless year,
> Husband and children! one by one, by sword
> And ravenous plague, all perished: every tear
> Dried up, despairing, desolate, on board
> A British ship I waked, as from a trance restored.

She responds in true Wordsworthian fashion to the calming influence of nature, in this case represented by the sea, but is finally turned adrift. When she reaches dry land she is eventually taken to a hospital, since she does not speak 'the beggar's language' and is thus unable to support herself. She becomes more in tune with this language later on:

> My heart is touched to think that men like these,
> The rude earth's tenants, were my first relief:
> How kindly did they paint their vagrant ease!
> And their long holiday that feared not grief,
> For all belonged to all, and each was chief.
> No plough their sinews strained; on grating road
> No wain they drove, and yet, the yellow sheaf
> In every vale for their delight was stowed:
> For them in nature's meads the milky udder flowed.

These vagrants are nature's statesmen because, against all the odds, they manage to cling to the simple virtues. Wordsworth is suggesting that, when both local and national communities are dislocated, only those who remain on the margins can keep these crucial values alive. The vagrant finally realises that she must to her own self be true:

> . . . But, what afflicts my peace with keenest ruth
> Is, that I have my inner self abused,
> Foregone the home delight of constant truth,
> And clear and open soul, so prized in fearless youth.

Times may change, but values should remain the same.

It is sometimes suggested that this particular poem offers a savage critique of unjust wars on both the home and foreign fronts, but Wordsworth's treatment of the internal structure of rural society is, once again, evasive. Indeed, it has many similarities with 'Michael' in this respect. Michael may have been splendidly isolated, but at least he was able to die on his own estate. He was probably even buried in the 'family mold', yet, if the plough had ripped up the ground immediately after Luke's fall from Wordsworthian grace, then Michael too might have been forced onto the roads and margins of rural society. His 'domestic affections', instead of being fixed and tangibly located in a particular place, would have become completely internalised. The hum of contented industry was in fact replaced by an 'utter solitude' after his death. The solitaries and outcasts keep alive the values which would otherwise have died with Michael and been buried forever in the 'family mold'. Dorothy Wordsworth recorded in her *Journal* for 2 June 1802 one of the many visits to their backdoor by beggars:

> Yesterday an old man called, a grey-headed man, above 70 years of age. He said he had been a soldier, that his wife and children had died in Jamaica. He had a Beggar's wallet over his shoulders, a coat of shreds and patches altogether of a drab colour – he was tall, and though his body was bent he had the look of one used to have been upright.[11]

The vagrant's father had a 'bending body' and the leech gatherer, in 'Resolution and Independence', is 'bent-double'. Those who manage against all the odds to keep 'upright', like the discharged soldier in Book Four of *The Prelude*, are still arrestingly abnormal. Wordsworth's travelling circus of freakish outcasts may appear to offer a critique of the unacceptable face of rural society, yet they merely endorse the same propagandist interpretation of social changes as 'Michael' tries to sell us. We are certainly presented with a rural wasteland. The last of the human flock meagrely shuffle about trying to remember what the good old days were really like. The brothers Ewbank are described as 'the last of all their race' in 'The Brothers'. It is almost as if a nuclear bomb has been dropped on the landscape. This is precisely the problem. Wordsworth is so busy depicting the effects of such bombs, that he can conveniently ignore the explosion taking place within rural society itself. The landscape and its inhabitants are attacked from the outside by bombs such as commerce, gentrification, 'dissolute cities' and even the Napoleonic wars. Yet there was an economic bomb, which was being exploded right under his nose. As it was being detonated by the local aristocracy and gentry, we do not hear a great deal about it.

It is also worth stressing that, like Michael, these solitaries and outcasts were only expected to be independent in carefully prescribed dependent situations. Dorothy's description in her *Journal* for 22 December 1801 of an encounter with yet another beggar illustrates how these outcasts were expected to conform:

> As we came up the White Moss we met an old man, who I saw was a beggar by his two bags hanging over his shoulder, but from a half laziness, half indifference, and a wanting to *try* him if he would speak I let him pass. He said nothing, and my heart smote me. I turned back and said You are begging? 'Ay', says he. I gave him a halfpenny. William, judging from his appearance joined in I suppose you were a sailor? 'Ay,' he replied. 'I have been 57 years at sea, 12 of them on board a man-of-war under Sir Hugh Palmer.' Why have you not a pension? 'I have no pension, but I could have got into Greenwich hospital but all my officers are dead.'[12]

This game of beggarman's bluff represents a means test, in every sense of the word. Dorothy felt not only willing but able to '*try*' this particular beggar. He should, after all, have put himself in a dependent position straight away. That was the rule of the social game. The beggar, who had probably heard that the Wordsworths usually liked their money's worth as well, decided it was not worth making a pitch. As far as Dorothy was concerned, this represented a defiant and independent gesture. Her heart may have been smitten by compassion, but she wanted to control this compassion on her own terms. So she immediately forced the discharged seaman into the obligatory subservient role. Once money had actually been told into his hand, he was under an obligation to tell William about his life and hard times. William, at first anyway, treated him as any overseer of the country poor would have done. There is, incidentally, no evidence to suggest that this particular beggar had any connection with small statesmen living or dead, but his treatment may still be related to Wordsworth's prescriptive attitude towards Michael and his kind. The poems themselves contain evidence of this attitude. Michael knows his place. He also knows a great deal about patience, perseverance and frugality. If external evidence is required, then examples of pastoralism in performance, like the drama which took place at Moss Side on 22 December 1801, ought to be considered. Wordsworth's pastoralism is riddled with paradoxes: the independent are expected to be dependent and the outcasts are expected to conform.

FACE-TO-FACE

The real problem with Wordsworth's representation of rural society is that the poachers are transformed into the gamekeepers. The Lowthers and their kind are either explicitly or implicitly held up as shining examples to all other gamekeepers, yet they were not averse to economic poaching expeditions. The 1818 election addresses show Wordsworth at his most explicitly conservative, although *Lyrical Ballads*, *The Prelude*, and indeed most of the poems on which his inflated poetic reputation is based, carry at least the seeds of this conservatism within them. Hannah More, Legh Richmond and Mary Mitford all sang the praises of the small, face-to-face community. Wordsworth chimed in with them. He found, rather surprisingly, welcoming faces at Cambridge, but failed miserably to respond to

London street theatre. He describes his bumpkin's progress in Book
Seven of *The Prelude*: .

> Here there and everywhere a weary throng,
> The comers and the goers face to face,
> Face after face; the string of dazzling wares,
> Shop after shop, with symbols, blazoned names,
> And all the tradesman's honours overhead:
> (ll.171–5)

It was the London Corresponding Society which threatened to re-
place 'face to face' with 'members unlimited', or 'face after face'.
Wordsworth is lost in the streets of London town because the good
old days when everybody knew each other and their place appear to
have gone forever:

> How often, in the overflowing streets,
> Have I gone forwards with the crowd, and said
> Unto myself, 'The face of every one
> That passes by me is a mystery!'
> Thus have I looked, nor ceased to look, oppressed
> By thoughts of what and whither, when and how,
> Until the shapes before my eyes became
> A second-sight procession, such as glides
> Over still mountains, or appears in dreams;
> And all the ballast of familiar life,
> The present, and the past; hope, fear; all stays,
> All laws of acting, thinking, speaking man
> Went from me, neither knowing me, nor known.
> (ll.594–606)

The city is 'dissolute' because it dissolves personal identity.
Wordsworth is swept into the ebbing and flowing tide of street life
against his will. He is carried along by the crowd and feels as if he is
drowning. His identity and will are being submerged. He is being
literally reduced to a part of the mainstream. This passage is often
interpreted as a great poet's affirmation of individual, nay human,
values, which is both of its time and for all time. Wordsworth is all
for reason when he stands there feeling 'oppressed' in those city
streets. Such interpretations accept Wordsworthian propaganda as
the whole truth. They firmly believe, for instance, that familiarity
does not breed contempt. They do not question assumptions that
villages and policemen are good things. Like the village bobby,

Wordsworth only feels at home when he knows all the faces on his patch or manor. He can then successfully interrogate them with 'thoughts of what and whither, when and how' as they pass by. This rescues him from drowning, but it means that most other people are swamped by a parochial paternalism. George Canning, the Tory politician, struck a Wordsworthian note when he defended the counter-revolutionary legislation which had been passed in the wake of Peterloo during the 1820 election campaign:

> Ancient habits, which the reformers would call prejudices; preconceived attachments, which they would call corruption; that mutual respect which makes the eye of a neighbour a security for each man's good conduct, but which the reformers would stigmatise as a confederacy among the few for the dominion over their fellows – all these things make men difficult to be moved on the sudden to any extravagant and violent enterprise. But bring together a multitude of individuals having no permanent relation to each other, no common tie, but what arises from their concurrences as members of that meeting, a tie dissolved as soon as the meeting is at an end; – in such an aggregation of individuals there is no such mutual respect, no such check upon the proceedings of each man from the awe of his neighbour's disapprobation. . . .[13]

Political meetings ought to be put down because they were not ballasted up with the familiar. Pastoral suggests that all communities, including the political one, are made up of friends and neighbours. They are face-to-face societies, which are based on a 'common tie' and a 'mutual respect'. Yet our village was not really their village. Similarly, for all his parade of homely, folksie togetherness, Canning was in fact trying to justify some ruthlessly paternalistic legislation. The implementation of the Six Acts against the radical movement is another example of pastoralism in performance.

Wordsworth retreats from the 'overflowing streets' of the big city to the safe, secure and predictable community of the Lake District. He is not oppressed by the 'little Family of Men', who gather under Helvellyn's watchful eye for a country fair. He sets the contrasting scene at the beginning of Book Eight of *The Prelude*:

> Booths are there none; a staff or two is here;
> A lame man or a blind, the one to beg,
> The other to make music; hither, too,
> From far, with basket, slung upon her arm,
> Of hawker's wares – books, pictures, combs and pins –
> Some aged woman finds her way again,

> Year after year a punctual visitant!
> The showman with his freight upon his back,
> And once, perchance, in lapse of many years
> Prouder itinerant, mountebank, or he
> Whose wonders in a covered wain lie hid.
>
> (ll.25–35)

The 'Ancient habits' and 'preconceived attachments' that have been built up 'year after year' provide the perfect antidote to the sea of metropolitan faces. Friends and neighbours have been looking forward to the event all year. The fair is given an economic dimension. A heifer gets a new master and some sheep are put in a pen and sold. A 'sweet lass of the Valley' rather shyly tries her hand at flogging some apples and pears. Yet country fairs, in the Lake District and elsewhere, were also places where the 'little Family of Men' bought and sold each other. Wordsworth was obviously feeling far too fragile after being oppressed up in London to want to deal with economic oppression. Perhaps the mountain mists actually obscured all but the quaint and folksie from neighbour Wordsworth's eye.

The 1800 Preface to *Lyrical Ballads* may be related to the ruthlessly folksie conservatism which controls Books Seven and Eight of *The Prelude*. The poetic soul is, once again, in full flight from the city. We are pompously informed that 'the great national events which are daily taking place, and the encreasing accumulation of men in cities' is reducing the mind 'to a state of almost savage torpor' (p. xviii). This was to be Mary Mitford's line thirty years later as well. Parochial patriotism was much safer than an interest and involvement in national and international issues. An hour a day listening to the nightingales keeps Tom Paine at bay. As the city apparently corrupts language and literature by producing a craving for sensationalism, Wordsworth retreats back to the land. The cottage becomes a linguistic and philosophical castle:

> Low and rustic life was generally chosen because in that situation the essential passions of the heart find a better soil in which they can attain their maturity, are less under restraint, and speak a plainer and more emphatic language; because in that situation our elementary feelings exist in a state of greater simplicity and consequently may be more accurately contemplated and more forcibly communicated; because the manners of rural life germinate from those elementary feelings; and from the necessary character of rural occupations are more easily comprehended; and are more durable; and lastly, because

in that situation the passions of men are incorporated with the beautiful and permanent forms of nature.

(p. xi)

The low life may really be the high life. The rustics are at least rooted in the good earth like the flowers of the field. This earth does not move in a sensationally extravagant fashion, so there is permanence and continuity. A virtue can be made out of any necessity. Rural occupations are not hard work, but the best possible linguistic and philosophical training ground. A face-to-face community should never be regarded as constricting, since it provides nature's statesmen and scholars with all the opportunities they need to hone up their discourse:

> from their rank in society and the sameness and narrow circle of their intercourse, being less under the action of social vanity they convey their feelings and notions in simple and unelaborated expressions.
>
> (p. xii)

Joseph Arch and John Clare might have had a few 'simple and unelaborated expressions' to vent against this kind of patronising nonsense about the closed university of life. The Preface is certainly riddled with contradictions. Is this philosophical language the product of all rustic life, or does it just occur in specific areas like the Lake District? Pastoral poets may well have put their own words into the mouths of their jolly shepherds, but isn't neighbour Wordsworth doing exactly the same by refusing to recognise that rustics have an unfortunate habit of speaking in dialect? He has obviously written the sermons himself, before hiding them behind the stones. The most interesting contradiction concerns the way in which the Preface argues against previous versions of pastoral only to conclude that peasants are philosophers. Wordsworth's clothing may be 'severe and unadorned', but it is sheep's clothing none the less. As such, it provided excellent cover for aristocratic wolves. Pastoral platitudes about the 'sedentary power' of aristocratic estates being the bulwark of poor old Michael's small estate disguised the sharp practices of real estate.

From Roger Sales, *English Literature in History 1780–1830: Pastoral and Politics* (London, 1983), pp. 52–69.

NOTES

[While John Lucas (essay 4), John Barrell (whose essay 7 follows) and to a degree David Simpson (essay 3), might all be nominated Marxist critics, it is Roger Sales who unambiguously reminds us that Marxism fundamentally threatens much that is normally taken for granted in other traditional critical approaches. Sales's book was, not surprisingly, given a rough ride by most reviewers; his approach uncompromisingly insists on the primacy of economics and class when it comes to the analysis of literature, and the assessment of literary figures. Unlike other critics represented here, he views any tendency to fall into the Romantic habit of idealising the figure of the poet with profound suspicion, just as he rejects any idea of 'culture' as a sacred preserve. His attack on Wordsworth's personal integrity is in fact a way of challenging a whole set of value-judgements underpinning capitalist society and its cultural superstructure. Sales forces us back to the text and the context to check our own reading of, in this instance, 'Michael'; there is no harm at all in being made to look again at the assumptions which may have informed our interpretation. Ed.]

1. *The Letters of William and Dorothy Wordsworth: The Middle Years*, ed. E. de Selincourt (Oxford, 1937), p. 784, from a letter to Daniel Stuart dated 7 April 1817. Wordsworth's conservatism is also apparent in another letter to Stuart dated 22 June 1817, pp. 791–4.

2. *The Prose Works of William Wordsworth*, ed. W. J. B. Owen and Jane Worthington Smyser (Oxford, 1973), vol. 3, p. 160. For further details about Wordsworth's activities, see letters to Lord Lonsdale in de Selincourt's *The Middle Years*.

3. *The Early Letters of William and Dorothy Wordsworth 1787–1805*, ed. E. de Selincourt (Oxford, 1935), pp. 261–2.

4. All quotations from *Lyrical Ballads*, ed. R. L. Brett and A. R. Jones (London, 1965), pp. 226–40.

5. For more details on the economic and social structure of the Lake District, see E. Hughes, *North Country Life in the Eighteenth Century: Cumberland and Westmorland 1700–1830* (Oxford, 1965).

6. *The Early Letters of William and Dorothy Wordsworth 1787–1805*, ed. E. de Selincourt (Oxford, 1935), p. 262.

7. Quotations from the 1805–6 version in *The Prelude: A Parallel Text*, ed. J. C. Maxwell (Harmondsworth, 1957).

8. Quoted by Mary Moorman, *William Wordsworth: A Biography. The Early Years 1770–1803* (Oxford, 1957), p. 497.

9. Oscar Wilde, 'The Decay of Lying', in *The First Collected Edition of the*

Works of Oscar Wilde 1908–1922, ed. Robert Ross (London, 1969), vol. 2, p. 21.

10. Quotations from *Lyrical Ballads*, R. L. Brett and A. R. Jones (London, 1965), pp. 67–82. For the interesting textual history of this poem, see *The Salisbury Plain Poems of William Wordsworth*, ed. Stephen Gill (Brighton, 1975), pp. 3–16, 119–209.

11. *Journals of Dorothy Wordsworth*, ed. Mary Moorman (Oxford, 1971), pp. 129–30.

12. Ibid., p. 71.

13. *The Speeches of the Rt. Hon. George Canning During the Election in Liverpool* (London, 1820), p. 42.

6

Wordsworth's Crazed Bedouin: 'The Prelude' and the Fate of Madness

ROSS WOODMAN

I

In the 1799 *Prelude*, Wordsworth describes himself at the age of five as in the 'twilight' rather than at the dawn of 'rememberable life' (I.298).[1] In both the 1805 and 1850 versions, the phrase is dropped, though in his 'Immortality' ode another version is suggested when for 'twilight' Wordsworth substitutes 'shades of the prison-house' that, like the twilight, begin to descend upon 'the growing Boy' (ll.67–8). Memory as darkness, twilight, imprisonment, forgetfulness finds for Wordsworth its oxymoronic equivalent in the Platonic myth of pre-existence in which birth itself becomes 'a forgetting' (l.58). As natural objects ('the earth, and every common sight') begin to register upon the senses, the soul's 'celestial light' (ll.2–4) darkens into twilight, fading finally into 'the light of common day' (l.76). For Berkeley, Wordsworth substitutes Locke, 'celestial light' becoming a '*tabula rasa*'. Perhaps for this reason, the growing boy of 'Tintern Abbey' bounding 'o'er the mountains . . . / Wherever nature led' is described as 'more like a man / Flying from something that he dreads, than one / Who sought the thing he loved' (ll.70–2). He dreads the descending darkness that is 'rememberable life'. In the 'Immortality' ode, he stands before that life as 'a guilty Thing surprised' (l.147). Wordsworth surprised by guilt is his sudden realisation of what had

112

been abandoned or forgotten in the active surrender to nature and 'the language of the sense', a surrender that had left him in 'Tintern Abbey' and the Preface to the *Lyrical Ballads* rather 'well pleased' (ll.107–8) with himself. The nurse of his moral being in 'Tintern Abbey' becomes the 'homely Nurse' (l.81) in the 'Immortality' ode who does all she can to make her foster child forget his heavenly origin. Rather than bind time to eternity, she binds day to day, imprisoning the poet for a crime he had not known he had committed until he was able to read the record of it in what he himself had written. His crime, as Coleridge recognised, was his defence of the 'language of the sense'.

In his Preface to the *Lyrical Ballads*, Wordsworth argued that he had chosen low and rustic life because, living in daily communion with the beautiful and permanent forms of nature, peasants, children, outlaws and idiots spoke a far more philosophical language than that which is frequently substituted for it by poets 'who think that they are conferring honour upon themselves and their art in proportion as they separate themselves from the sympathies of men, and indulge in arbitrary and capricious habits of expression in order to furnish food for fickle tastes and fickle appetites of their own creation' (Owen, vol. 1, p. 124). By 'philosophical' Wordsworth here has in mind the philosophy of Locke who argued that, since all knowledge 'terminated in things', it must arise from the mind's direct encounter with things through the medium of the senses. Ridding the mind of any innate ideas, reducing it to a *tabula rasa*, Locke demonstrated how man can gain a real knowledge of the external world and, through that knowledge, properly fit himself to it. Not, however, until he was well into the third book did he suddenly realise that, in the composition of his *Essay Concerning Human Understanding*,[2] it was not the senses with which he was directly dealing, but with writing. The *tabula rasa* was the white sheet of paper on which, by dipping his pen into ink, he was making marks that were signs or traces of the action of his mind. What in writing, in the marks upon the page, he was in touch with was not the external world of things but mind itself. 'I must confess', he writes, ' . . . that when I first began this discourse of the understanding, and a good while after, I had not the least thought that any consideration of words was at all necessary to it.' Yet, since words rather than things were what directly confronted him in the act of composition, he had to conclude that though knowledge 'terminated in things, yet it was, for the most part, so much by the intervention of words that they seemed scarce separable from our general knowledge. At least they interpose themselves so much between our understandings and the truth which it would contemplate and apprehend that, like the *medium* through which visible objects pass, their obscurity and disorder does not seldom cast a mist before our eyes and impose upon our understandings' (Bk 3, ch. 9, 87–8).

Language, he realised, was 'like the *medium* through which visible objects pass'. It was, that is, like the senses which were now as a *medium*, however, far superior to language because, as a result of the mechanical equipment invented for experiment in the laboratories of the Royal Society, they were less obscure, less subject to disorder, less likely to distort the understanding. The lingering 'obscurity and disorder' of language casting 'a mist before our eyes' and imposing 'upon our understanding' is rhetoric, the poetic diction that Wordsworth was determined to eradicate, and Locke, by implication, identified with the unassisted senses ill-equipped to make accurate observations. 'But yet, if we would speak of things as they are,' Locke continues, 'we must allow that all the art of rhetoric, besides order and clearness, all the artificial and figurative application of words eloquence hath invented, are for nothing else but to insinuate wrong *ideas*, move the passions, and thereby mislead the judgment, and so indeed are a perfect cheat;[3] . . . they are in certainty, in all discourses that pretend to inform or instruct, wholly to be avoided and, where truth and knowledge are concerned, cannot but be thought a great fault either of the language or the person that makes use of them.'

Avoidance, however, was not that easy, as Locke reading what he just had written must have realised, the 'great fault' being precisely what he was at that very instant indulging in, and, as writing, enjoying. As if confessing his pleasure, Locke with considerable irony (itself a form of rhetoric) continues: '*Eloquence*, like the fair sex, has too prevailing beauties in it to suffer itself ever to be spoken against. And it is in vain to find fault with those arts of deceiving wherein men find pleasure to be deceived' (Bk 3, ch. 10, 106).

Locke here could be Milton in a lighter vein writing about Adam and Eve after the fall, himself as Adam deceived by Eve though finding pleasure in it, choosing her rather than truth. He could also, however, be a romantic writing about the psyche which, because it lured the poet away from a 'termination in things', he sought to exorcise by reducing it to a *tabula rasa* even as Shelley in *Alastor* reduced the dream maiden embracing the Visionary to 'vacancy' and Keats, subjecting his Lamia to the cold stare of Apollonius, reduced her to nothing at all.

Wordsworth's poetical practice, as Coleridge demonstrated, was far different from his poetical theory. Unlike Locke, his real interest was in the essential passions of the human heart as they manifested themselves more deeply or instinctively in the state of nature. Locke's interest was in the empirical methodology of the newly con᷈ ᷈uted Royal Society. Locke's nature was not Wordsworth's: Loc⫶ ᷈s object was to render the mind a true picture of nature, a clea᷈ mirror in which nature and its operations could behold itself; Wordsworth's object was to render nature a true picture of the mind, a clear mirror in which the mind and its operations could behold itself. As rhetoric, both poet and philosopher were deeply committed to metaphor as opposed to metonymy, an identification of mind and nature as the mirror images of each other. For both of them the language of metaphor became the problem because in the exploration of it they were confronted by the nihilism that constitutes metaphor: the mind as nothing but nature, nature as nothing but mind. Thus the problem of language becomes the problem of metaphor, understood as the power to fuse, to obliterate difference, a problem to which, as de Man has shown in *Blindness and Insight*,[4] literature directly addresses itself. By locating language in fiction rather than empirical reality, metaphor, like the other forms of rhetoric that originate in it, constitutes, de Man suggests, magic or spell understood as the reflexiveness of language, its identity with itself, as manifest most directly in incantation. Shakespeare's Macbeth, for example, rises as king out of the incantation of the witches, kingship becoming for him an evil spell. He is possessed by metaphor and the spell is not broken until his head is removed. What is revealed in his severed head held up as a warning is the danger of metaphor for the writer who is possessed by it. Shakespeare's *Macbeth*, like all his plays, is at once an enactment of metaphor and an exorcism of it that culminates in *The Tempest*.

De Man, therefore, rightly concludes that there can be no demystification of literature because literature is 'demystified from the start' (p. 18). As such, he further concludes, literature remains a primary source of knowledge because as a self-acknowledged fiction deconstructing the illusions to which fiction as truth gives birth it keeps us in the presence of a nothingness which is finally for him the

object of knowledge itself. Against the confrontation of that nothingness metaphor would initially arm us only in the end to bring us to
an encounter with it that is not nothingness itself but the knowledge
of it. It is, in Wordsworth's *Prelude*, the mind 'caught by the spectacle' of its own blindness unable to read the label 'of the utmost we
can know' (VIII.643–5), or unable to read the 'monumental letters'
made 'fresh and visible' from 'year to year / By superstition of the
neighbourhood' (XII.241–3). It is the metaphor of nature as 'the
speaking face of earth and heaven' (v.13) becoming suddenly the
'ghastly face' of a drowned man rising 'bolt upright' (v.449–51)
which Cynthia Chase describes as 'an effaced figure unable to articulate any lesson'.[5]

Though in his 'Immortality' ode Wordsworth would by metaphor
idealise, with Plato's and Milton's help, this nothingness by identifying it with an 'imperial palace' (l.84) that in early childhood survived
in however a ghostly fashion as a 'celestial light' which appeared to
apparel 'the earth and every common sight', he knew in retrospect
that, like Macbeth possessed by a spell, he was in some sense de-
luded. That delusion, as he describes it in his Fenwick note to the
poem, lay in part in his conviction that, whatever might become of
others, he himself would be translated like Enoch and Elijah to
heaven. He would not, that is, die. At the same time, however, his
conviction of his own immortality was, as metaphor, a deliberate
disguise against death. Several times while going to school, he confesses, he would grasp the nearest wall or tree to recall himself from
what he calls 'the abyss of idealism' to reality because, as he says, he
was afraid of the process, a process that in the poem itself becomes
in another, more sinister, metaphor identified with the grave where
we in waiting lie, a metaphor so horrible that Coleridge persuaded
him to remove it (*Biographia Literaria*, 2.140–1). Metaphor in
Wordsworth's Ode is a fictional armour against the fact of death
which as fiction continually deconstructs itself. It is precisely this
reading of his Ode that Wordsworth explores in the Cartesian dream
of the Arab. Wordsworth in a cave by the sea reading Cervantes'
demystification of metaphor-making becomes in the dream a shell
which he puts to his ear to hear.

> An Ode, in passion uttered, which foretold
> Destruction to the children of the earth
> By deluge, now at hand.
>
> (V.96–8)

In *Of Grammatology*,[6] Derrida explores the tangible evidence of nothingness haunting Rousseau, as it haunted Wordsworth, driving him to constellate, in and as rhetoric, what is not there. Wordsworth in his 'Elegiac Stanzas' describes that constellated nothingness – his own extinction metaphorically idealised as pre-existence – as the 'gleam' or trace of 'the light that never was, on sea or land, / The consecration, and the Poet's dream' (ll.15–16), a dream that, if pursued to the point where the figural becomes the actual, conducts not only to blindness ('when the light of sense / Goes out' [vi.600–1]), but, as in 'Resolution and Independence', to 'despondency and madness' (l.49). Wordsworth standing upon the pinnacle of self-deification at the age of seventeen, which is the controlling metaphor of the 1799 *Prelude*, is also Chatterton, 'the marvellous Boy' (l.43), dead by his own hand at the same age. The attempt to constellate through language this 'gleam', Derrida's 'fabulous scene'[7] of metaphor-making, is an act of conjuration. Shelley, who understood this better than most romantics, therefore images Wordsworth writing his 'Immortality' ode ('O joy! that in our embers / Is something that doth live' [ll.129–30]) as a

> . . . dark magician in his visioned cave,
> Raking the cinders of a crucible
> For life and power, even when his feeble hand
> Shakes in its last decay. . . .
> *(Alastor*, ll.682–5)

Conjuring what is not there leaves as a kind of haunting its ghostly traces upon an otherwise empty page.

Still with Rousseau in mind, Derrida (p. 8) describes these marks or signs as the traces of a hypothetical 'full speech, that was fully *present* (present to itself, to its signified, to the other, the very condition of the theme of presence in general)'. Like Wordsworth, who follows here in Rousseau's footsteps to leave traces of his own, Rousseau in *Emile* affirms the 'Poet's dream' – 'a natural language common to all' – as the 'language of children before they begin to speak', a language that is 'inarticulate' though it has 'tone, stress and meaning' (p. 247). Such a language 'fully *present*', Wordsworth suggests in *The Prelude*, was most audible 'when the fleshly ear / . . . Forgot her functions, and slept undisturbed' (ii.416–18). Less audible than the dreaming sleep that is man's initial post-natal condition, though still pre-linguistically present, it can be heard again in the 'mock apparel' with which as words Hartley Coleridge at the age of six 'fittest to unutterable thought / The breeze-like motion and the self-born carol' (ll.2–4). In much the same form this pre-linguistic language as the 'mock apparel' of the unutterable can be heard and understood by Betty Foy in the 'burrs' (l.377) of her idiot son.

In 'The Idiot Boy', Wordsworth, in a manner that taxed even Coleridge's impressive credulity, boldly implies that Johnny is a pre-Homeric, pre-linguistic poet who, like the Boy of Winander (dead at the age of twelve in the 1850 *Prelude*, ten in the 1805), speaks the language of the crowing cocks ('to-whoo, to-whoo' [l.450]). Such a poet is a performer of miracles, a shaman who, like Johnny, through actions that serve as body-speech, unconsciously commands the sick to rise and walk. Thus old Susan Gale lying on her sick bed suddenly declares, 'I'll to the wood'. 'The words scarce said', the poem continues, 'Did Susan rise up from her bed, / As if by magic cured' (ll.424–6).

Defending in a manner that belied his own more rational judgement Wordsworth's conviction that his idiot boy spoke a more philosophical language than most poets, Coleridge acknowledged that Wordsworth's genius had tapped a 'freshness of sensation which is the constant accompaniment of mental, no less than bodily convalescence'. He had, he was persuaded, 'rescue[d] the most admitted truths from the impotence caused by the very circumstance of their universal admission' (*Biographia Literaria*, I.81–2). He had tapped a pre-linguistic world of sensation as immediate and direct as 'the eternal act of creation in the infinite I AM' (I.304). Out of his own need to come to grips with that achievement – a need directly related to his own bodily and mental convalescence – emerged his understanding of the imagination in both its primary and secondary senses, though particularly in the primary sense as the act of perception itself. Wordsworth's poetry, he announced, was as fresh as if all that it contained 'had then sprang forth at the first creative fiat' (I.80). He had as a poet felt as metaphor the riddle of the world and in his poetry he had helped to unravel it.

It was, however, for Wordsworth, one thing to feel the riddle of the world, to be, that is, directly in touch with the 'fabulous scene' of metaphor-making; it was another thing entirely to unravel it, a task far more suited to Coleridge than to himself, though even Coleridge would admit that it had stolen from his own nature 'all the natural man' ('Dejection', l.90). To unravel became for Wordsworth in some sense a crime against nature; it meant to pull apart, to dismember, to permit the 'meddling intellect' to mis-shape 'the beauteous form of things' ('Tables Turned', ll.25–7). It also meant to read ('Close up those barren leaves' [l.30]). Derrida casts considerable light on Wordsworth's dilemma, particularly as it took shape under the direct influence of Coleridge's 'abstruser musings'.

In 'Cogito and the History of Madness',[8] Derrida describes writing as a 'structure of deferral' in which what he calls the 'absolute excess' that constitutes the 'fabulous scene' from which writing emerges to leave its trace is tranquillised into a rational structure in order to exclude madness. In that exclusion of madness, philosophy, Derrida argues, 'betrays itself (or betrays itself as thought)' to enter what he calls 'a crisis and a forgetting of itself' like Wordsworth's account of birth as 'a sleep and a forgetting'. 'I philosophise', Derrida writes, 'only in *terror*, but in the *confessed* terror of going mad. The confession is simultaneously, at its *present* moment, oblivion and unveiling, protection and exposure: economy' (p. 62). By economy, he means, as Gayatri Chakravorty Spivak points out in her introduction to her translation of *Of Grammatology* (p. xlii), not a reconciliation of opposites (absence and presence), but, rather, a maintaining of disjunction.

In the writing of *The Prelude*, Wordsworth became increasingly aware of this disjunction between what he calls himself as narrator who is present to himself as a forming and hardening ego (Keat's 'egotistical sublime') and what he calls 'some other Being' (II.33) who is always in some sense absent, and perhaps most absent when almost present as in the concluding lines of the first book when Wordsworth confesses that his song is loth to quit

> Those recollected hours that have the charm
> Of visionary things, those lovely forms
> And sweet sensations that throw back our life,
> And almost make remotest infancy
> A visible scene, on which the sun is shining.
> (I.631–6)

The 'some other Being' is metaphor or 'charm' rendered almost 'visible' by incantation or 'song'. It is essentially a voice, usually identified with wind or water (a 'gentle breeze' [l.I] that can become 'a tempest' [l.46], or a gentle river with 'alder shades and rocky falls, / . . . fords and shallows' [ll.272–3] that can become 'the mighty flood of Nile / Pour[ing] from his fount of Abyssinian clouds / To fertilise the whole Egyptian plain' [VI.614–16)]). It is, above all, the unacknowledged hero of the first books, more particularly of the 1799 *Prelude*. Beyond that, it is the unacknowledged legislator of the 1805 and 1850 versions.

The struggle in *The Prelude*, between these 'two consciousnesses' (II.32) is rhetorically the conflict between metaphor as voice and allegory as the en-graving or in-scribing of the voice as epitaph. Metaphor operates in a world of Heraclitean flux where the law of perpetual change is the law of life, a world of radical instability, of continuous metamorphosis presided over by a magician, Hermes in Greece, Mercurius in Rome, Merlin in Britain. Allegory, on the other hand, struggles to arrest and stabilise metaphor by taking it out of the timeless, undifferentiated world associated with the imaginal life of a child and grounding or burying it in time. The relationship between them may, therefore, perhaps be best summed up in Wordsworth standing 'a long half hour together . . . / Mute, looking at the grave in which [the Boy of Winander] lies' (V.396–7). The muteness is not only Wordsworth's silence; it is as epitaph the 'lengthened pause / Of silence' when the owls no longer answer the boy's 'mimic hootings'. That silence, however, perhaps like Wordsworth's 'long half hour together' (together with the boy?), is not as death-like as it might at first appear, for sometimes in that silence the boy 'hung listening' and was rewarded with 'a gentle shock of mild surprise'. Instead of mere mimicry (copies of natural sound, the voice as the literal or actual voice of nature), it becomes figurative. The 'voice / Of mountain torrents' is 'carried far into the heart' or 'the visible scene / . . . enter[s] unawares into his mind. / With all its solemn imagery, its rocks, / Its woods' (V.374–88). The whole spectacle, in short, becomes 'a correspondent breeze' (I.35), 'a prospect in the mind' (II.352), a living rather than dead epitaph. Metaphor, that is, continues to live in the allegory, as indeed metaphor must, for it is, by definition, the resurrected form of the literal or the copy. Rhetoric with its tropes enacts its own life in ways that the author cannot fully control, language as language writing itself.

Thus in constructing a figurative life out of a literal or historical one, Wordsworth in *The Prelude* gradually confronts in what de Man calls 'the rhetoric of temporality'[9] the making of a shrine where metaphor becomes epitaph and *The Prelude* itself an elegy to an unwritten epic. The process of memory becomes a memorial, a burial, which, subject to the rhetoric of elegy, contains the possibility of some 'future restoration' (XII.286). The 'spots of time' that are 'scattered everywhere' throughout *The Prelude*, 'taking their date from our first childhood,' (XII.208–25) are metaphors that feed and propel the allegory to the limited degree it can absorb them. As metaphors, these 'moments' are signs of renovation, which, because of the temporality that allegory reimposes in a different, rhetorical form, can never become what they aspire to be: a 'metaphysics of presence'. For this reason, de Man concludes, 'the secularised allegory of the early romantics . . . necessarily contains the negative moment which . . . in Wordsworth [is] that of the loss of self in death or in error' (p. 207). This pattern inherent for de Man in the 'rhetoric of temporality' is already evident in the opening lines of the first book.

In the opening section of the 1805 *Prelude* (ll.1–115), the narrator as captive (the defining allegorical stance) comes 'from a house / Of bondage' (ll.6–7) to greet the 'welcome stranger' (equally the metaphorical stance). In terms of the allegory that Wordsworth is already shaping through a release from the literal into the figural, the narrator is encountering the essential energy of an otherwise imprisoned imagination that immediately begins its metaphoric work by transforming the narrator's habitual or historical self (Wordsworth coming from London, Bristol, or even Gosler) into the figurative dimension of an allegorical life. The messenger is the releasing metaphor that sets the allegory in motion. As such, it is the poem's unconscious or unknown author whom the narrator must now come to know.

Not surprisingly, the meeting between a newly-released captive and a spirit not unlike Shakespeare's Ariel is at once a greeting and a collision. On the one hand, the captive as 'renovated spirit' (in the 1850 version) is clothed in the 'priestly robe' of 'poetic numbers' and singled out, by virtue of that apparel, 'for holy services' (ll.52–4). On the other hand, however, he cannot cope with this sudden transformation that metaphor imposes. The messenger who anoints him with his priestly vocation is also, like all metaphors, a rather sinister figure: 'a tempest, a redundant energy, / Vexing its own creation' (ll.37–8). Unable finally to deal with the 'trances of thought and mountings of the mind' (l.19) that comes fast upon him, the narrator seeks 'a respite to this passion' (l.60) in what he calls in the 1850 version 'the sheltered and the sheltering grove' (l.69) (adding 'the sheltering' to 'the sheltered'). In this place of burial, Wordsworth in true elegiac fashion rises as the sun sets, the acorns dropping from their cups to the bare earth prefiguring an oak grove that, as a metaphor of his natural cathedral, *The Recluse* (as subtle and as varied as the one he is actually in), would never be accomplished.

Having buried the metaphor in the sheltered grove, the figurative life of Wordsworth descends again to the literal. Making a new trial of strength, he falls back upon a mechanical image entirely alien to the figurative world he will eventually inhabit and hopefully be able to read. What will become the blended murmur of a nurse's song and a flowing river sending a voice along his dreams becomes, in the absence of his messenger, a harp defrauded of its 'Aeolian visitations', leaving 'the banded host / Of harmony dispersed in straggling sounds' (ll.95–8). Settling down in his chosen vale to prepare himself for 'such an arduous task' (l.147) as the opening lines imposed, he finds himself reviewing the literature of the past in search of a subject until at last, confronted by his own emptiness ('much wanting, so much wanting') he recoils and droops and seeks repose 'In listlessness and vain perplexity' (ll.265–7). Precisely at this point (l.269) the messenger intervenes again, this time as a babe in arms rocked to sleep by its nurse's song that blended its murmurs with 'the fairest of all rivers', a song which echoes, however distantly, the 'gentle breeze' of the first line that brings with it a blessing. More significant, however, is the fact that the 1799 *Prelude*, complete in itself (and as a prelude the most complete of the various versions), begins with the welcoming of the babe as messenger, further to develop as metaphor as the nurse becomes nature itself, the relationship of mind to nature becoming as metaphor the madonna and child, Wordsworth's closest evocation of what Derrida calls 'full speech, that was fully *present* . . . the language of children before they begin to talk'.[10] Wordsworth, it would appear, has unveiled in his first book the 'fabulous scene' of metaphor-making by moving back to what he calls 'days / Disowned by memory' (ll.614–15). Not surprisingly in what constitutes the most powerful evocation of presence after Rousseau, Wordsworth as narrator can declare: 'my mind / Hath been revived' (ll.637–8). That 'mind' is the figurative mind whose life is the life of metaphor and whose history is a continuous allegory,[11] an allegory which as writer Wordsworth must learn to read by recognising in it the 'other Being' for whom he acts as scribe. That recognition, as perhaps is by now apparent, involves accepting metaphor as also a 'dark magician' full of dark disguises that only an equally dark interpreter can read and understand. The 'Babe in arms' (l.276) is also the Devil's child, who can, and in France almost does, drive the poet to madness.

II

The captive 'coming from a house / Of bondage' to greet the 'welcome messenger' in the opening lines of the 1805 *Prelude* is, in its larger epic context, the poet invoking his muse. As metaphor, the muse is initially 'this gentle breeze / That blows from the green fields and from the clouds / And from the sky' to beat against the poet's cheek. The breeze as metaphor or muse is not, therefore, 'merely a faithful copy, existing in the mind, of absent external things'. It is, rather, the 'operations of the mind upon those objects, and processes of creation or of composition, governed by certain fixed laws' (1815 Preface III. 30–2). Those operations, Keats's 'greeting of the spirit', are metaphorically present as invoked in the breeze as the half-conscious messenger conferring its blessing upon all that it touches. Its initial gentleness is the mind's pleasure in its own inward action, described by Wordsworth in his 1815 Preface as a 'slight exertion' (III.30) of the imagination. Wordsworth invoking the breeze as muse is at the very outset of his epic calling attention to his subject: the mind itself as his 'haunt and the main region of [his] song' (Prospectus, 40). More than that: he is enacting the marriage of the mind to 'this goodly universe / In love and holy passion' as that marriage is present not in 'Paradise, and groves / Elysian', which are a 'history only of departed things, / Or a mere fiction of what never was', but in 'the simple produce of the common day' (ll.47–55). It is present in the breeze caressing the poet's cheek.

A problem, however, immediately arises. Every exertion of the imagination, no matter how slight, that moves the mind away from a 'faithful copy' in the direction of the figurative is, in some sense, an act of deception, which, as Wordsworth points out in his note on 'The Thorn', can lead to superstition unless one remains conscious of the actual workings of the mind. The breeze is made to 'seem' (l.2) other than what it is, even as, for example, the mountain in the boat-stealing episode is made to seem as if it were striding after the boy 'as with voluntary power' or 'with a purpose of its own' or a 'measured motion like a living thing' (I.379–84). Metaphor in this respect constitutes a 'vain belief' ('Tintern Abbey', l.50) or what Shelley in his Preface to *Alastor* calls an 'illustrious superstition' (l.69).

Locke's rejection of rhetoric or 'eloquence' as the mind's irresponsible pleasure in its own delusory activity, a pleasure that required radical correction by the imposition of various instruments to correct distortion and ensure in the future accurate observations, is based, of course, upon the assumption that reality resides in 'things' and that all knowledge must therefore terminate in them. It assumes that mind, as distinct from nature, has in itself no reality like that of nature. Left to its own pleasurable activity (the imagination as pleasure principle), the mind, far from producing a faithful copy of a horse and rider, will produce a centaur. 'He that thinks the name centaur stands for some real thing imposes on himself and mistakes words for things', Locke writes (Bk 3, ch. 10, 104). Wordsworth, however, in creating a half-conscious breeze is not mistaking words for things. He does not confuse the figurative and the literal. He is, rather, at this point affirming the pleasures of writing, a pleasure which Locke affirms only to reject it as a form of seduction, Wordsworth's messenger being for him a temptress with whom it is in vain to find fault 'so long as men find pleasure to be deceived'. Locke's attack on rhetoric is a Puritan attack (in the new guise of empiricism) on pleasure.

The figurative as opposed to the literal has, for Wordsworth, its source in what he calls in his 1800 Preface, 'the grand elementary principle of pleasure, by which [man] knows, and feels, and lives, and moves' (I.140). Wordsworth's defence of poetry is, above all, a defence of the pleasure principle as the most immediate and direct affirmation that the mind, as the observer of its own creative power, grants to its own activity. Pleasure, that is, is the mind's affirmation of itself, the blessing that it confers upon itself in the presence of its own activity. That pleasure it expresses directly in and as metaphor, the mind's pleasure in itself becoming a captive greeting a messenger, a breeze beating against a cheek. These tropes are, for Wordsworth, not mistaken for things; they are the direct evidence of an inward state described by Shelley as 'the mind in creation' (*Defence*, ll.503–4). Unlike Locke, who wrote under the illusion that in the immediate and sensual presence of the words upon the page he was also in the presence of 'things', Wordsworth, as poet, confronting writing as writing, had no illusions about what writing is. He was, that is, in the presence of figuration, of metaphorical language, experiencing it as the blessing which the mind in creation confers upon itself. Wordsworth's joy is in words, not things.

And yet the problem remains: the pleasure affirms a fiction. Quarrelling with Wordsworth's failure to distinguish between the language of poetry and prose, Coleridge in his *Biographia Literaria* writes:

A difference of object and contents supplies an additional ground of distinction. The immediate purpose may be the communication of truths; either of truth absolute and demonstrable, as in works of science, or of facts experienced and recorded as in history. Pleasure, and that of the highest and most permanent kind, may *result* from the *attainment* of the end; but it is not itself the immediate end. In other works the communication of pleasure may be the immediate purpose; and though truth, either moral or intellectual, ought to be the *ultimate* end, yet this will distinguish the character of the author, not the class to which the work belongs.

(2. 12)

As metaphor – a half-conscious gentle breeze conferring a blessing by striking a cheek – *The Prelude* in its opening lines locates itself in 'the class to which [as poetry] it belongs'. Pleasure is the immediate end and it is, therefore, immediately achieved. The initial utterance, 'Oh', not yet a word, but a pre-linguistic sound (an emission of breath or 'gentle breeze') like Johnny's 'burrs', constitutes for the poet the release of utterance itself that takes him immediately into a figuration of himself that only later, as figuration, becomes allegory in the service of the ego, becomes character. At that point, metaphor absorbed into allegory, 'truth, either moral or intellectual', becomes the immediate rather than the ultimate end, displacing metaphor thereby and relocating poetry in a class to which as poetry it does not properly belong. Poetry placed in the service of truth, 'either moral or intellectual', is poetry subjected to 'the character of the author' rather than to itself. Keats immediately recognised Wordsworth's subjugation of poetry to truth when he attacked the presence in his poetry of what he called the 'egotistical sublime', contrasting it to 'negative capability' which, as in Shakespeare, resulted in a purer form of poetry because the author, as author, had no character at all. Coleridge makes the same point when, in his remarks to Mrs Barbauld, he condemns the moral stanzas of his *Rime*, which he may have included in response to Wordsworth's complaint that his ancient mariner lacked a character. He also makes it when he rejects allegory in favour of symbol.

What distinguishes the 1799 version of *The Prelude* from its 1805 and 1850 extensions is the relative absence of allegory. The hero, like Coleridge's mariner, has no ego, remaining as yet blessedly unconscious of his own creative power. As *The Prelude* develops into a continual allegory, however, Wordsworth as its narrator will have to provide the hero with an ego structure that at once judges and, with reservations, affirms the egoless child of the first two books. Unlike the extensions of *The Prelude*, the unconscious in the 1799 version is not yet answerable to consciousness; metaphor has not yet been relocated in the more limited confines of allegory. The poetry, that is, remains answerable largely to itself rather than to the character of the author.

Metaphor, as Derrida suggests, has what Shakespeare calls its 'hiding-places' (XII.279) of power in the 'fabulous scene' of writing itself, which allegory largely suppresses or buries within what Derrida calls a 'white mythology' that constitutes betrayal, absence, oblivion and protection, the psychological function of which, as an ego or allegorical structure, is to protect the author against the terrors of madness. Wordsworth in the first version of *The Prelude* largely protects himself from these terrors not by constructing a 'white mythology' to contain them, but by distancing himself as narrator from what he is narrating, locating the action of the mind in a scene that is and remains 'disowned' by the 'memory' that is allegory's domain. Those days that as rhetoric constitute the catachresis to which Locke so stoutly objected are as metaphor the planting in the 1805 version of 'snowdrops among winter snows' (l.644) or the rendering of his own 'remotest infancy / A visible scene on which the sun is shining'. Wordsworth, that is, is presenting catachresis as Derrida's 'full speech, that was fully *present* (present to itself, to its signified, to the other, the very condition of presence in general)', which, of course, is precisely the way that Derrida, deconstructing Rousseau, presents it. In celebrating the infant babe already unconsciously constructing the nature he perceives through the projection onto it of the mother's love, Wordsworth is at the same time apologising for what he calls his 'best conjecture' (II.233) that, as 'an infirmity of love for days / Disowned by memory' could mislead him into a belief that what the infant perceives is what is there in nature rather than the celestial apparel he imposes upon it as it issues as light from his mother's eye. Wordsworth in the first books of *The Prelude* has shaped a creation myth.

The Recluse, as Wordsworth originally conceived it with the help of Coleridge, was intended as hymn to the creation, a hymn to man's creative power as that power works through the medium of the senses to produce not nature itself ('a termination in things') but a rhetorical world that, like the presence of the Convent of Chartreuse, 'bodie[s] forth the ghostliness of things' (VI.428) by granting to that 'ghostliness' ('things' as separate from the action of the mind) 'a speaking face of earth and heaven': nature as figure, rhetoric, figuration. 'He was', as Coleridge later describes the original plan for *The Recluse*, 'to treat man as man, – a subject of eye, ear, touch and taste, in contact with external nature, and informing the senses *from* the mind, and not compounding a mind out of the senses' (*Table Talk*, 21 July 1832).

What went wrong? The question has been raised so often in so many different contexts that one suspects that it is the wrong question. Let me, however, suggest an answer more implicit than explicit in many already offered: allegory oppressively intervened. Truths 'either moral or intellectual' became, particularly in *The Excursion*, Wordsworth's immediate rather than ultimate end. The 'character of the author' assumed control. The result was something closer to prose, or a poetry virtually indistinguishable from it, for which Coleridge must assume considerable responsibility. His conviction that Wordsworth could and should write 'THE FIRST GENUINE PHILO-SOPHIC POEM' (2.156) was grounded in his theological conception of the imagination that, in theory if not in practice, bound the imagination to truth.

Coleridge's view of the primary imagination that rendered the act of perception a 'repetition in the finite mind of the eternal act of creation in the infinite I AM' imposed upon Wordsworth the very 'priestly robes' that incongruously appear in the opening lines of the 1805 *Prelude*. As theological rather than imaginal apparel, associated with truth rather than fiction, with the 'infinite I AM' rather than a wind god or an oracular voice, they become, in the primal context of immediate pleasure, 'these poisoned vestments', described by Wordsworth in his third essay on epitaphs, '. . . which have power to consume and to alienate from his right mind the victim who put them on' (*The Prose Works*, vol. 2, pp. 84–5). The 'welcome messenger' of the opening lines is not a bishop but a wind god, a conjurer, who, like the voice issuing from the shell (itself the sea-cave in which the dreamer sits as in Shelley's 'still cave of the witch Poesy' ['Mount Blanc', l.44]), is 'many gods' with 'voices more than all the winds' (v.106–7). For the narrator coming from the bondage of the habitual self, it is obviously overpowering; the 'trances of thought and mountings of the mind' that 'come fast upon [him]' become a 'tempest, a redundant energy / Vexing its own creation'. In the dream of the Arab that assembles onto itself the entire action of *The Prelude*, the 'tempest' becomes a 'mighty blast of harmony' issuing from a shell, itself the sea-cave or cave of winds that, despite the destruction it foretells, Wordsworth must, as crazed Bedouin, struggle to preserve.

Wordsworth's dream text, based, as Jane Worthington Smyser has pointed out,[12] on three dreams that Descartes had during the night of 10 November 1619,[13] throws considerable light upon the priestly apparel in the opening lines of *The Prelude*. In the three dreams, which Descartes interpreted both awake and as he slept, Descartes was persuaded that the Spirit of Truth had descended upon him and guided him into all truth. In the first dream the Holy Spirit descended in the form of a whirlwind which filled him initially with terror. In the second dream it descended as a thunderbolt, which, when he awakened, seemed to fill the room with sparks of fire. In the third and confirming dream in which his terror was appeased, it descended in the guise of two books, a dictionary showing the unity of the sciences, and a volume of poetry that, transcending the reason of the philosophers, was itself a direct revelation of the spark of divinity in man. Believing the dreams and the revelation they contained to be 'the most important thing in his life', he vowed to make a pilgrimage on foot from Venice to Lorette, a vow which he fulfilled some five years later.[14] Like Wordsworth, Descartes, as a result of what he considered a mystical experience, believed he was 'a renovated spirit singled out . . . for holy services' (I.53–4).

In her account of the dream text, Jane Smyser suggests that the 'studious friend' who told Wordsworth the dream (Wordsworth not claiming it as his own until 1839) was Michael Beaupuy rather than Coleridge, because, as she argues, Wordsworth would never have used the third person in speaking of Coleridge 'since throughout the poem Coleridge is intimately addressed in the second person' (p. 272). Coleridge, however, rather than Beaupuy is the more likely candidate, though for quite obvious reasons Wordsworth took care not to equate in the poem the crazed Bedouin whose reason was couched 'in the blind and aweful lair / Of such a madness' (v.151–2) with Coleridge. And yet, precisely as the Spirit of Truth descended upon Descartes, Coleridge in a letter to Godwin (25 March 1801) describes Wordsworth descending upon him. 'If I die, and the Book-sellers will give you anything for my life be sure to say – "Wordsworth descended on him, like the Γνωθι σε αυτον [know thyself] from Heaven. . . ."' More than that: comparing himself to Wordsworth (who made him know, that he himself 'was no poet'), he describes himself as 'once a Volume of Gold Leaf, rising & riding on every breath of Fancy – but I have beaten myself back into weight & density, & now I sink in quick-silver, yea, remain squat and square on the earth amid the hurricane, that makes Oaks and Straws join in one Dance, fifty yards high in the Element.'

The dream text of the Arab, I suggest, enacts in the most profound and startling manner the controlling metaphor of *The Prelude*: the symbiosis of Coleridge and Wordsworth as joint-authors of the apocalyptic poem describing the descent of the New Jerusalem as an action within the mind itself. That poem, doomed to die before it was complete, found its proper burial, memorial or epitaph in and as *The Prelude*. In the dream text, enchanter and Holy Spirit (the 'sweet breath of Heaven' [I.33]) meet in that permanent disjunction that as allegory is the necessary Derridean betrayal to protect the narrator from madness by means of 'some philosophic song / Of Truth that cherishes our daily life' (I.230–1). Though tempted like Milton (and like Descartes) to bind himself to the 'I AM that I AM' who met Moses 'on the secret top / Of Oreb' (*Paradise Lost*, I.6–7) (and almost meets Wordsworth on the top of Snowdon), Wordsworth in the end absorbs the metaphor into a fitting epitaph.[15]

Metaphor as metaphor belongs to 'days / Disowned by memory' that from a moral point of view can lead men astray by an 'infirmity of love' (I.614). It belongs to the polymorphous perverse babe at its mother's breast and to the incestuous union that is its strongest metaphor. Thus, when Wordsworth announces the theme of *The Recluse* in the metaphor of the descent of the New Jerusalem adorned as a bride to meet the bridegroom, Wordsworth's apocalyptic theme has all the strength of a metaphoric usurpation that rejects the moral taboos, including union with a Mother Nature as well as his union with Coleridge. He is voicing at once John's vision in Revelation and 'the language of children before they begin to speak'. He is proclaiming what Hartman calls an 'ur-fiat',[16] understood as Derrida's 'full speech' or 'original language' that is present only as absence, a 'fiat' described by Hartman as calling not for an object of desire, but in Wordsworth's words 'something evermore about to be'. The mood of the phrase, Hartman persuasively suggests, 'at once goads and restrains the reality-hunger of an infinite will desiring omnipotent and manifest fulfilments' (p. 199). In Coleridge's words, he is contemplating in his announcement of his apocalyptic theme 'the ANCIENT of days and all his works with feelings as fresh, as if all had then sprang forth at the first creative fiat' (I.80). Precisely here in Coleridge's ultimately paralysing identification of the first creative fiat of 'the ANCIENT of days' with the act of perception itself resides the blindness that Wordsworth rightly feared, though it was far more a blindness arising from insight than from any failure of the physical organ. The 'first creative fiat' brought into play everything that Derrida identities with '*différance*'.[17]

Hartman in his widely influential reading of Wordsworth explores what he calls 'a silenced ur-fiat' in Wordsworth's poetry, the substitution of *akedah* (or binding) for apocalypse,[18] which as rhetoric is the substitution of allegory (a moral and intellectual convenant imaged as a descent from a pinnacle to a 'populous') for metaphor (unconscious man in a non-convenantal state often imaged as a pre-existence). What distinguished the one from the other in Derrida's reading of Rousseau's uncovenanted man in the state of nature is the prohibition against incest, the prohibition against the apocalyptic marriage which Wordsworth announced as the theme of his un-written *The Recluse*. That prohibition, properly understood, is the prohibition against the union of mind and nature as a single undifferentiated body that would as union constitute oblivion or nothingness. Mind and nature face to face as one face (the 'workings of one mind, the features / Of the same face' [VI.637–8]) is God alone in the void described by Wordsworth as 'the Uncreated' (II. 413). Nietzsche, prefiguring his own madness, attempts an invocation of it in his account of a feeding herd. 'Man', he writes,

> cannot see them without regret, for even in the pride of his humanity he looks enviously on the beast's happiness. . . . He may ask the beast – 'Why do you look at me and not speak to me of your happiness?' The beast wants to answer – 'Because I always forget what I wished to say': but he forgets this answer too, and is silent; and the man is left to wonder.
>
> He wonders also about himself, that he cannot learn to forget, but hangs on to the past: however far or fast he runs, that chain runs after him ['More like a man / Flying from something that he dreads, than one / Who sought the thing he loved']. . . . A leaf is continually dropping out of the volume of time and fluttering away – and suddenly it flutters back into the man's lap. Then he says, 'I remember . . . ' and envies the beast, that forgets at once, and sees every moment really die, sink into night and mist, extinguished forever. The beast lives *unhistorically*; for it 'goes into' the present, like a number, without leaving any curious remainder.[19]

Metaphor is the attempt to live '*unhistorically*', to go perpetually into the present, 'like a number, without leaving any curious remainder'. It is an attempt, in Derrida's words, whose source is Nietzsche, to recover a 'full speech, that was fully *present* (present to itself, to its signified, to the other, the very condition of presence in general)'. It is a presence that Wordsworth will approximate in a babe at the mother's breast or his idiot Johnny, or even himself as a five year old making 'one long bathing of a summer'd day' (I.290). It is a presence which Nietzsche, bursting through the bounds of 'the human, all too human', entered as madness. Wordsworth, on the other hand, 'could wish his days to be / Bound each to each by natural piety'. That binding is the allegory which *The Prelude* becomes and, in the Book on 'Books', he attempts for the first time to read. The 'welcome messenger' of the opening lines becomes in the dream of the Arab the crazed Bedouin who as 'tempest' or 'redundant energy' he had withdrawn from in fear, the 'characters of danger and desire' (I.471–2) being nature's living inscription. Rather than put on his 'priestly robes' as a deliberate disguise, Wordsworth in the dream confronts the Arab as he struggles to decipher his own text. The dream becomes what de Man calls 'a scene of reading'.[20]

III

Essential to any understanding of Wordsworth's rhetorical figuration of his life (at once figured and disfigured) is the permanent and necessary disjunction between the 'two consciousnesses' that only nothingness can repair. Metaphor, so long as it continues to function as a creative agent, must continue to unbind what 'natural piety' would join together. What allegory would join together let metaphor put asunder constitutes a law of poetic composition. Allegory is *akedah*, the binding of the covenant, the taboo against incest, the moral centre as ultimate end rendered immediate. The child as metaphor, as *puer aeternus*, in fathering the poet unfathers the man because he is as metaphor, as *puer*, wedded to the Great Mother conjured in infancy in what for the allegorical or moral man is an 'infirmity of love', an unholy 'passion'. The *puer* as poet is the criminal, the outcast, the revolutionary who, far from being apparelled in 'priestly robes', decked out for 'holy services', is in the village church the 'uninvited guest / Whom no one owned', sitting like Satan in silence 'fed on the day of vengeance yet to come' (*Paradise Lost*, x.293–9). The world that the unconscious child constructs in the 1799 *Prelude* constitutes an unconscious process of self-deification

('Of genius, power, / Creation and divinity itself / I have been speaking' [III.171–3]) that leaves him at seventeen enthroned upon a pinnacle like Jehovah viewing his creation. That God-like metaphor contains as allegory the seeds of a horrendous crime. That crime, the 'independent intellect' (XI.244) which passes 'unalarmed Jehovah- with his thunder' (Prospectus, 33), repeats the action of Satan in *Paradise Lost* turning the Paradise of childhood into Milton's hell. Precisely this fate is recounted by the narrator in the books on the revolution as he moves uneasily back and forth between the literal and the figurative unable to locate himself in either because he cannot decide where as a revolutionary in a failed and foreign revolution he either in fact or in figure belongs. Though metaphor would conduct him one way, subverting the ego's demands, allegory as an ego defence ('as far as angels are from guilt' [IX.145]) de- manded another. His 'egotistical sublime', seemingly secure within the barricades that allegory erects, struggled with the help of the conscious will (Coleridge's 'secondary imagination') to maintain his stationing of himself as 'Adam, yet in Paradise / Though fallen from bliss' (VIII.659–60). The result, a radical conflict between the 'two consciousnesses' that dialectically shape *The Prelude*, was a night- mare bringing the poem close to collapse, a collapse that he examines more as metaphor than as allegory in the dream of the Arab:

>   . . . the hour of sleep
> To me came rarely charged with natural gifts,
> Such ghastly visions had I of despair
> And Tyranny, and implements of death;
> And innocent victims sinking under fear,
> And momentary hope, and worn-out prayer,
> Each in his separate cell, or penned in crowds
> For sacrifice, and struggling with forced mirth
> And levity in dungeons, where the dust
> Was laid with tears. Then suddenly the scene
> Changed, and the unbroken dream entangled me
> In long orations, which I strove to plead
> Before unjust tribunals, – with a voice
> Labouring, a brain confounded, and a sense,
> Death-like, of treacherous desertion, felt
> In the last place of refuge – my own soul.
>   (x.400–15)

In the dream of the Arab, Wordsworth struggles to resolve the nightmare of opposition by finding a *modus vivendi* between the moral demands of allegory and what, in terms of those demands, have become the terrors of metaphor, terrors inherent in the experience of desire as fear. Metaphor, too much suppressed or too long buried as the self-deifying vision of his first seventeen years recedes, now turns around to reveal its dark face, a face that would reduce allegory as a scene of reading to 'a label on a blind man's chest', which is the original version of line 618 in the 1805 account of his encounter with the blind beggar. 'I thought', he originally wrote,

> That even the very most of what we know,
> Both of ourselves and of the universe,
> The whole of what is written to our view,
> Is but a label on a blind man's chest.

If the scene of reading is to become again anything more than this, if *The Prelude* itself is not to find its fitting emblem in a *mise en abyme*[21] (an 'abyss structure' in which the poet confronts directly the nothingness that in the 'Immortality' ode rhetoric disguises as 'celestial light') then Wordsworth must affirm with Blake the dialectic of the imagination which requires that opposition remain 'true friendship' (Blake, *Marriage of Heaven and Hell*, 42).

In his account of the drowned man (yet another of his disfigurations in Book v), Wordsworth suggests that he could accept 'a spectre shape / Of terror' with 'no soul-debasing fear' because even by the age of nine his inner eye had already seen such sights 'among the shining streams / Of faery land, the forests of romance' (v.450–5). Yet, in the reversal of the revolution in a reign of terror and an imperial conquest that made him for a time a traitor to his country, Wordsworth could not hallow 'the sad spectacle / With decoration of ideal grace'. He could not, that is, preserve his 'dignity', his 'smoothness, like the works / Of Grecian art, and purest poetry' (v.456–9). Faery lands, now forlorn, had opened onto perilous seas, described as 'the devouring sea' in his 1805 introduction to his 'Residence in France' and changed to 'the ravenous sea' (ix.4) in the final 1850 version. He could not, that is, transform the literal into a work of Grecian art any more than he could comfortably wear 'priestly robes'. Wordsworth's world of metaphor was Gothic, unruly, expansive, accommodating, aspiring and retreating, gargoyles about its portals and devils in sacred places. It lacked, as metaphor, the grace of 'purest poetry' to become instead a 'mighty blast of harmony' issuing from 'voices more than all the winds'. Wordsworth in the dream of the Arab is struggling, as *The Prelude* continues to grow even against his will, to accommodate himself to the pressure of metaphor that continued to assert itself as the work of 'single and determined bounds' (the 1799 *Prelude*) became a 'work / Of ampler or more varied argument / Where [he] might be discomfited and lost' (I.642–5), as now indeed he was. Like Keats, though perhaps less consciously, Wordsworth in Book v realised that the emergence of the psyche, rather than the ego, as the hero of the action necessarily brought with it the destruction of Grecian form. A temple to the psyche, to 'Soul-making', was inherently Gothic rather than Greek. Wordsworth in the dream of the Arab is finding in a scene of reading that is simultaneously a scene of writing a new centre, neither a madman nor a sublime egotist, but a soul in the process of making itself. He is confronting what Keats in *The Fall of Hyperion* calls 'this warm scribe my hand' (I.18). The scene of writing becomes a scene of reading; fiction as fiction demystifies its illusory claims to truth while at the same time opening up the 'deluge' that in writing is always 'now at hand' (v.98).

In the scene of reading-writing that is the Bedouin dream dwells the dawning realisation that not Wordsworth but the imagination is authoring itself by bringing itself to consciousness. The dynamics of a continual allegory always threatened by its own extinction (the extinction of *The Recluse* as a presence in *The Prelude*) is not governed by a moral consciousness harnessed to the will, nor is it harnessed to the 'secondary imagination' struggling to 'idealise and to unify' the texts as an incarnation of the Logos or Word. The admonishments from another world are less the admonishments of the 'I Am that I Am' addressing Moses on Mount Horeb ('genius, power / Creation and divinity itself') than the admonishments of rhetoric understood as a secret collusion between allegory and metaphor in the interests of 'Soul-making'. Above all, and again as rhetoric, it is a reminder that poetry has its immediate source and its immediate end not in moral or intellectual truth, but in the pleasure the mind receives from its own creative activity and the contemplation of it, described by Coleridge as the pleasurable activity of the journey itself (*Letters*, p. 14). Only in the recognition of that activity, which is the scene of reading superimposed upon the scene of writing, can writing survive its oblivion as mark or sign; only in this way can the face of the page, like the face of nature become a 'speaking face' addressing the poet as reader even as nature addresses him as reader. The 'waters of the deep' that the crazed Bedouin tells

Wordsworth are 'gathering upon us' (v.130–1) are indeed the 'mind turned round / As with the might of waters' (vii.644–5). Wordsworth in that instant sees again the 'gentle breeze' become a 'tempest, a redundant energy / Vexing its own creation'. This time, however, he does not seek respite in 'the sheltered and the sheltering grove'. The very tempest propels him on as it propels the crazed Bedouin whom, in a metaphorical sense, he now becomes. The 'monumental letters' from which he once fled, the 'written paper' attached to the breast of a blind beggar which seemed 'an apt type / . . . Of the utmost we can know, / Both of ourselves and of the universe' (vii.645–7), become in the dream the moving pen interpreting its own marks. The pen as metaphor, as a consciousness reading itself.

'Monumental letters' as 'a written paper' telling a blind man's story is the dark side of an apocalyptic event, the imagination's 'strength / Of usurpation' that in putting out the light of sense reveals in a flash the 'invisible world'. The counterpart of this 'written paper' attached to the breast of a blind beggar is Wordsworth and his companion following a 'conspicuous invitation to ascend / A lofty mountain' where they meet a peasant from whose mouth (not unlike the 'written sheet') they learn that, far from climbing higher, they must in fact descend, that their 'future course, all plain to sight, / Was downward, with the current of the stream'. Loth to believe what they so grieved to hear ('for still [they] had hopes that pointed to the stars'), they questioned the peasant 'again and yet again'. 'But every word', Wordsworth concludes,

> that from the peasant's lips
> Came in reply, translated by our feelings,
> Ended in this, – *that we had crossed the Alps*.
> (vi.571–91)

Precisely in recording this encounter with 'low and rustic life' that spoke a more philosophic language than poets artificially aiming at the sublime, Wordsworth experienced the imagination's 'strength / Of usurpation'. The peasant, with his barely understood peasant speech, by defeating a 'mounting of the mind' by pointing in an opposite direction, released as rhetoric rather than as fact a presence beyond the reach of sense, even as a happy shepherd or idiot boy can awaken some vanishing gleam of a celestial world. Wordsworth's 'imperial palace', the apocalyptic imagination, is a peasant whose 'speaking face' directs him in what appears to be the opposite direction. Wordsworth's encounter with a peasant pointing in a literal direction became in the act of composition an encounter with metaphor itself.

The 'fleet waters of a drowning world' are, in the metaphorical world of the dream of the Arab, also 'a bed of glittering light' diffused over 'half the wilderness' (v.128–9). Absence in a system of metaphor is the trace of a presence. The 'mind in creation' inhabiting a metaphorical world of perpetual metamorphosis courts, as de Man recognised, annihilation, the presence of nothingness. That presence Wordsworth more than once apparelled in 'celestial light' as a protection against the terror of the deep, the *mise en abyme*, leaving on the page the traces of his fear in the guise of an affirmation of his insatiable desire, the 'something evermore about to be'. The outcome as writing was Derrida's '*present* moment, oblivion and unveiling, protection and exposure: economy'.

Wordsworth following the crazed Bedouin over the illimitable waste (a rather more frenzied vision of Adam and Eve leaving Paradise 'waved over by that flaming brand, the gate / With dreadful faces thronged and fiery arms' [*Paradise Lost*, XII.644–5]), is, like Milton's couple, in search of 'economy', a place to settle, a place to engrave or inscribe metaphor in however frail a shrine. He is searching for a way of going on with writing by learning how to live with the abysm that is always waiting, the abysm that metaphor throws up to remind us that it is there, even as Coleridge's chasm in 'Kubla Khan' flings up momently the sacred river. Allegory as the ego's defence against metaphor is not the only way. Metaphor, properly understood as a scene of reading, is soul. What metaphor reveals, Keats realised, is what allegory attempts to understand. Soul, that is, is a 'spark of divinity',[22] Wordsworth's 1799 *Prelude*, granted a personal identity: the narrator at last in the full psychic sense not a god or a devil, but a person.

The fear, shared by all poets, that the 'hiding-places' of creative power may as 'Old Ocean' dry up, leaving it 'singed and bare' and man, not extinguished, but surviving, 'abject, depressed, forlorn, disconsolate' (v.28–34), is real enough. In Wordsworth's case the more real as he witnessed what he considered the spectacle of Coleridge's ruin and the near-dissolution of *The Recluse*, which rendered the extended *Prelude* perhaps no more than a futile rescuing endeavour. Between the imagination's 'strength / Of usurpation' and its sudden disappearance (Coleridge's constant complaint), the act of composition becomes a precarious occupation. Wordsworth is not alone as a poet in his discovery that the 'still cave of the witch Poesy' in which he allegorically sits perusing the quixotic nature of metaphor is 'pavilioned upon chaos' (*Hellas*, l.772). He consciously numbers himself, however, among the greatest, Milton and Shakespeare included, in his decision to follow the Bedouin to the end, whatever that end may be. The vows originally made for him on a summer day during the long vacation (IV.334–5), Wordsworth now affirms for himself as he awakens from the dream, having managed, with all its necessary disfigurements, to read his poem, up to a point, in a new light that yet remains as 'Soul-making' one more refraction of its prismatic shape.

Thus, 'full often' during the continuing course of writing-reading (inscribing) *The Prelude* as a continuous allegory that has finally no end other than writing itself, Wordsworth takes 'from the world of dream / This Arab phantom' as his wind god or inspiration, giving him 'a substance' through the inscription of a voice to become thereby, as in the dream, his scribe. He fancies him 'a living man', a recluse whose 'internal thought' is 'protracted among endless solitudes' (V.141–8). He projects him, as he projects the infant rocked to sleep by the blended music of singing nurse and murmuring river which launches the 1799 *Prelude*: a 'foretaste, a dim earnest' (I.280), though of 'tempest' rather than 'calm'. He is not, therefore, the recluse that Coleridge images as the hero of their joint-labours: 'a man in mental repose, one whose principles were made up, and so prepared to deliver upon authority a system of philosophy' (*Table Talk*, 21 July 1832). As Keats recognised, 'Coleridge . . . would let go by a fine isolated verisimilitude caught from the Penetralium of mystery, from being incapable of remaining content with half knowledge' (21 December 1817). This incapability Wordsworth sought to resist by turning, as Coleridge himself turned, to the phantom world of dream where metaphors, like fish swimming in a stream, might be 'caught from the Penetralium of mystery'.

Far from pitying him, as indeed Coleridge as an addicted dreamer pitied himself, Wordsworth now, having read the dream, feels 'reverence . . . to a being thus employed' (v.150), particularly because of the reason or method he now discerns (Keats's 'negative capability') that lies couched in what otherwise, without the saving grace of allegory understood as reading, would indeed be madness. By virtue of his reading of this crucial dream, Wordsworth renews his poetic faith. He shares the 'maniac's fond anxiety' (v.160); he accepts as poet Don Quixote as himself. Thus, when overcome by the 'strong entrancement' (v.162) of a *mise en abyme* ('an event so dire, by signs in earth / Or heaven made manifest' [v.158–9]), he will think not of the leech-gatherer but of the Coleridge or 'Arab phantom' (v.142) buried in himself, even as the Boy of Winander resides and does not reside in the grave by which 'a long half hour together' Wordsworth sometimes stood, listening perhaps 'to notes that are / The ghostly language of the ancient earth' (II.308–9).

From *Studies in Romanticism*, 27 (Spring 1988), 3–29.

NOTES

[Ross Woodman's article invites us to reflect once more on the critical approach of Geoffrey Hartman; but Hartman is here placed alongside two of the most influential theorists of the poststructuralist school of thought, Paul de Man and Jacques Derrida. Woodman's interest is primarily in language, and although the critical language he himself employs can be difficult – it is language constantly reflecting on itself, a recipe for convolution – one very important fact is clearly established in the essay, that is, the consciousness writers of the eighteenth century possessed of language as a profoundly problematic medium. He is therefore also illustrating why twentieth-century literary theorists such as de Man and Derrida have played so important a part in the critical debate on Wordsworth.

You will need to brush up on your grammatical terms to read and fully understand this essay, but having done so, you will find the account that emerges of the inner life of the text in question is as intriguing as the implications that follow for the inner life of the poet who produced it. Ed.]

1. All references to *The Prelude* are taken from *The Prelude: 1799, 1805, 1850*, ed. J. Wordsworth, M. H. Abrams and S. Gill (New York, 1977). All references to other poems are taken from *Poems*, ed. John C. Haydon (Harmondsworth, 1977), 2 vols. All references to the prose are taken from *The Prose Works of William Wordsworth*, ed. W. J. B. Owen and Jane Worthington Smyser (Oxford, 1974). All references to Blake's poetry are taken from *The Complete Poetry and Prose of William Blake*, revised edition, ed. David V. Erdman with Commentary by Harold Bloom (Berkeley, 1982). All references to Coleridge's poems are taken from *The Poems of Samuel Taylor Coleridge*, ed. E. H. Coleridge (London, 1960).

    All references to the *Biographia Literaria* are taken from the Bollingen edition, ed. James Engell and W. Jackson Bate (Princeton, 1983). All references to Coleridge's letters are taken from *Collected Letters of S. T. Coleridge*, vol. 2, ed. Earl L. Griggs (Oxford, 1956). All references to *Table Talk* are taken from *The Table Talk and Omniana of Samuel*

Taylor Coleridge (London, 1917). All references to Keats's poetry are taken from *The Poems of John Keats*, ed. Jack Stillinger (Cambridge, Mass., 1978). All references to Keats's letters are taken from *Letters of John Keats*, ed. Robert Gittings (London, 1975). All references to Shelley's poetry and prose are taken from *Shelley's Poetry and Prose*, ed. Donald H. Reiman and Sharon B. Powers (New York, 1977). All references to Milton's poems are taken from *The Student's Milton*, ed. F. W. Patterson (New York, 1933).

2. *An Essay Concerning Human Understanding*, ed. Peter H. Nidditch (Oxford, 1975).

3. Adieu! the fancy cannot *cheat* so well
   As she is fam'd to do, *deceiving* elf.
   Keats, 'Ode to a Nightingale' (italics mine), ll.73–4.

4. Paul de Man, *Blindness and Insight: Essays in the Rhetoric of Contemporary Criticism* (2nd edn, Minneapolis, 1983).

5. Cynthia Chase, 'Accidents of Disfiguration: Limits to Literal and Rhetorical Reading in Book V of *The Prelude*', in *Studies in Romanticism*, 18 (1979), 565.

6. Trans. Gayatri Chakravorty Spivak (Baltimore, 1976).

7. 'White Mythology', trans. F. C. T. Moore, in *New Literary History*, 6 (1974), 7–77: 'It is metaphysics which has effaced in itself the fabulous scene which brought it into being, and which yet remains, active and stirring, inscribed in white ink, an invisible drawing covered over in the palimpsest' (p.11).

8. Jacques Derrida, *Writing and Difference*, trans. Alan Bass (Chicago, 1978).

9. Paul de Man, 'The Rhetoric of Temporality', in *Blindness and Insight* (Minneapolis, 1983), pp. 187–228.

10. Jacques Derrida, *Of Grammatology* (Baltimore, 1976), p. 247.

11. 'A man's life of any worth is a continual allegory – and very few eyes can see the mystery of his life – a life like the scriptures, figurative – which such [literalist] people can no more make out than they can the Hebrew Bible' (Keats writes to his brother [19 February 1819]).

12. Jane Worthington Smyser, 'Wordsworth's dream of Poetry and Science: *The Prelude* V', in *PMLA*, 71 (1956), 269–75.

13. Descartes' threefold dream is described in Baillet's *Vie de Descartes* (1691). In *New Studies in the Philosophy of Descartes* (London, 1963), Norman Smith translates Bailet's account which is based on a manuscript by Descartes which he entitled *Olympica*. The translation appears in Appendix A, pp. 33–9.

14. For an interesting reading of Descartes' dreams that bears directly upon Wordsworth's withdrawal from the imagination's 'strength/Of usurpation', his subjugation of the excesses of metaphor to the moral confines of allegory, his fear of the madness to which the 'divinity in man' may conduct, see Jacques Maritain's *The Dream of Descartes* (New York, 1944). Maritain contrasts the Incarnation with 'the anthropotheistic conception which insists that man be made god, and which ordinates everything to this conquest of divinity' (p. 186). The Cartesian heritage, which he locates initially in Descartes' three dreams, lies, Maritain argues, in this anthropotheistic conception.

15. In 'The Stone and the Shell: The Problem of Poetic Form in Wordsworth's Dream of the Arab', in *Mouvements premiers: Etudes critiques offertes à George Poulet* (Paris, 1972) pp. 125–47, J. Hillis Miller, discussing Wordsworth's epitaphs, suggests that Wordsworth 'far from always believing that poetry exists primarily as spoken language, sometimes felt that a poem only comes into existence in a satisfactory form when it has not only been written down but inscribed permanently on the purdurable substance of a stone' (p. 129). That 'purdurable substance' is in the dream of the Arab set over against the shell which is identified with voice rather than writing. His desire is to give voice to the 'purdurable substance' of writing, of a stone.

   One can, I think, see in this desire the fear that his conversation with Coleridge, now less and less frequent, constituted a dissolution of *The Recluse*, no longer even a voice but the echo of a voice. Coleridge's account in 'To William Wordsworth' of 'the last strain [of Wordsworth's voice] dying' as it 'awed the air' powerfully evokes what Wordsworth in the dream heard as he put the shell to his ear. J. Douglas Kneale's 'Wordsworth's Images of Language: Voice and Letter in *The Prelude*', *PMLA*, May (1986), 351–61, offers a valuable analysis of what he calls 'the voice-letter alternation', in Wordsworth. Nature's 'speaking face' in which, as Kneale points out, 'natural phenomena tend to the image of voice', is, as metaphor, Coleridge's phantom face, the face of the 'Arab phantom'. Coleridge as subtext (co-author) is the 'welcome stranger', the 'wind' become a 'tempest', the voice 'more than all winds'. He is the metaphor that Wordsworth must eulogise and bury.

16. Geoffrey Hartman, 'Words, Wish, Worth: Wordsworth', in *Deconstruction & Criticism* (New York, 1979), p. 199.

17. *Différance* combines the verb *différer* as to differ in space and to defer (put off) in time. Mind and nature cannot inhabit each other as one space, nor can Coleridge and Wordsworth inhabit each other in time. Yet both are demanded by the 'ur-fiat', both are essential to the writing of *The Recluse*. Against the violence of this 'usurpation' (seen by Derrida as a form of philosophical totalitarianism, a 'metaphysics of presence'), Derrida presents what Spivak calls 'the counter violence' of *solicitation* (from the Latin *sollicitare*, meaning to shake the totality:

sollus, 'all', and *orere*, 'to move, to shake'). What is forbidden is the totality, the *archia*. The forbidden appears as an *aporia*, the Greek word for what Spivak calls a 'seemingly insoluble logical difficulty. . . . It is neither this nor that, or both at the same time' (p. xvi). *The Prelude* is constituted upon an *aporia*, upon the impossibility of metaphor: Wordsworth is not nature, nor is he Coleridge. Both are ghostly forms of himself, the absence of his identity with himself summed up in 'two consciousnesses', himself and 'some other Being'. Coleridge is the reigning metaphor of that 'other Being'.

18. Geoffrey Hartman, *Wordsworth's Poetry 1787–1814* (New Haven, 1971), p. 225.

19. Friedrich Nietzsche, *The Use and Abuse of History, Thoughts Out of Season, Part II* (New York, 1964), pp. 6–7.

20. Paul de Man, *Allegories of Reading: Figural Language in Rousseau, Nietzsche, Rilke, and Proust* (New Haven, 1979), p. 162.

21. For a discussion of an 'abyss structure' (*mise en abyme*) in *The Prelude*, see James Hulbert's explanation in his translation of Derrida's 'Coming into one's Own', in *Psychoanalysis and the Question of the Text*, ed. Geoffrey Hartman (Baltimore, 1978), pp. 114–48: 'the expression "mise en abyme" originally from heraldry where it denotes a smaller escutcheon appearing in the centre of a larger one is [used] to refer to a structure in which the whole is represented in miniature in one of the parts' (pp. 147–8). The dream of the Arab is just such a 'smaller escutcheon' in that deeply heraldic poem, *The Prelude*.

22. 'There are intelligences of sparks of divinity in millions – but they are not souls till they acquire identities, till each one is personally itself', Keats writes (14 February – 3 May 1819). The 'two consciousnesses' are a spark of divinity and a soul.

The Uses of Dorothy: 'The Language of the Sense' in 'Tintern Abbey'

JOHN BARRELL

I

This essay is about the language of Wordsworth's 'Tintern Abbey';
more specifically, about its two languages, the language of natural
description, and the language of the meditations which seem to be
produced by the contemplation of nature, of landscape; and I will be
saying something about the theory of language which seems to define
the distinction between them. As in my discussions of James Thomson
and John Clare, I will be working towards an attempt to re-present
that distinction, as one between the language produced by a subject
who remains (it is imagined) undifferentiated from nature, and the
language spoken by a subject who is imagined to have achieved an
identity fully differentiated from it. What was at stake in those earlier
discussions, and in the distinction between those two kinds of subjects in terms of nature and culture, was a class distinction, defined
in its simplest terms, of the different relation of different subjects to
the means of production. But 'Tintern Abbey' offers us an opportunity of conceiving that distinction in terms of gender also, so that this
essay can be read as taking off from my remarks, at the end of the
essay on Milton, on Coleridge's notions of syntax as gendered.[1]
Constructions of gender-difference very often supply or repeat the
terms in which class-difference is constructed: women are frequently

represented as different from men on the same terms as ignorant men are assumed to differ from educated men, or as, indeed, children are assumed to differ from mature male adults. I shall be asking, then, about the nature of the comparison the poem makes between the masculine subject who speaks the poem, and the feminine subject to whom a part of it, at least, is spoken. On this topic, my remarks will turn on the question of whether a woman can be assumed capable either of uttering or of understanding the language of meditation in the poem, and so on whether Dorothy Wordsworth can be assumed to be capable of understanding the lines addressed to her at its end.

In a chapter of his book *Articulate Energy*, Donald Davie attempts to describe what he feels to be risks taken by the language of *The Prelude*. He begins by pointing out that 'Wordsworth's world is not pre-eminently a world of "things"', and that his language is not remarkable for its '"weight and mass"'. Because, he argues, Wordsworth had castigated some earlier poets, in the 'Preface' to the *Lyrical Ballads*, for 'giving no proof that they had ever truly *looked* at natural phenomena, it is often supposed that his own verse is full of such phenomena rendered in all their quiddity and concreteness'. This, argues Davie, is 'a sort of optical illusion. What Wordsworth renders is not the natural world but . . . the effect that world has upon him'; and in those passages of *The Prelude* where Wordsworth is trying to convey those effects, his words – such words as 'ties', 'bonds', 'influences', and 'power' – will carry his readers, only for so long as they do not 'loiter', only for so long as those words are taken as 'fiduciary symbols', as 'values of monetary exchange'. In short, 'Wordsworth's words have meaning so long as we trust them. They have just such meaning, and just as much meaning', as the term 'fiduciary symbols' suggests.[2]

I find this argument persuasive, not only for the language of *The Prelude*, but for its 'satellite-poem',[3] 'Tintern Abbey'. If we attempt to understand 'Tintern Abbey' by attempting to define clear conceptual meanings for the words in its abstract vocabulary – 'restoration', for example, or 'mystery', or 'affections', or 'recognitions', or 'something far more deeply interfused' – I believe we will fail; certainly we will not easily convince ourselves that there are any other words into which those ones can adequately be translated. But the problem goes further than that, as we will see if we consider a word which, in its singular and plural forms occurs no less than nine times in the 160 lines of the poem, the word 'thought'. Now clearly one point the poem is concerned to claim is that 'lofty' cliffs somehow give rise to 'lofty' thoughts, and that with the passage of time these lofty thoughts become more present to us than lofty cliffs can now be; and it is concerned to ask how these things happen. We might be more persuaded of the truth of that notion, perhaps, if we could arrive at a clear idea of what it is that Wordsworth thinks of as 'thoughts'. Is thinking one of a range of various activities of the mind, such as hoping, believing, imagining, feeling, or is it a term which includes some or all of those other activities? It is seldom if ever clear, and we may feel it matters that it *should* be clear, in view of the importance given to thinking as an activity characteristic of a certain kind of maturity, and of distance from immediate experience.

It is seldom if ever clear, also, what these thoughts are of, which are engendered by lofty cliffs, and how it is, therefore, that they can be described as 'lofty'. For though we get *some* idea, of course, of their content, the poem seems far more concerned to impress upon us the notion that these thoughts have such-and-such a character, than that they have such-and-such a content. Look, for example, as well as at the phrase 'lofty thoughts' in line 129, at 'elevated thoughts' in line 96; at 'my purest thoughts', in line 110; at the glowing, but still ungraspable, 'half-extinguished thought', in line 59; or at the 'thought' which endows, in time, the objects in the landscape with 'a remoter charm', in line 83. On two other occasions, the 'thoughts' are qualified by prepositional phrases, but it is by no means clear that it is their content, and not again their character, that is being represented. The 'healing thoughts / Of tender joy' in lines 145–6 may indicate that the content of Dorothy's thoughts will be joy, but as we probably think of joy as a feeling rather than as a thought, the phrase seems at least as likely to communicate that Dorothy will have thoughts of a tender, joyful character, or thoughts, of unspecified content, prompted by her tender joy. The 'thoughts of more deep seclusion', similarly, in line 7, may suggest thoughts *about* more deep seclusion, but the phrase hovers between suggesting that meaning, and suggesting that the 'steep and lofty cliffs' impress on the landscape thoughts proper to a seclusion yet more deep than the seclusion of the landscape itself – telling us, that is, something again about the kind of thoughts, not the content of them; but I will have more to say about this phrase later.

Perhaps the only time in the poem that the word 'thought' or 'thoughts' is used together with a clear suggestion of their content, is in lines 64–6, 'with pleasing thoughts, That in this moment there is life and food / For future years' – but even here, the parallelism around the caesura, 'present pleasure'/'pleasing thoughts', suggests that a sense-unit has already, in some sense, been completed at the end of line 64, by which time Wordsworth has told us, once again, of the character but not the content of the thoughts; and even when that content is revealed, the contrast, between the plural thoughts and the singular statement that defines them, seems to suggest that there is still a surplus on the side of the thoughts, that their entire content has by no means been manifested in the singular statement that follows.

We will find meaning in such words, Davie argues, only as long as we trust them; and it is a point made by the poem as well – which, for all its ratiocinative appearance, its deployment, repeatedly, of all those conjunctions by which we seek to display the connections in a rational process of thought, is still continually concerned to suggest that it proceeds not so much by the logical accretion of propositions, but by leaps of faith and trust. 'Perhaps', the poem suggests at line 32, the feelings of *unremembered* pleasure – and we must take it on trust that pleasures which cannot be remembered were indeed once experienced – have had some influence on acts of kindness which have also disappeared from the memory, and so can only be trusted to have occurred. He 'trusts' in line 36 that he may have owed to these feelings 'another gift'. That gift is a 'blessed mood', the visionary power of which at line 50 the poem appeals directly to us to confirm – we 'see into the life of things'.

But do we? – not only the fact that we do, but what we see, is to be taken on trust. The existence of that visionary power is acknowledged, in line 51, to be no more perhaps than a '*vain* belief, or a 'vain *belief*'; but the threat to the meditative direction of the poem offered by that concession is immediately pushed away, by the exclamatory assertion that, in any case, Wordsworth's spirit has, in oppressive circumstances, often turned to the River Wye. In line 66, the thought, 'That in this moment there is life and food / For future years', is redescribed as a hope, rather, and a remote one, which Wordsworth must 'dare' to entertain. His character as a youth in the Wye Valley we must, the poem makes clear, take on trust, for he cannot now 'paint' what then he was. In line 89, the notion that the gifts of maturity are an abundant recompense for the loss of youth is what Wordsworth 'would' believe, what he would like, or chooses, to believe. And so on: the poem sometimes declares, and sometimes concedes, that the doctrine that it offers to teach, that lofty cliffs are replaced by lofty thoughts, is the fruit of faith and hope, not of reason and demonstration, and that the content of this meditation, and the state of mind it attempts to represent, can only be the objects of our trust: they are open neither to be proved or disproved.

To explain his approval of, his enthusiasm for, a language whose meanings we must take on trust, Davie refers us to Coleridge's consideration of the 'Preface' to the *Lyrical Ballads* in *Biographia Literaria*.

> The best part of human language, properly so called, is derived from reflection on the acts of the mind itself. It is formed by the voluntary appropriation of fixed symbols to internal acts, to processes and results of imagination, the greater part of which have no place in the consciousness of uneducated man; though in civilised society, by imitation and passive remembrance of what they hear from their religious instructors and other superiors, the most uneducated share in the harvest which they neither sowed nor reaped.

Davie reminds us that 'this statement is made when Coleridge is objecting to Wordsworth's recommendation of rustic language', on the grounds, says Davie, that 'such language can provide only poor and meagre syntax'. For 'the rustic', continues Coleridge,

> from the more imperfect development of his faculties, and from the lower state of his cultivation, aims almost solely to convey insulated facts, either those of his scanty experience or his traditional belief; while the educated man chiefly seeks to discover those connections of things, or those relative bearings of fact to fact, from which some more or less general law is deducible.[4]

I have quoted the passage at rather greater length than is necessary to my immediate purpose, because some of what Coleridge says – which is, for the most part, the conventional wisdom of eighteenth-century theories of pastoral poetry – will be of relevance, if not now, then later on in this essay. For the moment, let us concentrate on what Davie concludes from these quotations, that Coleridge's point is that if a language is deficient in 'fixed symbols' for 'internal acts' of the mind, 'it will also be deficient in syntax'. Thus when Wordsworth in *The Prelude* or 'Tintern Abbey' 'abandoned rustic diction and took to rendering "internal acts", "processes and results of imagination"', he used for this purpose 'an elaborate syntax', and 'an important part of his vocabulary' came to be 'made up of fixed fiduciary symbols'.[5]

Davie has clouded things a little, I believe, by writing as though
Coleridge's term 'fixed symbols', means the same thing as his own
term, or rather the term he has borrowed from St-John Perse, 'fiduciary symbols'; and it may help us grasp the point of Davie's argument better if we distinguish between the two terms. For it may not
be true that a language which is rich in fixed symbols, voluntarily
appropriated to internal acts, will throw the burden of the meaning
of an utterance on to its syntax. By 'fixed symbols', 'voluntarily
appropriated', Coleridge has in mind the idea of words as arbitrary
signs, their meanings fixed by the meanings they have taken on in
earlier instances of their use, as opposed to the idea of words as
natural signs, their meanings fixed by some notionally natural connection between word and thing – if such signs, Coleridge seems to
suggest, form any part of language, it is the most primitive part. The
validation of the meaning of such arbitrary signs will not be within
any particular context in which they are used, but elsewhere, in an
agreement as to their meaning formed prior to any particular instance of their utterance; and such a compact could fix the meanings
of words that denote the *relation* of acts of the mind and the objects
of those acts, as well as the meanings of words denoting the separate
acts and objects.

The point that Davie is trying to make is better indicated by the
term 'fiduciary symbols', and by holding on to the notion that, in
Wordsworth's poetry, the meaning of such symbols depends not on
any agreement as to the meaning of words prior to their utterance in
any particular instance, but on the willingness to trust that they do
have some meaning, that they are promissory notes which, one day,
the bank will honour. This is a willingness that the poet creates in us
by, and during, his utterance; and it is such a notion of symbols, of
words whose meanings are not fixed, but whose relations with other
words the poet attempts to suggest as he utters them, that will throw
the weight of meaning in a poem on to its syntax, on to the relations
it proposes among the abstract nouns he is attempting to appropriate
to 'internal acts', to the 'processes', as well as the 'results', of imagination.

It is this notion of words as 'fiduciary symbols', as 'promissory
notes' which we trust the poet to honour in the future, that Davie is
concerned with as his discussion of *The Prelude* continues; and it
continues by attempting to establish the terms on which the readers
of the poem may be persuaded to take these symbols on trust during

their experience of reading it. The structure and texture of Wordsworth's blank verse, he argues, invites us to take that verse 'at a run, not pausing on the nouns for fear they congeal . . . but attending rather to the syntactical weave . . . What Wordsworth asks for . . . is for all his words to be considered only in their context.' 'These moods, exaltations, senses, sublimities, and faculties', he argues, will in themselves be no more clearly defined at the end of *The Prelude* than they are at any stage of our progress through the poem – and his choice here of the abstract nouns that for him typify *The Prelude* suggests that what he says of that poem may be applied to 'Tintern Abbey' as well, in which moods, senses, and the sublime, are quite as much a feature of the language. But though at the end of *The Prelude* we will arrive at no clear understanding, no clear definition of those terms, 'the poem will not be a botch'; for what will be clear at the end of the poem is the relation between them, the articulation. In short, argues Davie, 'this is poetry where the syntax counts . . . for nearly everything'.[6]

In no sense, then, will the *meanings* of the fiduciary symbols be fixed by Wordsworth's utterance; only, Davie suggests, the *relations* among them. What we learn to trust, as we read, is not that the poet will deliver, eventually, a clear conclusion or doctrine or statement of belief, one that we could abstract from the poem, translate into other terms, agree or disagree with. This is not a rhetorical poetry, in the sense that the poem is seen as a means to an end beyond itself, which, once the poem has arrived at it, will be separable from the process of its development. What we learn to trust is less the words themselves, perhaps, than the voice which speaks them: we learn to trust that the poet, even if he cannot explain them, is somehow in possession of the meanings of his abstract nouns, the proof of which is that he can propose a structure of relations among them, which is the structure of his syntax.

And the implication of Davie's argument is that we will agree to trust the poet's understanding only under certain conditions. One of these conditions is that the poem will continually *attempt* to adopt a ratiocinative mode, as if attempting to produce a conclusion which, when it is arrived at, would indeed be separable from the structure of the argument by which it was produced. It must adopt that mode as an earnest of its concern to satisfy our desire to attach fixed meanings to the nouns it employs, and thus to acknowledge our sense that only when the attempt, made in good earnest, has failed, will we be disposed to accept that the meaning of those nouns is beyond clear definition. And the second condition that this argument appears to propose is that there should be evident in the poem, alongside that ratiocinative mode and sometimes in apparent conflict with it, another mode of reflection, not concerned to provide explanations, but calling attention to itself as meditative, as ruminative, calling attention to the poem as a representation of the poet's mental experience, of what Wordsworth describes in the 'Preface' as 'the fluxes and refluxes', the ebb and flow, 'of the mind when agitated by the great and simple affections of our nature'.[7] The sincerity of the attempt at ratiocination will establish its failure as an honourable one, so that we will accept, along with Wordsworth, that all that is left to us thereafter is a ruminative mode, in which the mind proposes to itself, as its proper object of attention, not so much the meanings it seeks to generate, but its own movements in search of meaning.

II

Thus far Davie, and as will be clear from the attention I have bestowed upon his argument, I find it, with the reservation I have indicated, as suggestive in relation to 'Tintern Abbey' as I do in relation to *The Prelude*. What I want to do for the rest of this essay is to add two further conditions to those so far suggested as necessarily accompanying the demand that we take on trust the fiduciary symbols that are Wordsworth's abstract nouns. And the conditions I want to propose are such as will, I hope, help to situate the language of 'Tintern Abbey' in a specific historical context, in the context of late eighteenth-century beliefs about, and attitudes to, language, and to gender: beliefs and attitudes to which Wordsworth appeals, in his implicit demand that we take his words on trust, but to which he also refers explicitly, as we shall see. One of these conditions is that the poem's success – and a number of reviewers were enthusiastic about the poem, and used it as a stick to beat the 'lyrical ballads' proper – is achieved not *in spite of* its failure to define the meaning of its abstract nouns, but absolutely *because* of its refusal or failure to define them. That failure or refusal is welcomed not, perhaps, out of a belief that the meaning of the fiduciary symbols is too private, too much inherent in the experience of one individual to take on public meanings, but because the power of the poem, the power it communicates to us, is somehow dependent upon the refusal of the poem to communicate fixed meanings. That power, I shall suggest, was con-

ceived of as a masculine power, communicated specifically to male
subjects of language. It can be communicated to women only as a
promise, only as something they are always about to enjoy.

The first condition I shall consider towards the end of this essay.
The second is that we should believe that there is a relationship,
however irrecoverable, between the abstract and highly-articulated
language of the poem and another kind of language which is also
present in 'Tintern Abbey', as it is in *The Prelude* – the language of
natural description, or the language that names the objects in nature.
This language is conceived of as entirely unambiguous, but also as
lexically and syntactically impoverished. The first language, of course,
can be spoken only by a fully autonomous and individuated subject,
a subject who is male, educated, fully differentiated from sense and
nature; the second can be spoken also by subjects who are not male
or not educated or not either, and who are imperfectly differentiated
from nature. There seems to be no question of the nouns in this
second kind of language describing simply the 'effect' of the natural
world, or depending for their meaning on their context, or on any
complex of relations among them that requires to be articulated by
a complex syntax; so that, although they may crop up in complex
structures of ratiocinative or ruminative syntax, their appearance
always involves a temporary respite from that complexity.

Let us take, for example, lines 78–9, 'the tall rock, / The mountain, and the deep and gloomy wood'; or lines 98–100, 'the light of
setting suns, / And the round ocean, and the living air, / And the blue
sky'; or lines 104–5, 'the meadows and the woods, / And mountains';
or lines 159–60, 'these steep woods and lofty cliffs, / And this green
pastoral landscape'. These brief lists of natural objects appear as
islands of fixity and clarity in the troubled currents of Wordsworth's
syntax, and among the objects in these lists, the simplest of all
relationships is proposed – that made by the innocent conjunction
'and'. The simplicity of this connection is repeatedly emphasised by
continuing the lists of concrete nouns and noun-phrases over the
line-ending, so that the word 'And' can appear in the emphatic
position at the beginning of the line: '*And* the round ocean'; '*And*
mountains'; '*And* this green pastoral landscape'. This simple, repeated structure seems to be related to the structure we examined in
Thomson, whereby the eye, before it was revealed as the subject of its
sentence and of the landscape, was

> snatch'd o'er hill, and dale, and wood, and lawn,
> And verdant field, and darkening heath between,
> And villages embosom'd soft in trees,
> And spiry towns . . .

I am not trying to suggest, of course, that for as long as they appear, these lists of nouns are insulated from the operations of the intellect. But the kind of operation it seems appropriate to perform on them is well suggested in lines 15–17 –

> Once again I see
> These hedge-rows, hardly hedge-rows, little lines
> Of sportive wood run wild

– where the qualification, 'hardly hedge-rows', calls attention to the act of the mind involved in finding the right word or phrase for the objects of nature, in making the words of the poem more satisfactorily referential. We are dealing here with signs which, however liable to misrepresent the objects to which they refer, are treated, it seems, as if they can be *made* to represent them with some degree of exactness; and the pause in the momentum of the description, and then the act of redescription, serves to indicate how different this language is, whose proper objects are stable enough to be named with precision, from the language of moods, sublimities, presences.

It is to this language of natural description that Wordsworth refers, when he speaks at line 109 of 'the language of the sense' – a phrase which has caused considerable difficulty to a number of readers of the poem, no doubt because the function which Wordsworth ascribes to that language – which, together with nature, is claimed to be

> The anchor of my purest thoughts, the nurse,
> The guide, and guardian of my heart, and soul
> Of all my moral being

– seems a function altogether too grand, too awesome, to be performed by the language of natural description – if not by nature, which for Wordsworth can do almost anything. What then does Wordsworth mean by 'the language of the sense'? The first phrase we need to tackle here is 'the sense', a phrase which the *OED* does very little to illuminate. The only definition it offers is 'that one of the senses which is indicated by the context' – that is to say, the phrase occurs only when the context has already made clear which of the five senses it refers to, as in this example quoted from Goldsmith: 'Salts, metals, plants, ordures of every kind . . . make one mass of corruption, equally displeasing to the sense, as injurious to the health' – where the context clearly specifies 'the sense' as 'the sense of smell'. For the singular 'sense' without the definite article, however, the *OED* offers 'the senses viewed as forming a single faculty in contra-distinction to intellect, will, etc.', a meaning which corresponds to one meaning of *le sens* in French, and which amounts to the same definition as that which the *OED* offers for the plural form, 'the senses': 'the faculties of physical perception or sensation as opposed to the higher faculties of intellect, spirit, etc.'

It is clearly to this meaning of 'the senses' that Coleridge appeals, when he translates the Aristotelian maxim, 'nihil in intellectu quod non prius in sensu', as 'there is nothing in the Understanding not derived from the Senses'. But elsewhere, Coleridge translates the adage thus: 'there is nothing in the understanding which was not previously in the sense'; and elsewhere again, he writes that 'the REASON without being either the SENSE, the UNDERSTANDING or the IMAGINATION contains all three within itself' – where 'the sense' appears to have exactly the meaning of 'sense' or 'the senses' offered by the *OED*, as depending on a contradistinction of the sense from the intellect (Coleridge's 'understanding') and the other faculties.[8]

What then is 'the language' of the sense?[9] Once again, Coleridge offers us some help. He writes at one point of material nature as 'the so called elements, water, earth, air, and all their compounds', and notes that in writing thus he is using 'the ever-enduring language of the sense, to which nothing can be revealed, but as compact, or fluid, or aerial'. If the meaning of the phrase here remains opaque, it will seem less so when Coleridge writes that an 'infallible intelligence' (the Holy Spirit) 'may convey the truth in any one of three possible languages – that of sense, as objects appear to the beholder on this earth; or that of science, which supposes the beholder placed in the centre; or that of philosophy, which resolves both into a supersensual reality'. He is clearly rehearsing the same notion when he writes of the scriptures that they 'speak in the language of the Affections which they excite in us; on sensible objects, neither metaphysically, as they are known by superior intelligences; nor theoretically, as they would be seen by us were we placed in the Sun; but as they are represented by our human senses in our present relative position'.[10] The languages of science and metaphysics need not yet detain us, though the second can certainly be regarded as akin to the abstract language we have already located in 'Tintern Abbey'. The 'language of the senses' seems by this account to be either the literal language by which we name the objects we behold on earth; or the metaphorical 'language' of images, by which the senses, or the understanding operating on the data of sense, represent terrestrial objects to us.

It may indeed be the second of these, but only as a figurative extension of 'the language of the sense' as that by which we *name* the things we perceive. The 'understanding', according to one of Coleridge's many definitions (and we could use any one of them here) is 'the power of generalising the motives of the Sense [i.e.: sense-data] and of judging of the objective *reality* of all Appearances by their reducibility to a genus or class'. The understanding, it seems, produces things – let us say a red leather armchair – from the impressions of redness, shininess, comfort, curvilinearity – presented to it by the senses; from these it distinguishes the impressions of heat, brightness, and flickering motion which the senses receive at the same time, and composes these into the thing called the fire in front of which the chair is placed. But it can do this – it can produce objects out of sensations – only because it can *name* them ('let us *say* a red leather armchair', 'the thing *called* the fire'). 'In no instance do we understand a thing in itself; but only the name to which it is referred'; and so, 'in all instances, it is words, names, or, if images, yet images used as words or names, that are the only exclusive subjects of Understanding'.[11] The 'language of the sense' is then a phrase which can be used figuratively, to apply to the 'language' of images, only because it has already been used literally: for images, in this context, are 'used as words or names', to fix a bundle of impressions into an object. The 'language of the sense' is, first and foremost, the language by which we name the things, the material objects we perceive; though, to speak more accurately, we perceive only sensations, and only '*half*-perceive' objects, for we also 'half-*create*' them, by the operations of the understanding on impressions or sensations.

There is of course a danger in interpreting a phrase in a poem written by Wordsworth in 1798 by an appeal to the writings of Coleridge some twenty years later. But in this instance the danger seems minimal, in that there is not much in Coleridge's account of the language of the sense which he could not have learned from the mid eighteenth-century philosopher David Hartley, by whom he was much influenced in the 1790s; and so there is nothing in the account which Coleridge could not have communicated orally to Wordsworth, if Wordsworth himself had never looked at Hartley. In a famous passage of *The Prelude*, written in 1799, Wordsworth describes how a baby may be presumed to produce a unified image of an object, its nurse, by combining the various sensations it perceives; by combining, that is,

> In one appearance all the elements
> And parts of the same object, else detached
> And loth to coalesce

Thus the baby is at once the 'receiver' of the impressions of sense, and the 'creator' of the objects those impressions constitute.[12] The passage appears to derive, directly or indirectly, from a section in Hartley's *Observations on Man* (1749), in which Hartley attempts to show how 'the Names of visible Objects' are associated with 'the Impressions which these Objects make upon the Eye'. He argues that the association between names and things is produced by the fact that 'the Name of the visible Object, the Nurse, for Instance, is pronounced and repeated by the Attendants to the Child, more frequently when his Eye is fixed upon the Nurse, than when upon other Objects'. But, more interestingly, he argues that the ability to produce the complex, unified image of an object *depends* upon the baby's learning its name. It is by learning the word 'nurse' that the child learns to distinguish the nurse from the clothes she wears, for however often she changes her dress, the same word seems to name her; it is by learning that the word 'fire' names the fire in different places, and surrounded by different visible objects, that the child learns to separate the bundle of sensations that compose the object, the fire, from those which compose other objects. Much the same is true of how we learn what is common to a range of different objects: it is by the association of the word 'white' with the visible appearances of milk, linen, paper, and so on, that we learn to separate the quality common to those various objects from the qualities that distinguish them from each other. The language by which we learn to name objects is the means by which we learn to distinguish them; it is the first language we learn, and is 'confined to sensible things' – it is 'the language of the sense'.[13]

How is it, then, that Wordsworth can claim to ascribe so awesome a moral function to 'nature and the language of the sense'? This may appear to be fundamentally the same question as the one I posed earlier: how do 'lofty cliffs' produce 'lofty thoughts', thoughts that are elevated, 'pure', in that they are both somehow *above* nature, supernatural, and are also *morally* elevated. But that question has now been changed, by being associated with a question about language; and we could now rephrase it: how does the phrase 'lofty cliffs', or the ability to use such phrases, produce, or guide us towards, the phrase 'lofty thoughts', or the ability to deploy a phrase like that? How does the language of the sense not only produce, but foster in us, and guide us towards, the language of the intellect and of morality? And how does the language of the sense remain the anchor and guardian, not only of our purest thoughts and our moral being, but of the language by which we describe these spiritual objects of thought?

This question is posed also by Hartley, whose book is dedicated to arguing that the pleasures of sense and of the imagination – including those that we experience from the contemplation of natural beauty – must give way to, and be regulated by, 'the Precepts of Benevolence, Piety, and the Moral Sense'. The pleasure we take in 'a beautiful Scene', for example – say, the prospect of the Wye Valley near Tintern – 'ought to decline', 'by yielding, in due time, to more exalted and pure Pleasures' – say, 'the still, sad music of humanity', neither 'harsh nor grating'. The similarity of this scheme to that of 'Tintern Abbey' is obvious enough; but the important question for us is a question less of morality than of the 'natural history' of the individual: how does Hartley understand the process by which we learn the language of the intellect and of morality?

In the first place, Hartley argues, we learn the meanings of 'the names of intellectual and moral Qualities and Operations' in much the same way as we learn to find the unknown quality in an algebraic equation. That is to say, such names occur in connection with the names in the language of the sense; and by considering the relations of the words we do understand – those which describe 'sensible Impressions only' – with those we do not, we are enabled to arrive at our 'first imperfect Notions' of the names of such qualities and operations.[14] This is much the same as Davie's suggestion, that we understand Wordsworth's abstract nouns by trusting that they do have meaning, as we trust that x in an equation has value; by taking them 'at a run', and by considering them 'only in their context'. Our understanding of these names, Hartley continues, is further refined by encountering them in books, and in attempting to use them ourselves. But in the first place, we are led to understand the language of intellect and morality by its relation to the language of the sense, and in this light the language of the sense can be conceived of as the 'anchor' of the more 'elevated' language, the 'nurse' which fosters our understanding of it, and the 'guide' which leads us to that understanding.

But there is another light in which nature and the language of the sense can be seen to be all those things, to perform all the functions of anchor, nurse, guide and guardian, in relation to the language of intellect and morality. Like Locke, Hartley believed that complex ideas, such as the ideas of objects, are composed of bundles of simple ideas, separate sensations; and he believed further, that what he called 'decomplex' ideas, 'Ideas of Reflection, and intellectual Ideas', are produced by the association of complex ideas. But 'decomplex' ideas are unlike complex ones, in that they have no sensible images associated with them: we cannot refer the word 'intellect' to a visible image, as we can refer the word 'table' to the image of a table. As a result, the names attached to decomplex ideas are far more open to ambiguity, to being misunderstood, than are the names attached either to simple sensible qualities, like 'white' or 'sweet', or to complex ideas, like 'nurse' or 'table'. But in theory, the meaning of the names of decomplex ideas should be able to be fixed, by analysing those ideas themselves down to the simple ideas of sensation, of which ultimately they consist; and if we could do this, we would be able to arrive at 'the proper Use of those Words, which have no Ideas', to the great benefit of philosophy.[15] The ideas of nature, and the language of sensible impressions, are thus to be the fixed anchor by which floating 'Ideas of Reflection', of intellect and morality, and the language which describes them, are tethered to the solid ocean floor. They are the guardians of meaning, the guides by which meaning is to be comprehended; the tangible gold by which the value of the promissory notes of an abstract, intellectual, and moral vocabulary are, or should or might be, guaranteed.

It must of course be the unambiguous way in which the names in the language of the sense refer to their referents that makes nature and the language of the sense, as Wordsworth argues, anchor, nurse, guide, and guardian of his heart, and the soul of his moral being. Of his 'moral' being, because, within the meditative and contemplative language of this poem, in which morality is taken to be the exclusive property of whoever can be claimed to be the subject of nature, not the object of its determination, the capacity to feel for others is something 'learned', and is a function of the capacity to reflect, to have thoughts. 'Our thoughts', Wordsworth argues in the 'Preface', are 'the representatives of all our past feelings'; and in the same sentence it appears that feelings are 'influxes' from outside ourselves, are the sense-data named by the language of the sense.[16] So that however incommunicable and indefinable our thoughts may be – their character, as I tried to show earlier, can be communicated much more readily than their content – this empiricist belief that the basis of abstract ideas is in concrete experience is crucial to the poem's attempt to convince its readers that the language of thought has meaning because it is ultimately derived from objects of sense which admit of being rendered with precision and clarity. This assumed relation, in short, between the languages proper to intellection and to simple naming and description, is not only one of the conditions by which we may take 'fiduciary symbols' on trust – it is represented by Wordsworth as the essential condition for his own trusting of his thoughts.

III

Now that the problem – how do lofty cliffs produce lofty thoughts – has been represented at least partly as a problem of language, it admits of another solution, which was advanced not only by Hartley but by almost every empiricist philosopher of language in the eighteenth century who considered the relation between the language of sensible impressions and the language of intellection. For the question can now be put another way: how was the language of intellection produced out of the language of the sense? what is the natural history of the development of an abstract out of a concrete language? Hartley's version of the solution is to argue that 'if a Language be narrow, and much confined to sensible Things', as it will be in the infancy of a language, 'it will have great Occasion for Figures'[17] – in particular for figures of speech based on analogies between those ideas to which words are already attached, and those for which words are desired. The original, literal meaning of a word in the language of the sense can be extended, not only to other objects of sense, but to objects of intellection; and the fact that the same word can be applied to objects of both kinds may act to persuade us that perhaps the capacity of a word to be transferred from things to thoughts may impress upon us a sense of the reality of the relations between them, in such a way as to enable us to trust that abstract expressions do indeed have meaning. In this light, it seems important to the problem the poem is considering, that one of the most striking features of the language of the poem is *repetition*, by which the same word is used here literally, there figuratively, here as part of the language of the sense, and there as part of the language of 'intellectual and moral Qualities and Operations'. The word 'lofty' itself is an obvious example of such a transference; a more interesting one is 'deep', which, together with its derivatives, occurs six times in the poem.

Two of the instances of 'deep' seem to belong more to what we may regard as the language of the sense than to the language of reflection, though neither entirely escapes the more figurative meanings of the word evident in other instances of its use. 'The deep and gloomy wood' in line 79, and the 'deep rivers' of line 70, both occur in passages which I have suggested are moments of spatial arrest in the temporal movement of the ratiocinative and ruminative syntax. The literal, the topographical, the sensational meaning of the word in both cases is underlined by the fact that it occurs both times in the context of accounts of Wordsworth's primitive, appetitive enjoyment of nature, in the period of 'thoughtless youth', when the objects of the landscape had no need of 'a remoter charm / By thought supplied'. For, as we shall see, when the word 'deep' is used in a more thoroughly figurative sense, it is used to apply to a later, more mature phase of his development, when the kind of childish, thoughtless enjoyment he had once taken in nature, however much its loss is regretted, is represented as a superficial enjoyment, as compared with the more reflective, more melancholy enjoyment he now experiences.

This maturer enjoyment is characterised at once by his penetrating below the surface of nature, and by his own mind being penetrated far more deeply by what he sees or by what he once saw. To this opposition of the superficial and the youthful, on the one hand, and, on the other, the deep and mature, such a use of 'deep' as that in line 49 appeals – it is when our wild and greedy eyes are made quiet by the 'deep' power of joy that we see into the life of things. The most extreme use of 'deep' in this sense occurs in line 97: Wordsworth has felt, he claims, 'a sense sublime / Of something far more deeply interfused'. The whole phrase is the most extreme example in the poem of a notion that we have no alternative but to reject or to take on trust; and it calls attention to this by the word 'something', a frank admission of a failure to define, or of the impossibility of defining, the nature of that sense sublime. 'Deeply' here refers to an interiority so profound that the mere light of reason will certainly fail to illuminate its depths.

The first use of the word, in line 7, offers itself, by means of its ambiguity, almost as a kind of bridge between the extremes of literal and of figurative use. In the first place, the 'thoughts of more deep seclusion' may be thoughts about, or thoughts appropriate to, a scene which is yet more sequestered, yet more remote from the centres of civilisation, than Tintern Abbey is. They may be thoughts, that is, of a more deep seclusion than Wordsworth is now experiencing; and in this sense the word retains a literal notion of spatial separation, even if it operates in terms of a geography as much subjective as objective, a geography as much of thoughts as of maps, a 'landscape of the mind'. But this reading is complicated by the fact that the relation of 'deep seclusion' with 'a wild secluded scene' (line 6) invites itself to be read in terms of the opposition of wildness and depth that runs through the whole poem. Thus, to look on a 'wild' landscape, as Dorothy looks on it, with 'wild eyes' (line 120), and so to experience 'wild ecstasies' (line 139), is evidently to experience it at a superficial level which is entirely innocent of depth. The point is made clear by the insistence, in the second paragraph, that wild eyes must be made quiet, by the 'deep power of joy' (line 49), if they are to perceive things in their depth; it is made clear again by the prospect, announced in the last paragraph, of Dorothy's 'wild ecstasies' in nature maturing one day into a 'far deeper zeal / Of holier love' for nature (lines 155–6).

This opposition, then, of wildness and depth is an opposition between an immediate, superficial response to nature, and a response which, mediated by time and reflection, seems to occupy a deep interior space within the mature and reflective adult. In these terms, the 'thoughts of more deep seclusion' may be thoughts of a deeper seclusion than a merely 'wild seclusion', a merely geographical isolation in a natural landscape, can be: a regrettable but still salutary (or so Wordsworth would like to believe) seclusion of the subject from the immediate objects of experience. That suggestion is reinforced by the fact that the steep and lofty cliffs do not simply impress thoughts of more deep seclusion, they also 'connect / The landscape with the quiet of the sky'. The assertion at line 100, that the sense sublime dwells 'in the blue sky, and in the mind of man', so that sky and mind are associated, contributes to an attempt to develop out of the language of the sense another, figurative language, which will be able to describe ideas of reflection and morality. It is this extension which the ambiguous use of 'deep' at line 7 strives to achieve.

But these strategies of repetition and figuration can do no more than begin to provide names for intellectual operations and moral qualities. What they most obviously cannot do is to provide a syntax, a mode of connecting words in well-informed sentences, which both Davie and Hartley took as another essential condition for our trusting that abstract nouns had meanings, and by which Hartley believed we could arrive at an understanding, however imperfect, of those nouns. Can the poem do anything to account for the co-existence within it of a highly-articulated syntax which is descriptive, even mimetic of the operations of reflection and meditation, and the simple syntax of the language of the sense? And does it have anything to say about the historical process by which the first has developed out of the second?

The empiricist theory of language which Hartley and Wordsworth are heirs to derived the most substantial part of its intellectual legacy from the third book of Locke's *Essay Concerning Human Understanding* (1690). In particular, Hartley's concern to produce a philosophical language by rivetting each idea to its one appropriate name had been Locke's concern also, and the primary motive which led him to investigate the nature of language. And as a result, Locke's theory put far more stress on the naming function of language than on any other. He concentrated his attention on nouns and adjectives, and treated most other parts of speech, perhaps including verbs, as 'particles'. About these, he had almost nothing to say: they are, he says, 'marks of some action or intimation of the mind',[18] but he says no more than this, and nothing about syntax. 'It seems fair to conclude', remarks Stephen Land, that 'the only kind of word unmistakeably referred to by Locke in his thesis that words signify ideas is the "name". The formal properties of language have no significant place in Lockean semantics: by excluding from integral consideration all but the naming function Locke inevitably suggests that language is an aggregate of signs rather than a formal system.'[19] And there is every reason to associate with this suggestion the 'language of the sense' as it is referred to in 'Tintern Abbey': a language of names, with minimal formal connections between them, but of names which are nevertheless the 'anchor of our *purest* thoughts' – the word implies most abstract, most removed from sense, as well as most chaste, the thoughts of the 'purer mind', not of the heart, blood, or appetite, but thoughts which must finally be reducible to the language of the sense.

The history of empiricist British linguistics in the 150 or so years after Locke, Land argues, is a process of moving from a theory which conceived of language as an aggregate of signs, 'a collection of words', to one which conceived of it as a formal 'sign system':[20] a movement from an understanding of language in terms of signs to an understanding of it in terms of propositions; and Hartley's algebraic notion of syntax is a part of this development. And we can see the notion of trust, and of taking words at a run, that so engaged Davie, as essential to this new conception of language. We make utterances, or we listen to them, trusting that the formal relations the utterances produce will link together into meaning words which, separated from the contexts of discourse, can hardly be said to mean at all.

Now Locke's theory, and the development from that theory, with its concentration on the sign, to a theory which concentrated on the proposition, both lent themselves to being historicised, in the terms of that characteristically late eighteenth and early nineteenth-century notion of historical process which we sum up in the rule that ontogeny recapitulates phylogeny, that the development of the individual subject recapitulates the development of the race, or of mankind in general. Locke's theory itself could be historicised, by representing the naming of the objects of sense as the first stage of language; the ability to employ a vocabulary of abstract nouns, affixed to 'ideas of reflection', was an ability more likely to be discoverable in developed civilisations. Or the relation of signs to propositions could be historicised by the argument that the theory of language as an aggregate of signs does well enough as an account of the language of primitive peoples, who can express their fears and needs and appetites simply by naming the objects of desire or need, and so have small use for syntax – traces of that notion are evident in the passage I quoted earlier from *Biographia Literaria*, as well as in the 'Preface' to the *Lyrical Ballads*. As civilisation advances, primarily through the division of labour and the emergence of cultivated elites, the need to articulate the relations among signs increases, and an increasingly sophisticated system of syntax evolves. The language of John Clare, by this argument, will appear once again as a primitive language, its destiny to evolve into the more abstract and articulate language of

Thomson, as the destiny of its speaker is to become a civilised and so a differentiated subject, in control of, and able to organise, the words he uses, rather than being spoken by them.

Or the language of the sense or of Clare could be conceived of as a childish language, destined to mature into abstraction and sophistication as it developed towards the complexities of a propositional syntax able to express thoughts, reflections, rather than simply to name the objects of sense, need and desire. And it is this recapitulation of the history of civilisation in the history of the individual, I want to suggest, and the authority which such a notion of history commanded around 1800, that enables the transition in 'Tintern Abbey' from the deep shadowy ruminative tone of its central passages to the assured tone of certainty, of having achieved, having resolved something, at the end. The appeal to this history is made – or rather the linguistic and historical notions are summoned into the poem – by the description of 'the language of the sense' as, in particular, the 'nurse', the 'guardian' of Wordsworth's heart, and by the suddenly unproblematic account of Dorothy's future development, from wildness to depth, in the last paragraph of the poem – from the realm of the cultivated, the autonomous, the transcendent.

There is no problem foreseen in the process of Dorothy's development, which can now be seen as an entirely natural process: it is sense and Nature that lead from joy to joy, from the joy of wildness to the joy of depth; Dorothy's wild ecstasies will simply mature, like fruit or cheese, into a sober pleasure. It's all just a matter of growing up: nature and the language of the sense operate, in this process, not as what prevents but as what fosters that process; they are together the nurse and guardian who oversee the process, the guide who leads us from the experience appropriate to childhood to the experience appropriate to maturity. And yet the language of the sense remains present all the time, as the guarantor of meaning; of the meanings which, by the movement from signs to propositions, from 'animal' and 'thoughtless' youth to thinking loftily and deeply, to fully autonomous and differentiated subjectivity, we produce as adults, for these meanings are only *really* to be trusted because they are analysable into the language of the sense. Wordsworth himself has experienced a gap between the two kinds of experience and two kinds of language, the language of his 'former heart' and that of his 'purer mind'; and it was his loosening grip on the simple, and as it were pictogrammatic language that made him unable to 'paint' what once he was. There had seemed to be a problem of how to connect lofty cliffs and lofty thoughts, and the language of the sense seemed so far removed from the mature language of propositional syntax and fiduciary symbols that the first had seemed to function as an interruption of the other. But this gap he can now experience, on Dorothy's and so also on his own behalf, as a regular, and above all as a natural process of growth.

IV

But where does all this leave Dorothy? It is a fact that we should never lose sight of, in eighteenth-century Britain, that women were excluded from what was called the 'republic of letters', for the qualification for citizenship in that republic was the ability to reduce the data of experience to abstract categories, and women, it was commonly assumed, could think in terms only of the particular and the concrete. It was a common assumption among men, at least, that the language of women, whether educated or not, was thus relatively concrete and pictogrammatic as compared with that of educated men; because though they could recall, and arrange facts and images, to the degree necessary to use concrete nouns, they could not grasp the principles in terms of which such nouns were produced; they could not deploy with confidence an abstract language either far removed or entirely sundered from the world of things and of sensible ideas; and so they could not achieve that transcendent identity which is evinced in the production of an abstract and highly articulated language. One of the most popular English grammars of the early eighteenth century – a grammar based on the epistemological and linguistic theories of Locke – is divided (as were many contemporary grammars) between a large-print text which lays down the rules of grammar, and small-print notes which explain the principles from which the rules are derived. The text, the author explains, is all that need concern, as he puts it, 'children, women, and the ignorant of both sexes'[21] – the last category seeming to concede an ability to grasp principles, which has already been denied them by the inclusion of all women, whether educated or not, in the list of those who need not consult the notes.

We can be reasonably sure that Wordsworth would not openly or even privately have endorsed such an account of the intellectual 'imbecility' of women: in the late eighteenth century, and especially in the radical circles within which Wordsworth had moved in the 1790s, the *potential* of women to achieve the levels of rationality and transcendence which educated men achieved was being firmly asserted, most firmly by Mary Wollstonecraft. But we can also say with reasonable confidence that it was important for Wordsworth that the ability of women to grasp the principles of abstraction should be conceded only at the level of a potential, not an actual ability to do so. Thus in 'Tintern Abbey' Dorothy is promised future membership among the company of the intellectual, only for Wordsworth to withhold it for the time being, and perhaps indefinitely. I have said – for this is what the poem officially invites us to believe – that the transition from signs to propositions was made unproblematic, in the poem, by reference to the growth to intellectual maturity that Dorothy would surely accomplish: in 'after years' she will sober up, and her mind will become 'a mansion for all lovely forms' – I take it for general forms, for it is already a mansion for particular images of loveliness. How long a time is implied in the phrase 'after years' is not clear, but more, it seems, than the one-and-a-half years by which Dorothy was William's junior. Nevertheless, Dorothy will, it is promised or threatened, one day grow up, and learn to perceive nature in the quiet and intellectual terms which will indicate that her wild appetitive passions are now spent, and she has finally become a subject as fully differentiated from sense and nature as her brother, able to reflect upon her relations with nature, and not simply to respond to it.

In making this promise, however, Wordsworth is a victim of a conflict of his own interests, a conflict which requires Dorothy to perform a double function in the ratification of his achievement of a transcendent subjectivity. First, he needs to believe that Dorothy will grow up and sober up, for by doing so she will naturalise and legitimate his own loss of immediate pleasure in nature. The transition she makes, from the language of the sense to that of the intellect, will be an observable process, one which will recapitulate and historicise the transition Wordsworth has already made. But in the second place, the language of the sense, as presently employed by Dorothy, stands as a present and audible guarantee of the meanings in his own language of the intellect; it assures him of the secure foundation of his language in the language of the sense. Dorothy can perform these two functions, only if her potential for intellectual growth is acknowledged, but only if, also, that potential is never actualised. Wordsworth is quite explicit about this: the 'prayer' he begins to utter at line 120 –

> Oh! yet a little while
> May I behold in thee what I was once

– is no more or less than a prayer to nature to arrest Dorothy's development, and for his benefit. The danger, if nature does not answer his prayer, is not just that a mature and a fully autonomous Dorothy will drag the anchor by which Wordsworth's own language is secured to the language of the sense. For if, as I have suggested, Dorothy belongs for Wordsworth in a category which includes childhood, including his own, the language of the sense, and nature as something directly responded to, she also belongs in a category by which she becomes, child though she is, the 'nurse' of Wordsworth's heart. Her growth to autonomous subjectivity will not, as it turns out, simply recapitulate Wordsworth's own; it will precipitate, in him, a less comfortable subject-position than he now claims to occupy, in which he will be unguarded, unguided, un-nursed, where he will be without an audible guarantor of the fiduciary symbols that compose his own language, no longer able to appeal to Dorothy as the Bank of England, underwriting the value and meaning of the coins and banknotes he issues.

The paradoxes generated by Wordsworth's need are complicated, but not unfamiliar. Dorothy must be acknowledged as capable of growing up. But she must also remain a child, if she is to remain a nurse; and she must remain Wordsworth's nurse if Wordsworth himself is to remain a man. The point is reinforced if we glance back to the passage from *The Prelude*, and Hartley's *Observations*, which represent the nurse, not just as the guardian and guide of the male-child, but as the object of his perception, the material from which he produces complex ideas. From these in turn he will go on to produce the 'decomplex' ideas which the nurse is, at best, always only about to produce herself.

V

So much, then, by way of an account of one of the conditions for the taking on trust of Wordsworth's abstract vocabulary. I still need to say something about the other, which seems to contradict this first condition entirely. It was – for by now it has probably been forgotten – that we should believe that the power of the poem depends upon the very indefinability of Wordsworth's lofty thoughts, and that they occupy a vertiginous eminence, wrapped in a thick cloud which conceals any visible means of descent to, or ascent from, the world of nature and of sense. However securely those thoughts can be argued as deriving from the language of the sense, as being guaranteed by being reducible to that language, that does not mean to say that we can often, if ever, perform the act of analysis and reduction. And, more importantly, it was certainly not always believed at the end of the eighteenth century that we should even *wish* to be able to perform it. For while there was an intellectual satisfaction to be derived from the process of closing the gap between signs and propositions, by proposing a historical continuum between them, there was also an aesthetic pleasure to be derived from leaving open the gap between simple linguistic signs and those words, fiduciary symbols, whose meaning resisted analysis and definition. The nature of this pleasure was particularly the concern of theorists of the aesthetic category known as 'the sublime'; and it was as a poem which offered the pleasures and excitements of sublimity that 'Tintern Abbey' was recognised by a number of its early reviewers.

For most English readers contemporary with Wordsworth, the pleasure to be derived from the sublime of language had been defined largely by Edmund Burke, in his *Philosophical Enquiry into the Origins of our Ideas of the Sublime and the Beautiful,* first published in 1757. In his remarks on language, Burke made an important contribution to the process of qualifying the semantic account of language proposed by Locke. To put Burke's position as shortly as possible, he argued that we do not need to understand words by referring to the ideas they signified; and that in most uses of language it was impossible to do so. We do not understand the sentence, 'I shall go to Italy next summer', by referring the words to pictorial images. How many means of conveyance – foot, horse, coach, boat – would we need to conjure up the idea signified by 'going'; how many images are necessary to provide a referent for 'summer'? and how many summers do we need to try to visualise to understand the notion '*next* summer'? How many images of landscape and climate must be called up, to represent the sensible idea of 'Italy'? But more to the point, Burke argues that among the words which have the most affective power over us are what he called *compounded abstract* words – such words as 'virtue', 'liberty', 'honour' – which are almost impossible, in a connected train of conversation or reading, even to conceive of as being reducible to ideas of sense.[22]

We learn to use such words by attending to the contexts and occasions of their use, not by analysing them; and we can therefore generate contexts in which to use them without any clear under- standing of their meaning, even *within* particular contexts. Most important of all, the affective power of such compounded abstract words as are used to express the passions is crucially dependent, Burke suggests, on their obscurity and indefinability, on the fact that their connotative aura spreads beyond our ability to grasp its limits.[23] It is this sense of the limitless, of the infinite, of the *frisson* of the indefinable, of the sense of something too deeply interfused in our being to be fully illuminated by the light of analysis, that is the cause of our experience of the sublime of language. Wordsworth's use of the word 'sublime', in the context of passages of his most evidently passionate exaltation – the 'blessed mood', a gift of 'aspect more sublime' than the landscape; the sublime 'something' that dwells everywhere and so cannot be limited by being defined – is what justifies, or would have justified in 1798, his use of that vocabulary which so engaged Davie, no less than would the counter-claim, that this vocabulary is rooted in the language of the sense.

Only the last few pages of Burke's *Enquiry* are concerned with language: the bulk of it is a natural history of our experience of the sublime of vision. He argues, in brief, that obscure objects of vision are more affecting, more 'terrible', and so more sublime, than objects perceived with clarity. Darkness, extreme distance, extreme height, extreme depth – mountains, cliffs, abysses – these are objects the sight of which gives rise to sublime experience. And it seems to him to follow from this that language is a medium more capable of communicating sublime experience than the visual arts, just because language, which uses arbitrary signs, is necessarily more obscure, in that it cannot represent objects with the same clarity as can the natural signs which even the most obscure painting employs, as well as because it is often not concerned to conjure up ideas, in the sense of images, at all.

This argument also may offer a crucial context for an understand- ing of the language and development of 'Tintern Abbey'. Wordsworth begins the poem with the description of a landscape which evidently partakes of the sublime: it includes steep and lofty cliffs, which appeal to the vertiginous pleasure we take in whatever prompts our fear and our concern for self-preservation; it is 'wild', a crucial term in the sublime of landscape; it is observed with wild eyes, and it prompts wild ecstasies. Yet the first movement of the poem is to turn away from these merely visual experiences, and from what seemed to many in the eighteenth century to be an almost directly referential language of naming, towards an obscure and abstract language which, by virtue of its inability to find things to name, may be all the more affective. And only after that initial turning is the attempt made to connect the sublime of landscape and the sublime of language within a historical continuum from childhood to maturity, from determination by nature to freedom from determination.

Within the discourse of the sublime, 'the language of the sense' functioned as a marker of difference; in the historical discourse, it could function also as a marker of relation. For the sublime discourse invited the polite male to experience a peculiar satisfaction in contemplating the vast gap which separated him from those others, the uneducated rustic and the impressionable female, who could perform no very elaborate operations on the impressions they received. The historical discourse, concerned with how languages develop, in a people or in the individual, could drop a ladder down to those who remained 'merged in sense', apparently to invite them to ascend to share the autonomous subject-position at its top. But the two discourses could be knotted together, as they are in this poem, because both acknowledged that the gap between the language of the sense and what Coleridge called 'the best part of human language' was one of the most crucial issues which the theory of language was obliged to address. Thus both agreed that children, the vulgar, women, could be trusted to use such a word as 'table' with as much accuracy as the educated male, and could be expected to construct such sentences as 'table' might occur in with tolerable success. With words such as 'liberty' or 'virtue' – or 'restoration, or 'moral being', or 'sublime' itself – the case was evidently very different: such words could be well used only by the highly educated, in the highly-articulated syntax which only they could deploy.

The knotting together of these two discourses within 'Tintern Abbey' ensures that the invitation extended to Dorothy, to climb the ladder to the language of reflection, would not sound too sincere, and that the power to be derived from this knotting would not be put at risk. The polite needed the uneducated and impressionable to know and to keep their place, if they themselves were to remain in exclusive possession of the top spot. Dorothy may climb, one day she will, but for the moment . . . – this strategy reveals that the ladder is really an anchor chain, to provide the polite male with the private reassurance that his own articulate and artificial language is still securely tethered to the nature which he has escaped from and transcended, but which he must still appeal to, if he is to talk, not nonsense but 'sense'.

From John Barrell, *Poetry, Language and Politics* (Manchester, 1988), pp. 141–67.

NOTES

[*Poetry, Language and Politics* is made up of five distinct essays. However, as the opening of this essay – the last in the set – makes clear, John Barrell carries forward key ideas. He is essentially making use of recent developments in language theory to develop two important Marxist critical themes, the influence of class structure on the structures of writing, and the nature of the relationship between class-difference and gender-difference in literature.

In his discussion of the poet James Thomson (1700–1748), and John Clare (1793–1864) earlier in the book, we are offered a distinction between describing nature, and describing the more sophisticated process of *meditating* on nature. Barrell suggests that this distinction was understood to mean the difference between an existence 'undifferentiated from nature', and an existence marked by the possession of a distinct personal identity; it was from the vantage point of this latter, independent identity, that you could meditate on nature.

Progress from the simplicity of an animal existence to a mature, reflective personality is, Barrell suggests, expressed not only by reference to a child/adult difference, it is also 'gendered'. He suggests this at the end of his essay on Milton, he now develops the theme with reference to 'Tintern Abbey', and the roles within it of William and Dorothy Wordsworth. Ed.]

1. The essays referred to are: 'Masters of Suspense: syntax and gender in Milton's sonnets' (pp. 44–78); 'Being is perceiving: James Thomson and John Clare' (pp.100–36). [Ed.]

2. Donald Davie, *Articulate Energy* (London, 1955), pp. 106–7.

3. Herbert Lindenberger, *On Wordsworth's 'Prelude'* (Princeton, 1963), p. 44.

4. Samuel Taylor Coleridge, *Biographia Literaria*, ed. James Engell and W. Jackson Bate (London, 1983), vol. 2, pp. 52–3.

5. Donald Davie, *Articulate Energy* (London, 1955), p. 109.

6. Ibid., pp. 110–11.

7. *Lyrical Ballads*, ed. R. L. Brett and A. R. Jones (London, 1965), p. 247.

170 JOHN BARRELL

8. Samuel Taylor Coleridge, *Aids to Reflection*, ed. Thomas Penby (Edinburgh, 1905), p. 109n, and see *Biographia Literaria*, vol. 1, p. 141n; *Logic*, ed. J. R. de J. Jackson (London, 1981), p. 226; Coleridge, *Lay Sermons*, ed. R. J. White (London, 1972), p. 69.

9. In a famous essay on the meaning of 'sense' in *The Prelude*, in *The Structure of Complex Words* (London, 1951), pp. 289–305, William Empson identified Wordsworth's 'the sense' in the phrase we are considering as a new form, 'and the new form', he argues, 'must be supposed to imply some new meaning'. Thus 'the sense' could not mean simply 'the senses': 'even Wordsworth could not have got away with saying that the language of *the senses* was the soul of all his moral being'. It would take too many pages to take issue with the complex meaning Empson attributes to 'the sense' as Wordsworth uses it, in 'Tintern Abbey' and *The Prelude*; and it will have to be sufficient here to say that in none of the examples of the phrase Empson discusses does it seem to me that we need attribute any more complex meaning to 'the sense' than the one the *OED* attributes to 'sense' or 'the senses'; and that (as I hope this essay will demonstrate) Wordsworth could certainly 'have got away' with attributing to 'the language of the sense'(or 'sense' or 'of the senses') exactly the moral function that Empson says he could not.

10. Robert Southey and Coleridge, *Omniana*, ed. Robert Gittings (Fontwell, 1969), p. 347; Coleridge, *Confessions of an Enquiring Spirit* (London, 1886), p. 17; Coleridge, *Aids to Reflection*, ed. Thomas Fenby (Edinburgh, 1905), pp. 75–6.

11. Samuel Taylor Coleridge, *Lay Sermons*, ed. R. J. White (London, 1972), p. 60n; *Aids to Reflection*, p. 202.

12. Wordsworth, *The Prelude, 1799, 1805, 1850*, ed. Jonathan Wordsworth, M. H. Abrams and Stephen Gill (London, 1979). I quote from the 1799 version, Part 2, lines 278–80, 303.

13. David Hartley, *Observations on Man, His Frame, His Duty, and His Expectations* (London, 1749), Part 1, pp. 270–3, 292, 298.

14. Ibid., Part 2, p. 245; Part 1, pp. 422, 275, 277.

15. Ibid., Part 1, pp. 278, 76.

16. *Lyrical Ballads*, ed. R. L. Brett and A. R. Jones (London, 1965), p. 246.

17. David Hartley, *Observations on Man* (London, 1749), Part 1, p. 292.

18. John Locke, *An Essay Concerning Human Understanding* (London, 1690), III, vii, 4.

19. Stephen K. Land, *From Signs to Propositions: The Concept of Form in Eighteenth Century Semantic Theory* (London, 1974), p. 8.

20. Ibid., p. 189.

21. Anon., *A Grammar of the English Language* (London, 1711), 'Preface' (pages unnumbered). The division of eighteenth-century grammars into text and notes, each aimed at different kinds of readers, is discussed by Murray Cohen in *Sensible Words: Linguistic Practise in England 1640–1785* (Baltimore, 1977), ch. 2.

22. Edmund Burke, *A Philosophical Enquiry into the Origin of our Ideas of the Sublime and Beautiful*, ed. James T. Boulton (London, 1968), pp. 170, 164, 166.

23. Ibid., p. 175.

8

Sex and History in 'The Prelude' (1805): Books IX to XIII

GAYATRI CHAKRAVORTY SPIVAK

Whatever the 'truth' of Wordsworth's long life (1770–1850), Books IX through XIII of the 1805 version of his autobiographical poem *The Prelude* present the French Revolution as the major crisis of the poet's poetic formation. As one critic has put it, 'his allegiance to revolutionary enthusiasm was so strong that, when, as he saw it, the revolutionary government resorted to nationalistic war (and after he had set up residence with his sister, as they had so long desired), Wordsworth was thrown into a catastrophic depression that has led many modern critics to treat the Revolution (or having a child by and "deserting" Annette Vallon, one is never quite sure) as the trauma of his life.'[1] As this analysis reminds us, the 'revolution' in Wordsworth's life also involved two women. As in the critic's sentence, so also in *The Prelude*, the story of Annette is in parenthesis, the desertion in quotation marks. 'His sister' – and indeed Wordsworth does not name her – is also in parenthesis.

The consecutive parts of *The Prelude* were not consecutively composed. The account in the text is not chronological. I have taken the textual or narrative consecutivity imposed by an authorial decision as given. Such a decision is, after all, itself part of the effort to cope with crisis.

As I read these books of *The Prelude*, I submit the following theses:

(1) Wordsworth not only needed to exorcise his illegitimate paternity but also to re-establish himself sexually in order to declare his imagination restored.
(2) He coped with the experience of the French Revolution by transforming it into an iconic text that he could write and read.
(3) He suggested that poetry was a better cure for the oppression of mankind than political economy or revolution and that his own life had the preordained purpose of teaching mankind this lesson.[2]

My critique calls for a much more thorough reading of the history and politics of the French Revolution and the English reaction than I am able to provide here.

I sometimes use the Derridian words 'trace' and 'trace-structure' in the following way. In our effort to define things, we look for origins. Every origin that we seem to locate refers us back to something anterior and contains the possibility of something posterior. There is, in other words, a trace of something else in seemingly self-contained origins. This, for the purposes of my argument, 'is' the trace-structure.

The trace, since it breaks up every first cause or origin, cannot be a transcendental principle. It would thus be difficult to distinguish clearly between the trace as a principle and cases of the trace, such as writing or a stream. The trace-structure does not simply undermine origins; it also disrupts the unified and self-contained description of things. By isolating three theses in Wordsworth's work, I am inconsistent with the notion of the trace-structure. No discourse is possible, however, without the unity of *something* being taken for granted. It is not possible to attend to the trace *fully*. One's own self-contained critical position as attendant of the trace also refers back and forward. It is possible to read such references as one's 'history' and 'politics'. Since the trace cannot be fully attended to, one possible alternative is to pay attention to the texts of history and politics as the trace-structuring of positions, knowing that those two texts are themselves interminable.

WORDSWORTH'S EXORCISM OF ILLEGITIMATE
PATERNITY; SEXUAL SELF-ESTABLISHMENT TO RESTORE
IMAGINATION

It is commonly acknowledged that the story of Vaudracour and
Julia, as told in Book IX of *The Prelude* (1805), is a disguised version
of the affair between Wordsworth and Annette Vallon. The real
story is much more banal: Annette did not have a chance to begin
with. She was romantic and undemanding. Plans for marriage were
tacitly dropped over the years. No money was forthcoming even
after Wordsworth received his modest legacy. Annette got deeply
involved in the Royalist resistance and died poor at seventy-five. The
story is told in detail in Emile Legouis's *William Wordsworth and
Annette Vallon*.[3] 'It is only fair to add that Wordsworth made some
provision for his daughter from the time of her marriage in February,
1816. This took the form of an annuity for £30, which continued
until 1835 when the annuity was commuted for a final settlement of
£400.'[4] In 'Vaudracour and Julia' the woman is in a convent, the
child dead in infancy, and the man insane.

It is not my concern in this section to decide whether Wordsworth
can be excused or if Annette was worth his attentions. It is rather to
remark that, in these books of *The Prelude*, one may find textual
signs of a rejection of paternity, of a reinstatement of the subject as
son (rather than father) within Oedipal law, and then, through the
imagination, a claim to androgyny.

The acknowledgement of paternity is a patriarchal social acknowledgement of the trace, of membership in what Yeats called
'those dying generations'. Through this acknowledgement, the man
admits that his end is not in himself. This very man has earlier
accepted sonship and admitted that his *origin* is not in himself either.
This makes it possible for the man to declare a history. Wordsworth
the autobiographer seems more interested at this point in transcending or coping with rather than declaring history – in producing a
poem rather than a child. He deconstructs the opposition and co-
operation between fathers and sons. The possibility of his being a
father is handled in the Vaudracour and Julia episode. The
rememoration – the symbolic reworking of the structures – of his
being a son is constructed in the famous 'spots of time' passages.
Then, since mothers are not carriers of names, by means of nature as
mother, Wordsworth projects the possibility of being son *and* lover,
father *and* mother of poems, male *and* female at once.

I will try to show this projection through the reading of a few passages. But first I should insist that I am not interested in a personal psychoanalysis of William Wordsworth, even if I were capable of undertaking such a task. The thematics of psychoanalysis as a regional science should be considered as part of the ideology of male universalism, and my point here would be that Wordsworth is working with and out of that very ideology. If indeed one wished to make a rigorous structural psychoanalytic study, one would have to take into account 'the death of Wordsworth's mother when Wordsworth was eight'. One would have to plot not only 'the repressions, fixations, denials, and distortions that attend such traumatic events in a child's life and the hysteria and unconscious obsessions that affect the life of the grown man, and more than likely his poetic practice'[5] but also the search for 'the lost object' and the recourse to fetishism in the text as signature of the subject.

The story of Vaudracour and Julia begins as a moment of dissonance in the story of the French Revolution, marking a deliberate postponement or substitution:

> *I shall not, as my purpose was, take note*
> Of other matters which detain'd us oft
> In thought or conversation, *public* acts,
> And *public* persons, and the emotions wrought
> Within our minds by the every-varying wind
> Of *Record* or *Report* which day by day
> Swept over us; but I will here *instead*
> Draw from obscurity a tragic Tale
> *Not in its spirit singular indeed*
> But haply worth memorial.
> (IX. 541–50; italics mine)

Not only does the story not have its proper place or singularity, but its narrative beginning is given as two random and not sufficiently differentiated choices out of plural possibilities: 'Oh / Happy time of youthful Lovers! thus / My story may begin, Oh! balmy time . . .' (IX. 554–5). In the final version of *The Prelude* (1850), its revisions dating probably from 1828, the beginning is even less emphatic: '(thus / The story might begin)' is said in parenthesis, and the story itself is suppressed and relegated to the status of nothing but a trace of a record that exists elsewhere: 'So might – and with that prelude did begin / The record' (IX. 557–8 [1850]). If in the serious public business of *The Prelude* such a non-serious theme as love and desertion were to be introduced, the 1850 text asks, 'Fellow voyager! / Woulds't thou not chide?' (IX. 563–4).

The end of Book IX in both versions gives us an unredeemed Vaudracour, who, situated in an indefinite temporality, remains active as an unchanging pre-text at the same time as the prospective and retrospective temporality of Books X to XIII puts together a story with an end. The mad Vaudracour is 'always there':

> Thus liv'd the Youth
> Cut off from all intelligence with Man,
> And shunning even the light of common day;
> Nor could the voice of Freedom, which through France
> Soon afterwards resounded, public hope,
> Or personal memory of his own deep wrongs,
> Rouse him: but in those solitary shades
> His days he wasted, an imbecile mind.
> (IX. 926–33)

In this autobiography of origins and ends, Vaudracour simply lives on, wasting his days; the open-ended temporality does not bring his life to a close. In this story of the judgement of France, he remains unmoved by the voice of Freedom. In this account of the growth of a poet's mind, his mind remains imbecile. This is the counterplot of the origin of *The Prelude*, the author's alias. The author stands in contrast to, yet in complicity with, the testamentary figures of the endings of the later books, who are in fact sublated versions of Vaudracour.

At the end of Book X an acceptable *alter ego* is found. He is quite unlike the Vaudracour who marks the story of guilt. This is of course Coleridge, the Friend to whom *The Prelude* is addressed. Rather than remain suspended in an indefinite temporality, this sublated *alter ego* looks toward a future shaped by the author:

> Thou wilt stand
> Not as an Exile but a Visitant
> On Etna's top.
> (X. 1032–4)

Unlike the fictive Vaudracour in his uncomfortable suspension, Coleridge, now in degraded Sicily, *is* the parallel of Wordsworth, then in unruly France. Wordsworth had not been able to find a clue to the text of the September Massacres in Paris:

> upon these
> And other sights looking as doth a man
> Upon a volume whose contents he knows
> Are memorable, but from him lock'd up,
> Being written in a tongue he cannot read,
> So that he questions the mute leaves with pain
> And half upbraids their silence.
>
> (X. 48–54)

That failure seems recuperated in all the textual examples –
Empedocles, Archimedes, Theocritus, Comates – brought to bear
upon contemporary Sicily, precisely to transform it to a pleasant
sojourn for Coleridge. Imagination, a faculty of course denied to
Vaudracour's imbecile mind, is even further empowered:

> by pastoral Arethuse
> Or, if that fountain be in truth no more,
> Then near some other Spring, *which by the name*
> *Thou gratulatest, willingly deceived,*
> Shalt linger as a gladsome Votary,
> And not a Captive
>
> (X. 1034–98; italics mine)

As I will show later, the end of Book XI welcomes Coleridge as a
companion in an Oedipal scene, and the end of Book XII cites
Coleridge as guarantor that in Wordsworth's early poetry glimpses
of a future world superior to the revolutionary alternative are to be
found.

The end of Book XIII, the end of *The Prelude* as a whole, is a fully
negating sublation of Vaudracour. If *his* life was a waste of days, by
trick of grammar indefinitely prolonged, the poet's double is here
assured:

> yet a few short years of useful life,
> And all will be complete, thy race be run,
> Thy monument of glory will be raised.
>
> (XIII. 428–30)

If Vaudracour had remained unchanged by revolution as an imbecilic
mind, here the poet expresses a hope, for himself and his friend, that
they may

> Instruct . . . how the mind of man becomes
> A thousand times more beautiful than
> . . . this Frame of things
> (Which, 'mid all the revolution in the hopes
> And fears of men, doth still remain unchanged)
> (XII. 446–50)

Julia is obliterated rather quickly from the story. By recounting these successive testamentary endings and comparing them to Vaudracour's fate, which ends Book IX, I have tried to suggest that Vaudracour, the unacknowledged self as father, helps, through his disavowal and sublation, to secure the record of the progress and growth of the poet's mind. Let us now consider Wordsworth's use of Oedipal signals.

There is something like the use of a father figure by a son – as contrasted to acknowledging oneself as father – early in the next book (X. 467–515). Wordsworth recounts that he had felt great joy at the news of Robespierre's death. Is there a sense of guilt associated with ecstatic joy at *anyone's* death? We are free to imagine so, for, after recounting this excess of joy, Wordsworth suddenly recalls the faith in his own professional future felt by a father figure, his old teacher at Hawkshead. (As is often the case in *The Prelude*, there is no causal connection between the two episodes; however, a relationship is strongly suggested.) The memory had come to him by way of a thought of the teacher's epitaph, dealing with judgements on Merits and Frailties, written by Thomas Gray, a senior and meritorious member of the profession of poetry. This invocation of the tables of the law of the Fathers finds a much fuller expression in later passages.

In a passage toward the beginning of Book XI, there is once again a scene of disciplinary judgement. Of the trivium of Poetry, History, Logic, the last has, at this point in Wordsworth's life, seemingly got the upper hand. As for the other two – 'their sentence was, I thought, pronounc'd (XI. 94). The realisation of this inauspicious triumph of logic over poetry is given in a latent image of self-division and castration:

> Thus strangely did I war against myself
> . . . Did like a Monk who hath forsworn the world
> Zealously labour to cut off my heart
> From all the sources of her former strength.
> (XI. 74, 76–8)

Memories of the 'spots of time' bring enablement out of this predicament. The details are explicit and iconic.[6] The poet has not yet reached man's estate: 'When scarcely (I was then not six years old) / My hand could hold a bridle' (XI. 280–1). As he stumbles lost and alone, he accidentally discovers the anonymous *natural* inscription, *socially* preserved, of an undisclosed proper name, which is all that remains of the phallic instrument of the law:

> The Gibbet-mast was moulder'd down, the bones
> And iron case were gone; but on the turf,
> Hard by, soon after that fell deed was wrought
> Some unknown hand had carved the Murderer's name.
> The monumental writing was engraven
> In times long past, and still, from year to year,
> By superstition of the neighbourhood
> The grass is clear'd away; *and to this hour*
> The letters are all fresh and visible.
> (XI. 291–9; italics mine)

At the time he left the spot forthwith. Now the memory of the lugubrious discovery of the monument of the law provides:

> A virtue by which pleasure is enhanced
> That penetrates, enables us to mount
> When high, more high, and lifts us up when fallen.
> (XI. 266–8)

Many passages in these later books bring the French Revolution under control by declaring it to be a *felix culpa*, a necessary means toward Wordsworth's growth as a poet: this is such a suggestion. Nothing but the chain of events set off by the Revolution could have caused acts of rememoration that would abreactively fulfil memories of Oedipal events that childhood could not grasp.

As in the case of the memory of the teacher's grave, a metonymic though not logical or metaphoric connection between the second spot of time and the actual father is suggested through contiguity. Here Wordsworth and his brothers perch on a parting of the ways that reminds us of the setting of Oedipus's crime: 'One of two roads from Delphi, / another comes from Daulia'.[7] Ten days after they arrive at their father's house, the latter dies. There is no logical connection between the two events, and yet the spiritual gift of this spot of time is, precisely, that 'the event / With all the sorrow which it brought appear'd / A chastisement' (XI. 368–70).

One might produce a textual chain here: joy at Robespierre's *judgement* (averted by a father figure); the self-castrating despair at Poetry's *judgement* at the hand of Logic (averted by a historical reminder of the *judgement* of the Law); final acceptance of one's own gratuitous, metonymic (simply by virtue of temporal proximity) guilt. Now, according to the canonical Oedipal explanation, 'Wordsworth' is a man as son. And just as the murderer's name cut in the grass can be seen *to this day*, so also the rememorated accession to manhood retains a continuous power: 'in this later time . . . unknown to me' (XI. 386, 388). It is not to be forgotten that the false father Vaudracour, not established within the Oedipal law of legitimate fathers, also inhabits this temporality by fiat of grammar.

Near the end of Book XI, Coleridge, the benign *alter ego* – akin to the brothers at the recalled 'original' event – is once again called forth as witness to the Oedipal accession. Earlier, Wordsworth had written:

> . . . I shook the habit off
> Entirely and for ever, and again
> In Nature's presence stood, *as I stand now*,
> A sensitive, and a creative soul.
> (XI. 254–7; italics mine)

Although the 'habit' has a complicated conceptual antecedent dispersed in the argument of the thirty-odd previous lines, the force of the metaphor strongly suggests a sexual confrontation, a physical nakedness. One hundred and fifty lines later, Wordsworth welcomes Coleridge into the brotherhood in language that, purging the image of all sexuality, still reminds us of the earlier passage:

> Behold me then
> Once more in Nature's presence, thus restored
> *Or otherwise*, and strengthened once again
> (*With memory left of what had been escaped*)
> To habits of devoutest sympathy.
> (XI. 393–7; italics mine)

History and paternity are here fully disclosed as mere traces, a leftover memory in parenthesis (line 396), or one among alternate methods of restoration (line 394–5). All that is certain is that a man, stripped and newly clothed, stands in front of Nature.

It is interesting to note that Wordsworth's sister provides a passage into the rememoration of these Oedipal events, and finally into the accession to androgyny. Unlike the male mediators who punish, or demonstrate and justify the law – the teacher, the murderer, the father, Coleridge – Dorothy Wordsworth restores her brother's imagination as a living agent. And, indeed, William, interlarding his compliments with the patronage typical of his time, and perhaps of ours, does call her 'wholly free' (XI. 203).[8] It is curious, then, that the predication of *her* relationship with Nature, strongly reminiscent of 'Tintern Abbey', should be entirely in the conditional:

> Her the birds
> And every flower she met with, could they but
> Have known her, would have lov'd. Methought such charm
> Of sweetness did her presence breathe around
> That all the trees, and all the silent hills
> And every thing she look'd on, should have had
> An intimation how she bore herself
> Towards them and to all creatures.
>
> (XI. 214–21)

The only indicative description in this passage is introduced by a controlling 'methought'.

Although Wordsworth's delight in his sister makes him more like God than like her – 'God delights / In such a being' (XI. 221–2) – she provides a possibility of transference for him. The next verse paragraph begins – 'Even like this Maid' (XI. 224). Julia as object of desire had disappeared into a convent, leaving the child in Vaudracour's hands. Vaudracour as the substitute of the poet as father can only perform his service for the text as an awkward image caught in an indefinitely prolonged imbecility. Dorothy as sister is arranged as a figure that would allow the poet the possibility of a replaying of the Oedipal scene, the scene of sonship after the rejection of premature fatherhood. If the historical, though not transcendental, authority of the Oedipal explanation, especially for male protagonists, is given credence, then, by invoking a time when he was like her, William is invoking the pre-Oedipal stage when girl and boy are alike, leading to the passage through Oedipalisation itself, when the object of the son's desire is legally, though paradoxically, defined as his mother.[9] Nature sustains this paradox: for Nature is that which is not Culture, a place or stage where kinships are not yet articulated. 'One cannot confound incest as it would be in this intensive nonpersonal regime that would institute it, with incest as represented in extension in the state that prohibits it, and that defines it as a transgression against persons. . . . Incest as it is prohibited (the form of discernible persons) is employed to repress incest as it is desired (the substance of the intense earth).'[10]

Wordsworth would here clear a space beyond prohibitions for himself. Dorothy carries the kinship inscription 'sister' and provides the passage to Nature as object choice; Wordsworth, not acknowledging paternity, has not granted Annette access to a kinship inscription (she was either madame or the Widow Williams). The text of Book XI proceeds to inscribe Nature as mother and lover. The predicament out of which, in the narative, Dorothy rescues him, can also be read as a transgression against both such inscriptions of Nature:

> I push'd without remorse
> My speculations forward; yes, set foot
> On Nature's holiest places.
> (X. 877–9)

The last link in this chain is the poet's accession to an androgynous self-inscription which would include mother and lover. Through the supplementary presence of Nature, such an inscription seems to embrace places historically 'outside' and existentially 'inside' the poet. We locate a passage between the account of the discovery of the name of the murderer and the account of the death of the father:

> Oh! mystery of Man, *from what a depth*
> *Proceed* thy honours! I am lost, but see
> In simple childhood something of the base
> On which thy greatness stands, but this I feel,
> That from thyself it is that thou must give,
> Else never canst receive. The days gone by
> Come back upon me from the dawn almost
> Of life: *the hiding-places of my power*
> *Seem open; I approach, and then they close;*
> I see by glimpses now; when age comes on,
> May scarcely see at all, and I would give,
> While yet we may, as far as words can give,
> A substance and a life to what I feel:
> I would enshrine the spirit of the past
> For future restoration.
> (XI. 329–43; italics mine)

We notice here the indeterminacy of inside and outside: 'from thy-
self' probably means 'from myself', but if addressed to 'mystery of
man', that meaning is, strictly speaking, rendered problematic; there
are the 'I feel's that are both subjective and the subject matter of
poetry; and, of course, the pervasive uncertainty as to whether memory
is ever inside or outside. We also notice the double inscription: womb
or depths that produce the subject and vagina where the subject's
power finds a hiding place. Consummation is as yet impossible. The
hiding places of power seem open but, upon approach, close. It is a
situation of seduction, not without promise. It is a palimpsest of sex,
biographic memorialisation, and psychohistoriography.

Dorothy is in fact invoked as chaperon when Nature is his
handmaiden (XIII. 236–46). And when, in the same penultimate
passage of the entire *Prelude*, she is apostrophised, William claims
for the full-grown poet an androgynous plenitude which would
include within the self an indeterminate role of mother as well as
lover:

> And he whose soul hath risen
> Up to the height of feeling intellect
> Shall want no humbler tenderness, his heart
> Be tender as a nursing Mother's Heart;
> Of female softness shall his life be full,
> Of little loves and delicate desires,
> Mild interests and gentlest sympathies
> (XIII. 204–10)

The intimation of androgynous plenitude finds its narrative opening in the last book of *The Prelude* through the thematics of self-
separation and autoeroticism, harbingers of the trace. The theme is
set up as at least twofold, and grammatically plural. One item is
Imagination, itself 'another name' for three other qualities of mind,
and the other is 'that intellectual love' (XIII. 186), with no grammatical fulfilment of the 'that' other than another double construction,
twenty lines above, where indeed Imagination is declared to be
another name for something else. Of Imagination and intellectual
love it is said that 'they are each in each, and cannot stand / Dividually'
(XIII. 187–8). It is a picture of indeterminate coexistence with a
strong aura of identity ('each in each', not 'each in the other';
'dividually', not 'individually'). In this declaration of theme, as he
sees the progress of the representative poet's life in his own,
Wordsworth seems curiously self-separated. 'This faculty', he writes,

and we have already seen how pluralised it is, 'hath been the moving soul / Of our long labour.' Yet so intrinsic a cause as a moving soul is also described as an extrinsic object of pursuit, the trace as stream:

> We have traced the stream
> From darkness, and the very place of birth
> In its blind cavern, whence is faintly heard
> The sound of waters.
>
> (XIII. 172–5)

The place of birth, or womb, carries a trace of sound, testifying to some previous origin. The explicit description of the origin as place of birth clarifies the autoerotic masculinity of 'then given it greeting, as it rose once more / With strength' (XIII. 179–80). For a time the poet had 'lost sight of it bewilder'd and engulph'd' (XIII. 178). The openness of the two adjective/adverbs keeps the distinction between the poet as subject (inside) and Imagination as object (outside) indeterminate. The autoerotic image of the subject greeting the strongly erect phallus that is his moving soul slides quickly into a logical contradiction. No *rising* stream can 'reflect anything in its "solemn breast"', let alone 'the works of man and face of human life' (XIII. 180–1). It is after this pluralised and autoerotic story of Imagination as trace that Wordsworth assures 'Man' that this 'prime and vital principle is thine / In the recesses of thy nature' and follows through to the openly androgynous claims of lines 204–10, cited above.

The itinerary of Wordsworth's securing of the Imagination is worth recapitulating. Suppression of Julia, unemphatic retention of Vaudracour as sustained and negative condition of possibility of disavowal, his sublation into Coleridge, rememorating through the mediation of the figure of Dorothy his own Oedipal accession to the Law, Imagination as the androgyny of Nature and Man – Woman shut out. I cannot but see in it the sexual-political programme of the Great Tradition. If, in disclosing such a programmatic itinerary, I have left aside the irreducible heterogeneity of Wordsworth's text, it is also in the interest of a certain politics. It is in the interest of suggesting that, when a man (here Wordsworth) addresses another man (Coleridge) in a sustained conversation on a seemingly universal topic, we must *learn* to read the microstructural burden of the woman's part.

From *Post-Structuralist Readings of English Poetry*, ed. Richard Machin and Christopher Norris (Cambridge, 1987), pp. 193–204.

NOTES

[This is the first part of Gayatri Chakravorty Spivak's essay, the scope of which goes far beyond the discussion of gender. The second part of the essay looks at the way Wordsworth coped with his experience of the French Revolution. He did so, Spivak argues, by turning it into a text; something, in other words, of which he became the master: he could both write it and read it. The third part of the essay argues that Wordsworth came to believe that poetry, and not political economy or revolution, would in due course rid mankind of oppression. The spirit in which these theses are proposed sounds playful, even mocking; their implications for reading Wordsworth, however, are serious. The destabilising tone of the writing reflects an ambivalence that is part of a poststructuralist strategy. The fact remains that Wordsworth 'the great poet' is being put down no less comprehensively than in Roger Sales's chapter (essay 5). The structure of the essay tends to imply that Wordsworth's inadequacy when it came to dealing with history and politics was only to be expected given his shortcomings in respect of gender politics. As in the previous essay by John Barrell, the interrelationship of gender and history is of central concern, though Spivak's handling of her material is far more self-consciously 'poststructuralist'. Ed.]

1. Wallace W. Douglas, *Wordsworth: The Construction of a Personality* (Kent, 1968), pp. 3–4.

2. Part One of the essay is reproduced here, dealing with the first of the three theses. See Editor's Note above. [Ed.]

3. Legouis's approach is so sexist and politically reactionary that the reader feels that it was Annette's good fortune to have been used by Wordsworth, Wordsworth's good sense to have treated her with exemplary pious indifference and no financial assistance, and his magnanimity to have given his daughter money in her adult life, to have allowed this daughter, by default, to use his name, and to have probably addressed her as 'dear Girl' in 'It is a beauteous evening', when, on the eve of his marriage to sweet Mary Hutchinson, Dorothy and William were walking with ten-year-old Caroline, *without* Annette, because the latter, 'although inexhaustibly voluble when she pours out her heart, . . . seems to be devoid of intellectual curiosity' (Emile Legouis, *William Wordsworth and Annette Vallon* [London, 1922], pp. 68, 33. Critical consensus has taken Wordsworth's increasingly brutal evaluation of the Annette affair at face value: 'In retrospect [his passion for Annette] seemed to him to have been transient rather than permanent in its effects upon him, and perhaps to have arrested rather than developed the growth of his poetic mind. . . . Consequently, however vital a part of his biography as a man, it seemed less vital in the history of his mind.' (*The Prelude, or Growth of a Poet's Mind*, ed. Ernest de Selincourt [Oxford, 1926], p. 573; this is the edition of *The Prelude* that I have

used. References to book and line numbers in the 1805 version are included in my text.) Female critics have not necessarily questioned this evaluation: 'What sort of a girl was Annette Vallon that she could arouse such a storm of passion in William Wordsworth?' (Mary Moorman, *William Wordsworth: A Biography* [Oxford, 1957], vol. 1, p. 178). More surprisingly, 'it would not be possible to read *The Prelude* without wondering why on earth Vaudracour and Julia suddenly crop up in it, or why Wordsworth does not make any more direct mention of Annette Vallon. Nevertheless, although one cannot help wondering about these things, they are not really what the poem is about' (Margaret Drabble, *Wordsworth* [London, 1966], p. 79). Herbert Read did in fact put a great deal of emphasis on Annette's role in the production of Wordsworth's poetry (*Wordsworth*, The Clark Lectures, 1929–30 [London, 1930]). His thoroughly sentimental view of the relationship between men and women – 'the torn and anguished heart [Wordsworth] brought back to England at the end of this year 1792' – and his discounting of politics – 'he was transferring to this symbol of France the effect of his cooling affection for Annette' – make it difficult for me to endorse his reading entirely (pp. 102, 134).

4. Herbert Read, *Wordsworth* (London, 1930), pp. 205–6. 'It is impossible to date *Vaudracour and Julia* accurately; we know of no earlier version than that in MS. "A" of *The Prelude*, but it is possible that the episode was written some time before 1804' (F. M. Todd, 'Wordsworth, Helen Maria Williams, and France', *Modern Language Review*, 43, [1948], 462).

5. Richard J. Onorato, *The Character of the Poet: Wordsworth in The Prelude* (Princeton, 1971), p. 409.

6. I refer the reader to my essay, partially on a passage from *The Prelude*, 'Allégorie et histoire de la poésie: Hypothèse de travail', *Poétique*, 8 (1971), for a working definition of the 'iconic' style. An 'icon' is created in 'passages where the [putative] imitation of real time is momentarily effaced for the sake of a descriptive atemporality [*achronie*]' (p. 430). Such passages in Romantic and post-Romantic allegory characteristically include moments of a 'temporal menace . . . resulting in a final dislocation' (p. 434). This earlier essay does not relate Wordsworth's 'iconic' practice to a political programme. Geoffrey Hartman's definition of the concept of a 'spot of time', also unrelated to a political argument, is provocative: 'The concept is . . . very rich, fusing not only time and place but also stasis and continuity', *Wordsworth's Poetry 1787–1814* (New Haven, 1964), p. 212.

7. *Sophocles I*, ed. David Grene (Chicago, 1954), p. 42.

8. For the sort of practical but unacknowledged use that Wordsworth made of Dorothy, see Drabble, *Wordsworth* (London, 1966), pp. 111 and *passim*. The most profoundly sympathetic account of the relation-

ship between William and Dorothy is to be found in F. W. Bateson, *Wordsworth: A Re-interpretation*, 2nd edn (London, 1954).

9. 'Femininity', in *The Standard Edition of the Complete Psychological Words of Sigmund Freud*, trans. James Strachey (London, 1964), vol. 22.

10. Gilles Deleuze and Félix Guattari, *Anti-Oedipus: capitalism and schizophrenia*, trans. Mark Seem *et al.* (New York, 1977), p. 161.

9

Genre, Gender, and Autobiography: Vaudracour and Julia

MARY JACOBUS

> The question of the literary genre is not a formal one: it covers the motif of the law in general, of generation in the natural and symbolic senses, of birth in the natural and symbolic senses, of the generation of difference, sexual difference between the feminine and masculine genre/ gender . . . of an identity and difference between the feminine and masculine.
>
> (Jacques Derrida, 'The Law of Genre')[1]

What has sexual difference to do with *The Prelude*? In particular, what can be said about the relation between the genre of Wordsworth's autobiographical poem and questions having to do with gender? My epigraph provides one approach to these questions. It comes from an essay whose already involuted paradoxes of classification and taxonomy need no further elaboration here (although I will be returning to Derrida in due course). Rather, Derrida's summary announces in brief the argument which I want to make apropos of *The Prelude* in particular, but also apropos of genre theory in general. Questions of genre involve both law and generation, or beginnings; both gender and sexual identity, or difference. My point of departure (and in a sense, my pretext) is provided by the Vaudracour and Julia episode

– an episode whose plot is for my purposes conveniently summarised by Derrida's summary; but I hope also to suggest ways in which that episode might serve as a rereading of current genre theory, especially in the light of Derrida's critical reflections on the (il)legitimising effects of 'the law of genre'. In other words, instead of reading the episode in the light of theories of genre, I want to read theories of genre in the light of an episode that involves questions of generation, law, and sexual difference as a central aspect of its narrative.

In doing so, I have in mind especially attempts such as Alistair Fowler's to bring notions of generic transformation to bear on literary history in *Kinds of Literature* (1982). Rather misleadingly subtitled *An Introduction to the Theory of Genres and Modes*, Fowler's book might well be seen as an instance of the refusal of theory, in the interests of conserving an ultimately dynastic view of literary history. Genre, in effect, does away with the need for theory since it organises literature in the forms in which we already know it; recognisability and an unbroken line of descent are the final criteria, and literary hierarchies remain fundamentally unchanged. The Vaudracour and Julia episode tells a story about illegitimacy, but, interestingly, the fate of the episode itself tells a story about literary hierarchy. I want to argue that the disreputable episode lost its place in Wordsworth's autobiography because it threatened to undo the legitimising efforts that went into the authorised version of *The Prelude*. One way to explore the (non)-relation between views of genre as different as those of Derrida and Fowler is to tell the story of the Vaudracour and Julia episode as it is told not only by Wordsworth himself, but by the textual history of *The Prelude*, and then as it in turn retells the story of the law of genre – a story which also necessarily engages questions of gender along with questions of theory.

'WITH THAT PRELUDE *DID* BEGIN / THE RECORD'

To begin at the end: the naming of Wordsworth's untitled posthumous poem by his widow can be seen as at once a legitimation, an act of propriety, and an appropriation. Here is his nephew Christopher's account of the naming of the 'anonymous' poem that became *The Prelude*, in the *Memoirs of William Wordsworth* (1851):

Its title, 'The Prelude', had not been fixed on by the author himself: the Poem remained anonymous till his death. The present title has been prefixed to it at the suggestion of the beloved partner of his life, and the best interpreter of his thoughts, from considerations of its tentative and preliminary character. Obviously it would have been desirable to mark its relation to 'The Recluse' by some analogous appellation; but this could not easily be done, at the same time that its other essential characteristics were indicated. Besides, the appearance of this poem, *after* the author's death, might tend to lead some readers into an opinion that it was his *final* production, instead of being, as it really is, one of his *earlier* works. They were to be guarded against this supposition. Hence a name has been adopted, which may serve to keep the true nature and position of the poem constantly before the eye of the reader; and 'THE PRELUDE' will now be perused and estimated with the feelings properly due to its preparatory character and to the period at which it was composed.[2]

Guarded against the supposition that it is a later work ('his *final* production'), the reader knows where the poem belongs ('one of his *earlier* works'), and to whom – the poet's family; more particularly, his widow ('the best interpreter of his thoughts'). The title, then, not so much prefixes *The Prelude* as serves to fix it, or 'to keep the true nature and position of the poem constantly before the eye of the reader'. The widow's afterthought prepares us to be prepared. But for what? How can we know 'the feelings properly due to its preparatory character' without knowing what comes afterwards? And what if its 'true nature' were to have been an end, and not a beginning – the 'tail-piece' to the unwritten *Recluse* which Coleridge had first envisaged? Or supposing the famous antechapel turned out to be an annex instead – 'the biographical, or philosophico-biographical Poem to be prefixed or annexed to the Recluse' (Coleridge again)?[3] At once an endless beginning and always an afterword to the life it narrates, Wordsworth's autobiography seems not to have a proper place after all. It belongs nowhere and has no fixed character, redundant to the non-existent text which its title is supposed to 'prelude'. In short, it is an impropriety, and one properly suppressed during the poet's lifetime.

It would be difficult to cut *The Prelude* from the record of Wordsworth's writings. But he did his best to excise another impropriety, also successfully suppressed during his lifetime. I mean, of course, his off-the-record love affair with Annette Vallon and the birth of their daughter Caroline:

Oh, happy time of youthful lovers, (thus
My story may begin) O balmy time,
In which a love-knot, on a lady's brow,
Is fairer than the fairest star in Heaven!
So might – and with that prelude *did* begin
The record; and, in faithful verse, was given
The doleful sequel.[4]

(1850: IX. 553–9)

The record thus begun and aborted was the story of Vaudracour and
Julia, published separately in 1820 and omitted altogether from the
1850 version of *The Prelude* in which these prelusive lines occur
('and with that prelude *did* begin / The record'). Removed from its
originally autobiographical context, 'The doleful sequel' became yet
another of Wordsworth's pathetic tales, a 'Poem Founded on the
Affections'. The note added in 1820 indicates that the story was
'written as an Episode, in a work [i.e. *The Prelude*] from which its
length may perhaps exclude it'.[5] But in a letter of 1805 to Sir George
Beaumont, Wordsworth makes it hard for himself to exclude anything from his ever-expanding autobiography. Offering, in his own
phrase, to 'lop off' any 'redundancies' that may later become apparent in the completed poem, he withdraws the offer in the same
breath: 'this defect [i.e. redundancy], whenever I have suspected it or
found it to exist in any writings of mine, I have always found
incurable. The fault lies too deep, and is in the first conception.'[6]
Contradictorily, Wordsworth seems to say that lopping off an incurable defect risks damaging an integrity which already includes redundancies. The cut would at once strike a blow to the integrity of the
work, and yet admits that it lacks integrity to start with, since the
'fault' or 'defect' lies in its first conception. A story of impropriety,
disowning, and cutting off as the result of a faulty conception, the
Vaudracour and Julia episode suffers the same fate as its hero –
surely the most lopped-off romantic lover since Abelard.

There is nothing in the 1850 version of *The Prelude* to tell us that
Vaudracour and Julia are both victims of an *ancien régime* whose
social and sexual codes of honour are founded on both the Name
and the Law of the Father – on paternity, property, and propriety.
Wordsworth contents himself with directing his imaginary reader
elsewhere for 'The doleful sequel' to the story, and at this point in the
1850 text substitutes a clumsy twenty-line paraphrase which is striking for its omissions: 'Thou, also, there mayst read', he tells Coleridge
(who may be presumed to have known the whole story anyway),

> how the enamoured youth [i.e. Vaudracour] was driven,
> By public power abused, to fatal crime,
> Nature's rebellion against monstrous law;
> How, between heart and heart, oppression thrust
> Her mandates, severing whom true love had joined,
> Harassing both; until he sank and pressed
> The couch his fate had made for him; supine,
> Save when the stings of viperous remorse,
> Trying their strength, enforced him to start up,
> Aghast and prayerless. Into a deep wood
> He fled, to shun the haunts of human kind;
> There dwelt, weakened in spirit more and more;
> Nor could the voice of Freedom, which through France
> Full speedily resounded, public hope,
> Or personal memory of his own worst wrongs,
> Rouse him; but, hidden in those gloomy shades,
> His days he wasted – an imbecile mind.
>   (1850: IX. 568–85)

To set the record straight: Vaudracour loses his liberty, his manhood, and his marbles because his noble father objects to a middle-class marriage (plebeian, as it becomes in 1820) with his childhood play-mate; these are not star-crossed lovers, but class-crossed, and the paternal prohibition which mobilises the law against Vaudracour means that the child he engenders outside marriage can never be legitimate – can never inherit the Name of the Father. The censored text of 1850 may tell us no more than the fact that by this time Wordsworth himself had become a Victorian father, a reading borne out by the 1820 denial of his earlier, more permissive speculation that the lovers had been carried away 'through effect / Of some delirious hour' (IX. 596–7; 'ah, speak it, think it, not!' is Wordsworth's expostulatory 1820 revision). But where beginning fictions are concerned, omissions like this tell tales. Modern readers of *The Prelude* know – too knowingly, perhaps – that the episode is a pretext; for Vaudracour read 'Heartsworth', or Wordsworth as lover; for Julia, read Annette.[7] But the biographical reading is a short cut. What should interest us is not so much the begetting of Caroline as the beginnings of *The Prelude*; not so much the (giving) life as the work.

In 1805, Wordsworth had introduced the episode as a digression from his main purpose in the Revolutionary books: 'I shall not, as my purpose was, take note / Of other matters . . . – public acts, / And public persons . . . – but I will here instead / Draw from obscurity a tragic tale' (IX. 544–51). This turning away from history, or domestication of epic, is prefigured at the start of *The Prelude* when Wordsworth's survey of mythic and historical themes for his projected poem comes home to 'Some tale from my own heart, more near akin / To my own passions and habitual thoughts' (I. 221–2). Although it too proved a false start, the untold 'tale from [his] own heart' is resumed in Book IX. The Vaudracour and Julia episode can be seen – not, I think, entirely fancifully – as the point from which *The Prelude* departs as well as a redundancy; as an opening as well as a cut. A history of error and transgression, the episode is also symptomatic of the errancy of Wordsworth's abandonment of historical and philosophical epic for that mixed and transgressive genre, autobiography. Here a pause for classification seems in order. Wordsworth's 1815 'Preface' includes under the heading of narrative the following taxonomy of genres or kinds: 'the Epopoeia, the Historic Poem, the Tale, the Romance, the Mock-heroic, and . . . that dear production of our days, the metrical Novel. The distinguishing mark of this class, Wordsworth goes on, 'is, that the Narrator . . . is himself the source from which everything primarily flows'.[8] Where does this leave his autobiography, which Wordsworth, we know, regarded as 'unprecedented' in literary history ('a thing unprecedented in Literary history that a man should talk so much about himself', as he wrote to Beaumont)?[9] Presumably, it leaves autobiography with tales and romances. In other words, Wordsworth's lapse into 'that dear production of our days, the metrical Novel' can scarcely be dissociated from his larger lapse in talking so much about himself. Cutting the Vaudracour and Julia episode makes amends for an error that cannot be cut, the altogether redundant, too talkative *Prelude*. Romance – which is well known to be in love with error – is censored in the form of the Vaudracour and Julia episode, so that autobiography can speak out at unprecedented length.

REVOLUTION, ROMANCE, AND SEXUAL DIFFERENCE

What kind of poem is *The Prelude*? We could settle for Coleridge's 'philosophico-biographical' and leave it at that as far as generic legitimacy goes. But I would like to press the question a little further. Genre might be called the Frenchification of gender, and it was in France that (having left his French letters at home, as they say in England) Wordsworth discovered the literal implications of engendering. We know that France appeared to him under the sign of romance as well as revolution; 'Bliss was it in that dawn to be alive' (X. 692), but also: 'O balmy time, / In which a love-knot, on a lady's brow, / Is fairer than the fairest star in Heaven!' (1850: IX. 554–6). In a strikingly proleptic passage, Wordsworth describes how on his first arrival in Paris in 1791 he gathered up a stone from the ruins of the Bastille 'And pocketed the relick in the guise / Of an enthusiast' (IX. 66–7). Yet, 'Affecting more emotion than [he] felt', he is less moved by this symbol of the Revolution than by a picture then on show in Paris as a tourist attraction, 'the Magdalene of le Brun' (IX. 71–80). Le Brun, associated with Versailles and Richelieu, and a rapturously penitent Magdalene popularly (but incorrectly) thought to portray Louise de la Vallière, the mistress of Louis XIV, seem on the face of it to represent aesthetic lapses on the part of an aspiring Republican. But the incident foretells the Vaudracour and Julia episode, later in the same book, in a number of significant ways. The painting's erotic religiosity would have provided an imaginary visual parallel for the tale of hapless lovers forced – like Louise de la Vallière, who retired to a Carmelite convent – to sublimate their passion in religious houses (Julia is consigned to a convent by her mother while, according to the Fenwick note, the final refuge of the real-life Vaudracour was the convent of La Trappe). Politically speaking, Wordsworth himself had fallen in love with a woman of royalist sympathies in a Loire landscape bearing the traces of royal erotic history ('that rural castle, name now slipped / From my re-membrance, where a lady lodged / By the first Francis wooed' IX. 485–7). Finally, the Vaudracour and Julia episode redeems sexual love as romance (this is no casual affair, after all) and rededicates it to revolution.

Two critics have recently and persuasively argued for the central-ity of the erotic motif in Book IX, offering their own readings of both le Brun's penitent Magdalene and the Vaudracour and Julia episode. For Alan Liu, elaborating what he calls 'the Genre of Revolution' in Books IX and X of *The Prelude*, the Magdalene is the female 'genius' of the revolutionary landscape; Wordsworth, writes Liu persuasively apropos of le Brun's painting,

> wants to see a revolutionary country in which liberation arrives, not with the pike-thrusts of violence, but with the soft, fluid undulations of a necklace spilling from a box, of clouds rolling through a window, or of the clothes, hair, tears, and body, of a woman flowing out of old constraints.

He points out that Wordsworth misread both the penitent Magdalene and revolutionary France.[10] For Ronald Paulson, drawing on Liu's argument that Wordsworth is trying to fit the French Revolution into an aesthetic category or literary genre in order to make it manageable, 'love itself is the symbol of revolution' and 'The act of love . . . an act of rebellion, or at least a scandalous act, in the context of a society of arranged marriages, closed families, and decorous art and literature'. The story thus becomes for Paulson 'the hidden centre' or 'displaced paradigm' of Wordsworth's revolutionary experience which he reads as follows:

> he falls in love with an alien woman (alien by class and nationality), challenges his father, runs away with her, but eventually succumbs to the external, paternal pressures. The act of loving with this slightly alien woman *is* the act of revolution.[11]

Thematically speaking, the Vaudracour and Julia episode clearly represents just such 'an act of rebellion, or at least a scandalous act' and it is no surprise that the later Wordsworth should have chosen to hush it up on political as well as personal grounds. But persuasive as these readings are, I want to risk an alternative reading, one which bears not only on the genre of *The Prelude* but on the gender of the poet (not to mention that 'slightly alien woman'). This is my justification for retelling the story which Liu and Paulson in their different ways have already told in the context of their common concern with genre and revolution in Books IX and X of *The Prelude*.

In brief, I want to suggest that the metonymic swerve of passion from fallen Bastille to fallen woman, from history to romance, puts a woman's face on the Revolution and, in doing so, makes a man of Wordsworth. Without 'a regular chronicle' of recent events, Wordsworth (he tells us) is unable to give them 'A form and body' (IX. 101–6); 'all things', he complains, 'were to me / Loose and disjointed' (IX. 106–7). Lacking a body ('the affections left / Without a vital interest', IX. 107–8), how can revolution engender desire? Chaotic, formless, and multitudinous, revolutionary uproar – the 'hubbub wild' of Milton's Pandemonium which strikes Wordsworth on his arrival (IX. 56) – mocks all attempts to textualise it for posterity: 'Oh, laughter for the page that would reflect / To future times the face of what now is!' (IX. 176–7), writes Wordsworth, dropping into the present tense. Superimposed on the faceless face 'of what now is' we find that of le Brun's stylised Magdalene, 'A beauty exquisitely wrought – fair face / And rueful, with its ever-flowing tears' (IX. 79–80). Le Brun's expressive theory of the passions was famous for transforming the face itself into an intelligible or speaking text. Embodied as a beautiful woman (whose expression, Liu points out, is closest to that of 'Ravishment' or 'Rapture' in le Brun's scheme), revolution becomes readable. Elsewhere, Wordsworth himself admits to having prized 'the historian's tale' only as 'Tales of the poets'; only as romance – 'as it made my heart / Beat high and filled my fancy with fair forms' (IX. 207–10). Once more seduced by fair forms as he encounters the reality of revolutionary France, Wordsworth substitutes the Vaudracour and Julia episode for the historian's tale. But, like the penitent Magdalene with her fair face, the episode gives form to more than the unreadable, risible text of history. The story of Vaudracour and Julia is also a means of constituting Wordsworth himself as an autobiographical subject, and, specifically, as a masculine one.

Paul de Man has written of the resistance of autobiography to attempts to make it look less disreputable by elevating it into a genre or mode and installing it 'among the canonical hierarchies of the major literary genres'; rather, autobiographical discourse becomes for him 'a figure of reading or of understanding that occurs, to some degree, in all texts'. He goes on: 'The autobiographical moment happens as an alignment between the two subjects involved in the process of reading in which they determine each other by mutual reflexive substitution'; as a figure of face (posited by language) and simultaneous defacement (since language for de Man is privative).[12] Because the woman's face images his own, reflecting the onlooker's desire much as the supposed Magdalene (Louise de la Vallière) might be thought to reflect that of Louis XIV, the autobiographer can come into existence as a specular image of the reader. When the page has a face, it can speak to the future; or at any rate to Coleridge – another of the autobiographer's self-constituting mirror images or faces in *The Prelude*.

Hence gender (sexual difference) establishes identity by means of a difference that is finally excised. What we end up with is not difference (that 'slightly alien woman') but the same: man, or man-to-man. Like the Vaudracour and Julia episode, and like the feminised genre of romance, woman becomes redundant. Her role is to mediate between men, as the role of romance is to mediate between history and the historian's tale or page. The real hero of this tale is in fact Beaupuy, Wordsworth's surrogate narrator for the Vaudracour and Julia episode, as well as his mentor and idealised revolutionary self (his name, tellingly, combines beauty and power – a masculine or beau ideal). Their 'earnest dialogues' beneath the trees of the Loire valley are compared to those between Dion and Plato (IX. 446, 415–16), or between student and teacher. But Wordsworth's thoughts soon wander from philosophic debate about freedom (Dion liberated Sicily from tyrannical rule) to tales of damsels more or less in distress – fantasies drawn from Ariosto, Tasso, and Spenser: 'Angelica thundering through the woods', 'Erminia, fugitive as fair as she', satyrs mobbing 'a female in the midst, / A mortal beauty, their unhappy thrall' (IX, 454–64). Beaupuy himself is an errant knight who wanders 'As through a book, an old romance, or tale / Of Fairy' (IX. 307–8), and chivalry turns out to be the motivating force for his political idealism even when he points to a present-day reality, the hunger-bitten girl feeding her heifer by the wayside (''Tis against that / Which we are fighting', IX. 519–20). Beaupuy's political pro-gramme, in fact, is none other than to transfer to the people 'A passion and a gallantry . . . Which he, a soldier, in his idler day / Had payed to woman' (IX. 318–20). As Gayatri Spivak has noted in her provocative analysis of 'Sex and History in *The Prelude*', the transfer constitutes 'an unwitting display of class and sex prejudice'.[13] This embodiment of the people as an unhappy female thrall in need of rescue suggests that their role (like that of the beauty surrounded by satyrs) is to mediate relations between men. Both politics (the people) and romance (woman) go under, leaving the philosophic dialogue addressed by one man to another; this dialogue Dorothy Wordsworth called 'the Poem addressed to Coleridge'[14] – a poem 'fair-copied' by the women of the Wordsworth–Coleridge circle, but not, or only rarely, addressed to them.

In the economics of chivalry, it is the woman who pays. Wordsworth, who in 1793 had called Burke's *Reflections on the Revolution in France* 'a philosophic lamentation over the extinction of Chivalry', knew the price. The Vaudracour and Julia episode reads like a critique of Burke's famous lament (inspired by the fate of Marie Antoinette) for the age of chivalry: 'It is gone, that sensibility of principle, that chastity of honour, which felt a stain like a wound, which inspired courage whilst it mitigated ferocity, which ennobled whatever it touched, and under which vice itself lost half its evil, by losing all its grossness . . .'[15] The Vaudracour and Julia episode translates 'that chastity of honour' as ruthless persecution of the lovers, even to the point where the father imprisons his son rather than recognise marriage to a commoner; even to the point of disregarding primogeniture rather than recognise an illegitimate child. Yet Wordsworth's own unmasking of the ideology which sustains the fictions of 'chivalry' – an ideology based on class and sexual inequality, and maintained by laws designed to perpetuate the interests of the upper classes – might be accused of participating in the values of an outmoded genre. If only by its contiguity with chivalric romance, the 'Tale' or 'metrical Novel' is anachronistic, identified with the values of the ruling class even when it tells of simple people, and complicit in the retreat from the specificity of history whereby romance conceals the social basis of the ruling class – its exploitation or oppression of the ruled.[16] Though Wordsworth claims for Beaupuy's narrative of Vaudracour and Julia 'The humbler province of plain history' (IX. 643), the story – based in part on Helen Maria Williams's *Letters Written in France in the Summer of 1790* (1790) – preserves all the self-consciously literary qualities of sensibility and pathos common in late eighteenth-century fiction and metrical tales.[17] Vaudracour himself is a man of feeling whose single act of violence (the murder of one of the men sent by his father to arrest him) accentuates his passivity and feminisation in the face of paternal authority. His final impotence, roused neither by 'the voice of Freedom, . . . public hope, / Or personal memory of his own worst wrongs' (1850: IX. 581–3) is the impotence of the pathetic tale itself to confront history, let alone revolution. Set in a pre-revolutionary era, it is a relic, literally a pre-text – its lovers for ever belated, as if caught in a time-warp from which *The Prelude* itself is able to escape by virtue of its impropriety or illegitimacy, that of a distinctively revolutionary non-genre, autobiography. Unlike Wordsworth (or for that matter the voluble Annette) who lived to tell his own tale, Vaudracour is silenced: 'From that time forth he never uttered word / To any living' (IX. 912–13). His imbecility is the autobiographer's unacted part. Though he had found it hard to get started on his epic, Wordsworth had not 'wasted' his days; his release from the past came not just through timely utterance but through an excess of talkativeness: 'a thing unprecedented in Literary history that a man should talk so much about himself'.

A FAMILY ROMANCE: OR, THE POLITICS OF GENRE

Oedipal interpretations of the Vaudracour and Julia episode are fuelled by Wordsworth himself when he writes of 'A conflict of sensations without name' which he experienced after his return from revolutionary France on finding himself unowned and silent in the midst of a congregation praying 'To their great Father' for victory against the French (X. 265–73). Oedipal conflict becomes synonymous with the French Revolution – 'in the minds of all ingenuous youth, / Change and subversion from this hour . . . that might be named / A revolution,' writes Wordsworth (X. 232–7). Paulson's Bloomian version of the Oedipal plot has Wordsworth staging a successful poetic rebellion against the literary father, Milton;' 'the struggle with (as Bloom would put it) his poetic father reflecting in microcosm the oedipal conflict of the Revolution itself . . . the rebellion against Milton [is] a successful version of the Vaudracour–Julia story in which the father *is* defied.'[18] For Spivak, in the most ambitious attempt so far to read the Vaudracour and Julia episode in the combined light of gender, politics, and psychoanalysis, Wordsworth's disavowal of paternity (his fathering of Caroline) is crucial to the plot of both *The Prelude* and the Great Tradition which has it that 'the Child is father of the Man', i.e. 'man as son'. Paulson's Wordsworth reverses the fate of Vaudracour, who remains by contrast for ever son not father – his marriage forbidden, his freedom curtailed, and his child illegitimate. Spivak's reading is less indulgent of the Oedipal plot, seeing it as a ruse that allows Wordsworth to play at mothers and fathers, thereby acceding to an androgyny which finally excludes women in the interests of a restored imagination. 'Suppression of Julia, unemphatic retention of Vaudracour as sustained and negative condition of possibility of disavowal, his sublation into Coleridge . . . Imagination as the androgyny of Nature and Man – woman shut out. I cannot but see in it the sexual-political programme of the Great Tradition.'[19] The plot, in short, is a (Great) Masterplot.

But what about the baby, to whom Vaudracour becomes so devoted after Julia's incarceration in a convent, and whom he curiously resembles in his own helplessness and dependence on Julia? When we recall the baby's omission from the 1850 text of *The Prelude*, we might pause to ask whether, in suppressing it, Wordsworth may not be providing us with another twist to the Oedipal narrative: that of the so-called 'family romance'. In his edition of *The Prelude*, Ernest de Selincourt takes time out to grumble about the Vaudracour and Julia episode in a footnote as 'among the weakest of [Wordsworth's] attempts in narrative verse'. 'Its most radical fault', he goes on, lies in that part which was probably true to fact, but farthest removed from his own experience, i.e. the character of the hero, with whose meek resignation it is as impossible to sympathise as with the patience of a Griselda. . . . Wordsworth completely fails in presenting a character so unlike his own; and the matter-of-fact detail which he supplies, often so effective and moving in his narratives, only makes *Vaudracour and Julia* more ludicrous, till in [the lines narrating the death of the baby] it reaches a climax of absurdity difficult to parallel in our literature.[20]

'A hero', writes Freud in *Moses and Monotheism* (1939), 'is someone who has had the courage to rebel against his father and has in the end victoriously overcome him.'[21] The antithesis of such a hero and therefore (for de Selincourt) unlike Wordsworth himself, Vaudracour can only be a woman, or a patient Griselda. For woman, read 'neurotic', since according to Freud in 'Family Romances' (1908) the failure to liberate oneself from the authority of one's parents determines one class of neurotic. Freud's essay goes on to identify a characteristic form of fantasy in children and in the erotic and ambitious fantasies of adolescents – one never yielded up by such neurotic individuals; namely, the fantasy of being a stepchild or an adopted child. In the Moses story, it is the aristocratic father who disowns his child or condemns him to death (a role taken by Vaudracour's implacable father in the *Prelude* episode). Vaudracour, then, assumes the role of nurse to himself as abandoned infant when disowned by the father. This may shed light on the unparalleled 'climax of absurdity' denounced by de Selincourt, lines describing Vaudracour performing 'The office of a nurse to his young child, / Which . . . by some mistake / Or indiscretion of the father, died' (IX. 906–8). Negligent nursing and negligent narrative coincide. Wordsworth's offhand aporia (is this a displaced suicide, a mercy killing, or an infanticide?) raises a bizarre line of questioning. Freud remarks on an interesting variant of the family romance in which a younger child robs those born before him of their prerogatives by imagining them illegitimate, so that 'the hero and author returns to legitimacy himself while his brothers and sisters are eliminated by being bastardised'.[22] When one recalls the lines which depict Vaudracour 'Propping a pale and melancholy face' (IX. 812) on one of Julia's breasts while the baby drinks from the other, this is a less far-fetched interpretation than might at first appear. Killing off the illegitimate child leaves Vaudracour (Wordsworth as Heartsworth) without a rival in his mother's affections, while simultaneously relegitimising him as his father's only son and heir.

A second aporia immediately follows the lines relating the death of the baby: 'The tale I follow to its last recess / Of suffering or of peace, I know not which –' (IX. 909–10). The last recess is presumably the grave – a 'sepulchral recess', like one of those included in the gothic edifice of which *The Prelude* is the antechapel. Literally, it is the end of the line; Vaudracour, the eldest son, dies without issue. The prominence of genealogy in the Vaudracour and Julia episode provides scope for the theoretical reversal I promised at the start. What light does the episode throw on genre theory, in particular, on the analogy given fresh currency by Alistair Fowler's *Kinds of Literature*, that of family resemblance? Preferring to see genres as characters or types rather than classes, Fowler invokes Wittgenstein's famous analogy between word-games and games in general: 'We see a complicated network of similarities overlapping and criss-crossing . . . I can think of no better expression to characterise these similarities than "family resemblances"; for the various resemblances between members of a family: build, features, colour of eyes, gait, temperament, etc., etc., overlap and criss-cross in the same way.' Fowler glosses this as follows: 'Representatives of a genre may then be regarded as making up a family whose septs and individual members are related in various ways, without necessarily having any single feature shared in common by all.'[23] (One recalls Wordsworth's grouping of different kinds of narrative according to a common line of descent: 'the Narrator . . . is himself the source from which everything primarily flows.') A 'sept', appropriately, is a clan or tribe claiming descent from a common ancestor. Though Fowler himself had earlier dismissed the view that genres form distinct classes (preferring to see genre in interpretative rather than taxonomic terms), the family analogy allows him to reintroduce qualities of distinctiveness, individuality, and integrity commonly associated with the concept of 'character' – a concept which buttresses our sense of the separateness of subjects against the dangers of (inter-)mixing. By means of the 'mutual reflexive substitution' or 'alignment between the two subjects involved in the process of reading' which de Man identifies as constitutive of autobiography, genre puts a face on theory. Is genre theory, then, no more than 'a figure of reading or of understanding', a means of stabilising the errant text by putting a face on it, and so reading into it a recognisable, specular image of our own acts of understanding? In this light, theories of genre become inseparable from theories of the subject, and hence inseparable from theories of writing. However mixed the genre or mixed-up the 'self', the source of writing ('the source from which everything primarily flows', in Wordsworth's phrase) is held finally to be a more or less integrated and coherent author, the individual named 'Wordsworth' who guarantees the stability and, finally, the legitimacy of the text by means of what Fowler elsewhere calls 'legitimate authorial privilege'.

The family analogy also throws light on what might be termed the politics of genre – a politics implicitly conservative. As Fowler himself goes on to point out, the basis of such family resemblances ('build, features, colour of eyes, gait, temperament, etc., etc.') is literary tradition; specifically, features such as influence, imitation, and inherited codes: 'Poems', writes Fowler, 'are made in part from earlier poems: each is the child . . . of an earlier representative of the genre and may yet be the mother of a subsequent representative.' The implications of this genealogical view of genre are clearly stated in Fowler's book: 'in the realm of genre, revolution or complete discontinuity is impossible'.[24] To break with literary tradition would be to break with the possibility of perceived resemblance. The result would be an unrecognisable text or a faceless page, like the one with which the French Revolution presented Wordsworth ('Oh, laughter for the page that would reflect / To future times the face of what now is!' (IX. 176–7). To get over the difficulty inherent in his privileging of continuity (how then does literary change occur?) Fowler elaborates the family analogy in the direction of genetic mutation: 'Naturally', he goes on, 'the genetic make-up alters with slow time.'[25] *Naturally?* By consecrating genre as part of the order of nature, while simultaneously emphasising the gradual evolution of genre in response to historical change, Fowler reveals himself to be a moderate (if not a conservative) rather than revolutionary, not only in the realm of genre theory, but in the realm of theory itself, where 'farouche structuralists' are said to be at work with 'mere bad effects of Yale formalism' and 'deconstruction is no more than a regrettable but unavoidable necessity' like 'political iconoclasm . . . inappropriately directed against legitimate authorial privilege'. Here Fowler sounds remarkably like Burke in *Prelude*, Book VII ('Exploding upstart Theory', 1850: VII. 529).[26]

The same could be said of Wordsworth, a Girondist Republican turned Tory, when it comes to literary tradition (and finally to politics too). We are back with Derrida's essay on 'The Law of Genre' – a law which Derrida ventriloquises as follows: 'genres should not intermix. And if it should happen that they do intermix, by accident or through transgression, by mistake or through a lapse, then this should confirm, since after all, we are speaking of "mixing", the essential purity of their identity.'[27] The Vaudracour and Julia episode, in which intermixing occurs 'by accident or through transgression, by mistake or through a lapse', says in effect: let genres (classes) mix; there is no such thing as illegitimacy (the unrecognised baby), since the only law Wordsworth will recognise is the law of nature (the gradual transformation of class systems by social or literary intermixing). The baby becomes 'Nature's rebellion against monstrous law' (1850: IX. 571). But so long as the notions of authorship and identity remain intact, the law itself remains unchallenged, albeit in a naturalised form; entrusting oneself 'To Nature for a happy end of all' (IX. 604) turns out to be a futile recourse for Vaudracour and Julia. Their child can have no name, no future. '*Pater semper incertus est, sed mater certissima*' ('paternity is always uncertain, maternity is most certain', the old legal tag invoked by Freud in 'Family Romances') means that legitimacy must still be bestowed by legal process; by the father, and not the mother.[28] As necessity is the mother of invention, 'Nature' may similarly become the mother of *The Prelude* – nature, in all its 'essential' impurity. But it is only when *The Prelude* has been named by the poet's family that it becomes legitimate, a recognised and recognisable literary text. In the last resort, nature proves to be merely the common-law wife of a Wordsworth who subsequently married within the family (thereby, incidentally, refusing the principle of exogamy which is also the principle of intermixture). If *The Prelude* as autobiography is Romanticism's rebellion against the law of genre, it is a rebellion which ultimately turns back to the order of the past in the interests of a readable text. Engendered by the illicit mixing of aristocratic and middle-class genres – 'the Epopoeia, the Historic Poem, the Tale, the Romance, the Mock-heroic, and . . . the metrical Novel'[29] – *The Prelude* simultaneously defies the Law of the Father and preserves it.

But the Vaudracour and Julia episode reminds us that there is no history without error; that genre is always impure, always 'mothered' as well as fathered, and the 'lodged within the heart of the law itself, [is] a law of impurity or a principle of contamination'. Although the episode may serve to question the authority of epic as history, it stops short of questioning the law; specifically the law of its own lopping-off from *The Prelude*. The Vaudracour and Julia episode ultimately remained (in Christopher Wordsworth's sense of the term) 'anonymous', nameless like Vaudracour's child and disowned like Vaudracour himself; hence, at once unauthored and unauthorised – a mere prelude to *The Prelude* proper. But just as we can see in *The Prelude* itself the playing out of possibilities that are occluded by the silencing of Vaudracour and the death of the baby in its 'pre-text', so we can see in Derrida's elaboration of 'the law of genre' the playing out of possibilities which Wordsworth himself must occlude in the interests of installing his poem (however unprecedented) in what he calls 'Literary history': 'The genre has always in all genres been able to play the role of order's principle: resemblance, analogy, identity and difference, taxonomic classification, organisation and genealogical tree, order of reason, order of reasons, sense of sense, truth of truth, natural light and sense of history'.[30] It might be argued that to appropriate *The Prelude* – a poem presumably innocent of poststructuralist literary politics – for Derridean literary theory merely repeats the proprietary gesture of Wordsworth's widow (' "THE PRELUDE" will now be perused and estimated with the feelings properly due to its preparatory character, and to the period at which it was composed').[31] Rather than simply refixing the face of genre with the face of Derrida, I would argue instead that the Vaudracour and Julia episode reveals what is at stake in all such acts of appropriation, naming, or legitimation: not the genre (or even the character) of literature, but the literariness of genre, or the character of the poet. As the 'fair form' that puts a recognisable face on the page of literary history and thereby makes it readable, genre allows us to find our own faces in the text rather than experiencing that anxious dissolution of identity which is akin to not knowing our kind; or should one say, gender? In the context of *The Prelude*, this would amount to finding the author lacking either in issue or in the distinctive masculinity which aligns his poem with epic struggle rather than with the pathos of the feminised metrical tale; which is to say, it would amount to finding *The Prelude* unreadable.

From Mary Jacobus, *Romanticism, Writing, and Sexual Difference: Essays on The Prelude* (Oxford, 1989), pp. 187–205.

NOTES

[The idea that it is possible to distinguish between types of writing, or genres, has long been a fundamental assumption within literary studies. Establishing the genre helps to establish the appropriate critical approach. In recent years much feminist criticism has explored the relationship between theories of genre and gender, with the effect of questioning assumptions inherent in the application of both terms. As with the essentially political basis of Lucas's and Sales's critical approach in essays 4 and 5, the concern for genre and gender which Jacobus and Spivak (essay 8) pursue has the effect of redefining 'literary studies' towards a more inclusive project best described as 'cultural studies'. For Jacobus, defining *The Prelude* as an autobiographical poem is to isolate and privilege one of many identifying genres suitable for the work. A 'cultural studies' approach consequently challenges not only the familiar ways of thinking about literature established by English Departments in schools and universities over many years, it also opposes the tendency to privilege any one of the so-called Humanities disciplines over the others. It is therefore appropriate that Jacobus should choose to analyse Wordsworth's embarrassingly 'disreputable' affair with Annette Vallon, an incident which threatened profoundly disruptive 'questions of generation, law, and sexual difference' for him personally, while at the same time it threatened to deconstruct the genre of his autobiographical poem. Ed.]

1. Jacques Derrida, 'The Law of Genre', *Glyph*, 7 (1980), 221.

2. Christopher Wordsworth, *Memoirs of William Wordsworth* (London, 1851), vol. 1, p. 313.

3. *Collected Letters of Samuel Taylor Coleridge*, ed. E. L. Griggs (6 vols, Oxford, 1956–71), vol. 1, p. 538; vol. 2, p. 1104.

4. William Wordsworth, *The Prelude 1799, 1805, 1850*, ed. J. Wordsworth, M. H. Abrams, and S. Gill (New York, 1979), 1850 text. [All further references are given in the text, where 1850 indicates the date of the version of *The Prelude* cited. Ed.]

5. *The Poetical Works of William Wordsworth*, ed. E. de Selincourt and H. Darbishire (5 vols, Oxford, 1940–9), vol. 2, p. 59.

6. *The Letters of William and Dorothy Wordsworth, The Early Years*, ed. E. de Selincourt, 2nd edn, revd C. L. Shaver (Oxford, 1967), p. 587.

7. See David Erdman, 'Wordsworth as Heartsworth; or, Was Regicide the Prophetic Ground of those "Moral Questionings"?', in D. Reiman, M. Jaye and B. Bennet (eds), *The Evidence of the Imagination* (New York, 1978), p. 15.

8. *The Prose Works of William Wordsworth*, ed. W. J. B. Owen and Jane Worthington Smyser (3 vols, Oxford, 1974), vol. 3, p. 27.

9. *The Letters of William and Dorothy Wordsworth, The Early Years*, ed. E. de Selincourt, revd C. L. Shaver (Oxford, 1967), p. 586.

10. Alan Liu, '"Shapeless Eagerness". The Genre of Revolution in Books 9–10 of *The Prelude*', *Modern Language Quarterly*, 43 (1982), 10. Liu offers a particularly suggestive analysis of the le Brun 'Magdalene'.

11. R. Paulson, *Representations of Revolution 1789–1820* (New Haven, 1983), pp. 265, 268–9.

12. See Paul de Man, 'Autobiography as Defacement', in *The Rhetoric of Romanticism* (New York, 1984), pp. 67–8, 70.

13. Gayatri Spivak, 'Sex and History in *The Prelude* (1805): Books Nine to Thirteen', *Texas Studies in Literature and Language*, 23 (1981), 341. It seems worth noting in the context of the Vaudracour and Julia episode that Freud, in 'A Special Type of Choice of Object made by Men' (1910) identifies the masculine fantasy of idealising, debasing and rescuing the beloved as a version of the wish to make her a (his) mother: see S. Freud, *The Standard Edition of the Complete Psychological Works*, trans. and ed. J. Strachey (24 vols, London, 1953–74), vol. 9, pp. 71–4.

14. *The Letters of William and Dorothy Wordsworth, The Early Years*, ed. E. de Selincourt, revd C. L. Shaver (Oxford, 1967), p. 664.

15. *The Prose Works of William Wordsworth*, ed. W. J. B. Owen and Jane Worthington Smyser (3 vols, Oxford, 1974), vol. 1, pp. 35, 56n.

16. See Patricia Parker's argument in *Inescapable Romance: Studies in the Poetics of a Mode* (Princeton, 1979), p. 9.

17. See F. M. Todd, *Politics and the Poet* (London, 1957), pp. 219–25. K. R. Johnston, *Wordsworth and The Recluse* (New Haven and London, 1984), pp. 178–80, argus that – like Helen Maria Williams's tale – Wordsworth's too may in its own way have been intended as a tract for the times, less sentimental than cautionary.

18. R. Paulson, *Representations of Revolution 1789–1820* (New Haven, 1983), pp. 273–5.

19. See Spivak, 'Sex and History in *The Prelude* (1805), *Texas Studies in Literature and Language*, 23 (1981), 331, 336, and 326–36 *passim*.

20. William Wordsworth, *The Prelude*, ed. E. de Selincourt, revd H. Darbishire (2nd edn, Oxford, 1959), pp. 592–3.

21. S. Freud, *The Complete Psychological Words* (London, 1953–74), vol. 23, p. 12.

22. Ibid., vol. 9, p. 240.

23. A. Fowler, *Kinds of Literature: An Introduction to the Theory of Genres and Modes* (Cambridge, Mass., 1982), p. 41.

24. Ibid., pp. 42, 32.

25. Ibid., p. 42.

26. A. Fowler, *Kinds of Literature: An Introduction to the Theory of Genres and Modes* (Cambridge, Mass., 1982), pp. 264–6.

27. Jacques Derrida, 'The Law of Genre', *Glyph*, 7 (1980), 204.

28. S. Freud, *The Complete Psychological Works* (London, 1953–74), vol. 9, p. 239 and n. For a brief political consideration of the role played by

'Nature' in the Vaudracour and Julia episode, see J. K. Chandler, *Wordsworth's Second Nature: A Study in the Poetry and Politics* (Chicago, 1984), p. 79.

29. *The Prose Works of William Wordsworth*, ed. W. J. B. Owen and Jane Worthington Smyser (3 vols, Oxford, 1974), vol. 3, p. 27.

30. Jacques Derrida, 'The Law of Genre', *Glyph*, 7 (1980), 228.

31. Christopher Wordsworth, *Memoirs of William Wordsworth* (London, 1851, vol. 1, p. 313.

Further Reading

There are many helpful, general introductions to Wordsworth studies. These include Geoffrey Durrant, *William Wordsworth* (Cambridge: Cambridge University Press, 1969); P. D. Sheats, *The Making of Wordsworth* (Cambridge, Mass.: Harvard University Press, 1973), a study of the early poetry; and John Purkis, *A Preface to Wordsworth* (London: Longman, 1982). Books on the Romantic Movement which include helpful discussions of Wordsworth include Jonathan Wordsworth, Michael C. Jaye and Robert Woof, *William Wordsworth and the Age of English Romanticism* (London: Rutgers University Press, 1987); J. R. Watson, *Romantic Poetry* (London: Longmans, 1985); Marilyn Butler, *Romantics, Rebels and Reactionaries* (London: Oxford University Press, 1982); J. R. Watson has also edited a collection of essays, *An Infinite Complexity* (Edinburgh: Edinburgh University Press, 1983).

Detailed information on Wordsworth's movements, and dates of composition and publication of the poetry are to be found in Mark L. Reed, *Wordsworth: The Chronology of the Early and Middle Years*, 2 vols (Cambridge, Mass.: Harvard University Press, 1967 and 1975).

There are two major biographies. Mary Moorman, *William Wordsworth: A Biography*, 2 vols (London: Oxford University Press, 1965–67); and Stephen Gill, *William Wordsworth: A Life* (Oxford: Clarendon Press, 1989). Readers in the 1980s and 1990s have perhaps become used to a somewhat less reverential attitude towards the poet and his poetry than that offered by Moorman; Gill's biography reflects the style and interests of more recent scholarship.

To these biographies should be added Ben Ross Schneider, *Wordsworth's Cambridge Education* (Cambridge: Cambridge University Press, 1957); and Robert Gittings and Jo Manton, *Dorothy Wordsworth* (Oxford: Clarendon Press, 1985). Gittings and Manton portray Wordsworth from an unusual and revealing vantage point; for once it is the women who hold centre stage. Gender is now an important feature of critical scholarship generally. The best of the feminist critics raise issues of gender that incorporate historical and linguistic issues. Particularly valuable are Mary Jacobus, *Romanticism,*

Writing, and Sexual Difference: Essays on The Prelude (Oxford: Clarendon Press, 1989); Cynthia Chase, 'The Accidents of Disfiguration: Limits to Literal and Rhetorical Reading in Book IV of *The Prelude*', in *Studies in Romanticism*, 18 (1979); Theresa M. Kelley, *Wordsworth's Revisionary Aesthetics* (Cambridge: Cambridge University Press, 1988); James A. Heffernan, 'The Presence of the Absent Mother in Wordsworth's *Prelude*', in *Studies in Romanticism*, 28 (1988); Margaret Homans, 'Eliot, Wordsworth, and the scene of the Sisters' Instruction', in *Critical Inquiry*, 8 (1981).

Further specialist studies of Wordsworth include Jonathan Wordsworth, *William Wordsworth: The Borders of Vision* (London: Oxford University Press, 1982), a comprehensive, scholarly account of Wordsworth's development as a poet, with a comprehensive bibliography; J. R. Watson, *Wordsworth's Vital Soul* (London: Macmillan, 1983), a discussion of religious and anthropological ideas in the poetry; Frederick Garber, *Wordsworth and the Poetry of Encounter* (Urbana: University of Illinois Press, 1971); D. Wesling, *Wordsworth and the Adequacy of Landscape* (London: Routledge, 1970); David Pirie, *William Wordsworth: The Poetry of Grandeur and Tenderness* (London: Methuen, 1982).

On *Lyrical Ballads* there is John E. Jordan, *Why the Lyrical Ballads?* (Berkeley: University of California Press, 1976); Stephen Prickett, *Coleridge and Wordsworth: The Poetry of Growth* (Cambridge: Cambridge University Press, 1970); Mary Jacobus, *Tradition and Experiment in Wordsworth's Lyrical Ballads* (London: Oxford University Press, 1976); Jerome Christensen, 'Wordsworth's Misery, Coleridge's Woe: Reading "The Thorn"', in *Papers in Literature and Language*, 16 (1980); *Wordsworth: Lyrical Ballads*, ed. Alun R. Jones and William Tydeman (London: Macmillan, 1972). *Lyrical Ballads* and the 1807 *Poems in Two Volumes* are discussed in J. F. Danby, *The Simple Wordsworth* (London: Routledge, 1960); the 1807 *Poems* are the subject of a Macmillan Casebook (1990), ed. Alun R. Jones.

On *The Prelude* there is H. Lindenberger, *On Wordsworth's Prelude* (Princeton: Princeton University Press, 1963); *Wordsworth: The Prelude*, ed. W. J. Harvey and Richard Gravil (London: Macmillan, 1972); there are helpful essays included in *The Prelude: 1799, 1805, 1850*, ed. Jonathan Wordsworth, M. H. Abrams and Stephen Gill (London: Norton, 1979). On Wordsworth's later poetry there is Bernard Groom, *The Unity of Wordsworth's Poetry* (London: Macmillan, 1966). Wordsworth's prose is discussed by W. J. B. Owen, *Wordsworth as Critic* (London: Oxford University Press, 1969); and Wordsworth's pamphlet, 'The Convention of Cintra' is the focal point of Gordon Kent Thomas's *Wordsworth's Dirge and Promise* (Lincoln: University of Nebraska Press, 1971).

Most if not all the above critics have been influenced by the work of Geoffrey Hartman. His later essays often make difficult reading. There is now an excellent selection of his work with a helpful Foreword by Donald G. Marshall, and a retrospective Introduction by Hartman himself, in *The Unremarkable Wordsworth* (London: Methuen, 1987); there is also *Beyond Formalism* (New Haven: Yale University Press, 1970); in addition Hartman has edited *New Perspectives on Coleridge and Wordsworth: Selected Papers from the English Institute* (New York: Columbia University Press, 1972).

Francis Fergusson, *Wordsworth: Language as Counter Spirit* (New Haven: Yale University Press, 1977); John Beer, *Wordsworth and the Human Heart* (London: Macmillan, 1978) and *Wordsworth in Time* (London: Faber & Faber, 1979); and G. Salvesen, *The Landscape of Memory* (London: Arnold, 1965), are all helpful books, tending to depict a less agonised and insecure poet than the one offered by Hartman, unlike David Pirie's *Poetry of Grandeur and Tenderness* (noted above) which develops Hartman's approach in readable and interesting ways. All these writers are particularly concerned with language, as is Jeffrey Baker, *Time and Mind in Wordsworth's Poetry* (Detroit: Wayne State University Press, 1980), and L. Newlyn, *Coleridge, Wordsworth, and the Language of Allusion* (Oxford: Oxford University Press, 1986).

A provocative summary of developments in Wordsworth criticism since the 'New Criticism' of the 1930s is to be found in M. H. Abrams, *Doing Things With Texts: Essays in Criticism and Critical Theory* (London: Norton, 1990), especially the chapter entitled 'On Political Readings of *Lyrical Ballads*'. Abrams is concerned to assess the consequences of applying the study of history to the study of poetry. Important examples of this approach are Arthur Beatty, *William Wordsworth, His Doctrine, Mind and Art in their Historical Relations* (Madison: University of Wisconsin Press, 1922); Crane Brinton, *Political Ideas of the English Romanticists* (London: Oxford University Press, 1926); Walter Graham, 'The Politics of the Greater Romantic Poets', in PMLA, 36 (1921); Carl Woodring, *Politics in English Romantic Poetry* (Cambridge, Mass.: Harvard University Press, 1970); F. M. Todd, *Politics and the Poet: A Study of Wordsworth* (London: Methuen, 1957); K. R. Johnston, 'The Politics of *Tintern Abbey*', in *The Wordsworth Circle*, 14 (Winter 1983).

Critics who have adopted this form of contextual approach, especially Beatty, Brinton and Graham, find a source of objectivity in history. This tradition is maintained in James K. Chandler, *Wordsworth's Second Nature: A Study of the Poetry and Politics* (London: University of Chicago Press, 1984), which emphasises the conservative, Burkean strain in Wordsworth. A more objective approach to the influence of the radical political milieu in which Wordsworth moved is to be found in Nicholas Roe, *Wordsworth and Coleridge: The Radical Years* (Oxford: Clarendon Press, 1988). The influence of eighteenth-century British political radicalism (prior to France and 1789) on Wordsworth is the subject of John Williams, *Wordsworth: Romantic Poetry and Revolution Politics* (Manchester: Manchester University Press, 1989).

None of the above books is markedly left-wing; in 'On Political Readings of *Lyrical Ballads*' it is most certainly the left-wing tendency of such criticism that Abrams is concerned with. The influence of Marxist theory on Wordsworth studies, though hardly overwhelming, has certainly stimulated important work. Texts worth noting in this respect are Heather Glen, *Vision and Disenchantment: Blake's Songs and Wordsworth's Lyrical Ballads* (Cambridge: Cambridge University Press, 1983); Jerome J. McGann, *The Romantic Ideology: A Critical Investigation* (Chicago: University of Chicago Press, 1983); Paul Hamilton, *Wordsworth* (Brighton: Harvester Press, 1986); V. G. Kiernan, 'Wordsworth and the People', in *Marxists on Literature*, ed. David Craig (Harmondsworth: Penguin, 1975); and John Barrell, *The Dark Side of the Landscape* (Cambridge: Cambridge University Press, 1980). E. P. Thompson, 'Eighteenth Century English Society: Class Struggle Without Class', in *Social History* (May 1978), offers a more general discussion of the issues.

One recent branch of historical literary criticism has come to be known as 'historicist'. What this broadly signifies is a merging of historical scholarship with poststructuralist theory, where critical 'objectivity' gives way to a far more open-ended, exploratory approach. In Wordsworth studies, this position has been worked through by Marjory Levinson, *Wordsworth's Great Period Poems* (Cambridge: Cambridge University Press, 1986); and David Simpson, *Wordsworth and the Figurings of the Real* (London: Macmillan, 1982), and *Wordsworth's Historical Imagination* (London: Methuen, 1987).

Introductory texts are crucial to a reading of structuralist, poststructuralist and historicist criticism. The best place to start is with Terry Eagleton, *Literary Theory* (London: Blackwell, 1983); a more detailed account of theory since the New Criticism is Frank Lentricchia, *After the New Criticism* (Chicago: University of Chicago Press, 1980); something of a foil to Lentricchia is Geoffrey Hartman, *Criticism in the Wilderness: The Study of Literature Today* (New Haven: Yale University Press, 1980). Very helpful on language theory in the eighteenth century is Chapter One in David Morse, *Perspectives on Romanticism: A Transformational Analysis* (London: Macmillan, 1981).

The following books and essays are essentially the product of the theoretical debate outlined by Lentricchia, Abrams, Hartman and Eagleton, although as Morse makes clear, it is a debate with roots in Wordsworth's own period, and before: Robert Rheder, *Wordsworth and the Beginnings of Modern Poetry* (London: Croom Helm, 1981); Cynthia Chase, 'The Ring of Gyges and the Coat of Darkness: Reading Rousseau with Wordsworth', and Timothy Bahti, 'Wordsworth's Rhetorical Theft', both in *Romanticism and Language*, ed. Arden Reed (London; Methuen, 1984); Jonathan Arac, 'Bounding Lines: *The Prelude* and critical revision', in *Post-Structuralist Readings of English Poetry*, ed. Richard Machin and Christopher Norris (Cambridge: Cambridge University Press, 1987); Don Bialostosky, *Making Tales: The Poetics of Wordsworth's Narrative Experiments* (Chicago: Chicago University Press, 1984); Eric C. Walker, 'Wordsworth: Warriors and Naming', in *Studies in Romanticism*, 29 (Summer 1990); Stephen K. Land, 'The Silent Poet', in *University of Toronto Quarterly*, 42:2 (Winter 1973); and John Turner, *Wordsworth's Play and Politics* (London: Macmillan, 1986).

Notes on Contributors

John Barrell is Professor of English in the School of English and American Studies, University of Sussex. His publications include *The Idea of Landscape and the Sense of Place 1730–1840: An Approach to the Poetry of John Clare* (Cambridge, 1972); *The Dark Side of the Landscape* (Cambridge, 1980), and *The Political Theory of Painting from Reynolds to Hazlitt* (London, 1987).

Geoffrey H. Hartman is Karl Young Professor of English and Comparative Literature at Yale University. His publications include *The Unmediated Vision: An Interpretation of Wordsworth, Hopkins, Rilke, and Valery* (London, 1964); *New Perspectives on Coleridge and Wordsworth: Selected Papers from the English Institute* (New York, 1972); and *The Unremarkable Wordsworth* (London, 1987).

Mary Jacobus is John Wendell Anderson Professor of English at Cornell University. Her publications include *Tradition and Experiment in Wordsworth's Lyrical Ballads* (London, 1976); and *Reading Women: Essays in Feminist Criticism* (New York and London, 1986).

John Lucas is Professor of English and Drama at the University of Loughborough. His publications include *The Literature of Change: Studies in the Provincial Novel* (Brighton, 1977); *English Poetry from Hardy to Hughes* (London, 1986); and *Romantic to Modern Literature: Essays and Ideas of Culture 1750–1900* (Brighton, 1982).

Nicholas Roe is a Lecturer in English at the University of St Andrews. Articles in *The Wordsworth Circle* include 'Citizen Wordsworth', 14 (Winter 1983); 'Wordsworth, Samuel Nicholson, and the Society for Constitutional Information', 13 (Autumn 1982); and for *Notes and Queries*, 'Wordsworth's Account of Beaupuy's Death' (September 1985).

Roger Sales is a Lecturer in English Studies at the University of East Anglia. In addition to *English Literature in History 1780–1830: Pastoral and Politics* (London, 1983), his publications include *Stoppard's 'Rosencrantz* *and Guildenstern are Dead'* (Harmondsworth, 1988); and he has edited *Shakespeare in Perspective* (London, 1982).

David Simpson is Professor of English at the University of Colorado. His publications include *Wordsworth and the Figurings of the Real* (London, 1982); *German Aesthetic and Literary Criticism: Kant, Fichte, Schelling, Schopenhauer, Hegel* (Cambridge, 1984); and 'Criticism, politics and style in Wordsworth's Poetry', in *Critical Inquiry*, 11 (1984–5), 52–81.

Gayatri Chakravorty Spivak is Longstreet Professor of English, Emory University, Atlanta, Georgia. She has translated Derrida's *Of Grammatology* (Baltimore, 1977). Other publications include 'Scattered Speculations on the Question of Value', in *Diacritics*, 15:4 (Winter 1985); and 'The Letter As Cutting Edge', in Shoshona Felman (ed.), *Literature and Psychoanalysis: The Question of Reading: Otherwise* (Baltimore, 1982).

Ross Woodman is Professor of English, University of Western Ontario. His publications include *The Apocalyptic Vision in the Poetry of Shelley* (Toronto, 1964).

Index